Promoting
Successful
Adoptions

SAGE SOURCEBOOKS FOR THE HUMAN SERVICES SERIES

Series Editors: ARMAND LAUFFER and CHARLES GARVIN

Recent Volumes in This Series

Promoting
Successful
Adoptions
Practice with Troubled Families

Susan Livingston Smith
Jeanne A. Howard

Sage Sourcebooks for

the Human Services

Sage Publications
International Educational and Professional Publisher
Thousand Oaks London New Delhi

For information:

Sage Publications, Inc.
2455 Teller Road
Thousand Oaks, California 91320
E-mail: order@sagepub.com

Sage Publications Ltd.
6 Bonhill Street
London EC2A 4PU
United Kingdom

Sage Publications India Pvt. Ltd.
M-32 Market
Greater Kailash I
New Delhi 110 048 India

Printed in the United States of America

Library of Congress Cataloging-in-Publication Data

Smith, Susan Livingston.
    Promoting successful adoptions: Practice with troubled families /
by Susan Livingston Smith, Jeanne A. Howard.
       p. cm.—(Sage sourcebooks for the human services series; v. 40)
    Includes bibliographical references and index.
    ISBN 0-7619-0656-8 (cloth: alk. paper)
    ISBN 0-7619-0657-6 (pbk.: alk. paper)
    1. Adoption—United States. 2. Special needs adoption—United States.
I. Howard, Jeanne A. II. Title. III. Series.
HV875.55 .S653   1999
362.73′4′0973—dc21   99-6361

This book is printed on acid-free paper.

99 00 01 02 03 04 05 7 6 5 4 3 2 1

Acquisition Editor:	Jim Nageotte
Editorial Assistant:	Heidi Van Middlesworth
Production Editor:	Denise Santoyo
Editorial Assistant:	Patricia Zeman
Typesetter:	Lynn Miyata

To the families who created us
and the families we created,
with appreciation for your encouragement and patience

CONTENTS

PREFACE

Adoption is a unique phenomenon that involves profound life events—the creation of life and the creation of families. Although only about 2% of Americans are themselves adopted, adoption touches the lives of many more. Adoptive parents, spouses, and children of adopted individuals, birth parents who relinquish children, and other family members all confront issues in their lives that are linked to adoption. Those of us who are not directly affected by adoption often underestimate its complexity and effect. When helping professionals work with families touched by adoption, they need adoption-related knowledge, sensitivity, and competence.

This book seeks to build on our own research on adoption disruption, adoption dissolution, and postlegal adoption services to provide a knowledge base for work with troubled adoptive families. We conducted a 4-year study of an adoption preservation program in Illinois that was developed to serve adoptive families at risk of child placement or adoption dissolution. We also completed a project for the U.S. Children's Bureau to synthesize the work of the approximately 65 postlegal adoption projects that it funded over a 6-year period. Through our research, we have come into contact with many adopted children and families struggling to heal from past losses and traumas. We have heard many painful stories of adoptive families' encounters with helping professionals that compounded their difficulties rather than relieved them. It is common for families seeking help from the Illinois Adoption Preservation Project to have seen many mental health professionals over a 5- to 10-year period without achieving any notable improvement in their family situations. In fact, some of these families felt that they had been harmed by professionals who encouraged them "to give their children back" (as if that were possible) or blamed parents for family problems.

There is a great need for social workers, psychologists, psychiatrists, residential treatment staff, teachers, and others who work with adopted children and families to understand the issues, dynamics, and strategies intrinsic to adoption preservation work. Such understanding is even more important for professionals working with special needs adoptive families. Our purpose is to present a comprehensive overview of adoption preservation work that is linked with the available empirical literature on adoption, theoretical knowledge underlying adoption practice, practice knowledge in this area, and the insights gained from our adoption preservation research.

This volume is grounded in both empiricism and practice wisdom. As researchers, we are familiar with the body of adoption research and the need for empirical testing of long-held assumptions. We also are social work educators with child welfare practice backgrounds. In addition, through our close relationships with adoption clinicians, we have gathered many practice-based insights related to adoption work. In this volume, we are seeking to integrate theoretical, research-based, and practice literature relevant to understanding the variety of issues intrinsic to post-adoption services. These issues include attachment, grief, identity, the effect of trauma, common family dynamics in troubled adoptive families, and other topics. All case material in this book reflects real family situations, although the identifying information has been modified to protect the confidentiality of the families.

It is important to recognize that the stories presented in this volume are not representative of all adoptions, or even of all special needs adoptions. The focus of this work is primarily troubled adoptions. All adoptive families must confront certain issues and tasks, which are discussed in this book. The majority of adoptive families are able to navigate their lives successfully without professional help. This is not to say that they may not benefit from special educational or therapeutic services from time to time as they confront specific adoption-related issues. It does mean that these issues do not pose extraordinary difficulties to their ongoing functioning as a family or as individuals. Yet, some adopted individuals and their families are not able to incorporate or to adjust to specific aspects of their adoption situation without the help of others having special understanding of adoption. This book is written for those families and the professionals working with them.

Like all authors, we bring a set of assumptions to our work. Our views on adoption have been formed through our own research, the research and experience of other professionals, and the stories of adoptive families. Over time, we have developed the following assumptions about adoption, assumptions that guide our research and this book.

First, we believe adoption to be a beneficial response to children in need of homes. We believe that society should promote adoption, particularly for children whose families have been proven unable to meet their basic needs. We believe that adoption typically is better for children than remaining in the child welfare system, and that every child deserves a permanent home.

Second, we believe adoption is best understood ecologically. The process of adoption and the status of being adopted interact with a host of factors that can protect a child or predispose a child to difficulty. A child's adoption through the child welfare system often is associated with difficult life events—loss of attachment figures, abuse and neglect, insecurity and powerlessness. The history and personality of the child interact with the history and personalities of other family members. Both interact with a host of systems in the environment—the extended family, the school system, the neighborhood, the church, and friends. Further, adoption takes place in the context of the larger society. Thus, families are influenced by societal perceptions of adoption as a means to form a family.

Not all adoptive families struggle unduly. Not all adopted children feel desolate or abandoned. Some adopted children and their families struggle mightily, however. Adoption is another aspect of family life, one that can pose significant challenges. It must be incorporated into the family's identity and functioning, as are differences such as divorce.

Third, we believe that society has an obligation to support adoptive families beyond the point of adoption finalization. This obligation appears particularly clear to us for those who come to adoption through the child welfare system. The challenges presented by many of these children will persist. We believe that the public child welfare agency, in concert with a range of community supports, should provide families with the resources they need to function effectively.

We now present the case for post-adoption services, along with an overview of the needs of adoptive families, common dynamics in troubled adoptive families, and a framework for understanding issues and interventions.

ACKNOWLEDGMENTS

Many people helped us make this book a reality. We would like to express our appreciation to the following individuals and organizations for their contributions to our work: the Illinois Department of Children and Family Services, for its vision and responsiveness in the development of adoption preservation services tailored to the needs of families; our colleagues, Mary Campbell, Judy Pence, Karla Uphoff, and Ivy Hutchison, for their ideas and assistance in the preparation of this volume; the adoption preservation workers who spent hours sharing insights and discussing the nature of this work with us, especially Linda Matesi Wolter, Janet Yelovich, and Dave Matthews; Gary Morgan, whose dedication to children has been an inspiration; and the adoptive families who have committed their lives to children who desperately needed families. Finally, we thank our husbands, Jim and Rhondal, whose tolerance and encouragement helped sustain us to the end.

Chapter 1

SPECIAL NEEDS DON'T DISAPPEAR
WITH ADOPTION
The Case for Post-Adoption Services

The phenomenon of adoption has changed dramatically in recent years. Wider availability and use of contraceptive measures, abortion, and a greater acceptance of single parenting have resulted in a declining number of infants available for adoption. In addition, the large numbers of maltreated children removed from birth homes and freed for adoption have led to the field of *special needs adoptions.*

With the development of the search movement among adopted individuals and birth parents, adoption policies have been modified to allow for more openness in the sharing of information. Research on adoption has shed light on many complexities involved in adoption and some of the unhealthy emotional consequences resulting from past adoption practices. As adoption practice has evolved, the fact that helping professionals need greater understanding of the issues confronting adoptive families has become evident. These professionals include the wide range of counseling providers (social workers, psychologists, and psychiatrists) as well as educators, attorneys, juvenile justice workers, staff in residential treatment centers and other mental health programs, and pediatricians.

National child welfare policies have produced major changes in adoption practice in recent years. In the late 1970s, the large number of children entering and drifting in foster care became a concern of child welfare experts. Several important studies highlighted the high cost of such care and the negative effect on children who remained in care for long periods without clear plans for their future (Bush & Gordon, 1982; Fanshel & Shinn, 1978; Maluccio, Fein, Hamilton, Klier, & Ward, 1980; Shyne & Schroeder, 1978; Vasaly, 1978). Fanshel and Shinn (1978) and others provide evidence that the longer a child is in foster care, the greater the likelihood that the child will continue in placement and the greater the likelihood that the child will lose contact with his or her original family. Growing concern about the plight of these children led to systematic attempts to reduce impermanence, efforts that became known as the *permanency planning movement.* Confidence in the ability to correct the system's problems led to the formalization of policy aimed at keeping children at home or, when necessary, providing permanent homes for children who could not be safely cared for in their original homes. This policy was codified in the federal Adoption Assistance and Child Welfare Act of 1980 (P.L. 96-272).

The permanency planning movement led to the termination of parental rights for growing numbers of abused and neglected children and placement of many of these children in adoptive homes. Adoption is seen as the ultimate answer for children who cannot grow up in their birth families. The field has become more bold in placing children who in previous years were viewed as unadoptable and consigned to the uncertainties of foster care. Like every new wave in child welfare, however, permanency planning has an undertow—these changes both solve and create problems. Thousands of children with special needs have found permanent homes through adoption; others have experienced adoption disruption (removal of the child from an adoptive placement before legal finalization) or dissolution (ending the adoption after legal finalization).

Special needs is a designation that varies from state to state but generally denotes conditions that make children harder to place—older age, minority or sibling group status, or medical, mental, or emotional problems. Categorizing a child as special needs means that the child is eligible to receive adoption subsidy. To some extent, special needs is an arbitrary distinction. For example, age limits for qualifying as special needs vary from birth for minority children in some states to age 12 for white children in a few states (Avery, 1998). The same child may be designated as special needs in one state and not in another. Some children who qualify as special needs may have experienced little maltreatment and minimal moves in care. These children may be developmentally on target and experience few adjustment problems throughout their childhood. The extent of adjustment problems among children who qualify as special needs adoptive placements is not known. In general, however, the term *special needs adoptions* is used across the country and in this book to refer to children who do indeed have special needs. Most of them have experienced maltreatment, interrupted attachments, and moves in care that present some challenges in their development. Also, some children who have not been categorized as special needs because their needs were not obvious at the time of their adoptive placements fit in this category.

The severity of damage among many children in our child welfare system has been underestimated, as has the complexity of forming a new family through adoption. The damage done to children from factors such as prenatal substance exposure or maltreatment may not be manifested until well after the adoption is finalized. Many families who parent these children are likely to have continuing needs, peaking at certain developmental periods or times of family stress. Two decades after the origins of the permanency planning movement, our knowledge about how to strengthen and stabilize adoptive families lags far behind our ability to find homes for special needs children.

TRENDS IN ADOPTION

As the number of newborns surrendered by unwed parents has declined in this country, the proportion of adoptees coming to adoption through other situations has increased. National adoption statistics indicate that about half of the approximately 114,000 adoptions each year are by relatives, and the other half are by nonrelated people (Flango & Flango, 1995). Adoptions of infants and children from other countries continue to make up a large percentage of nonrelative adoptions; however, the adoption of special needs children through public child welfare agencies has increased over the last two decades. In the mid-1990s, approximately 20,000 children with special needs were adopted each year (Child Welfare League, 1997). This number has increased dramatically since the Adoption and Safe Families Act of 1997, however.

Not only has there been a change in the type of adoptions occurring, but there also have been changes in society's view of adoption and adoption practice. Until very recently, adoption was shaped to a significant extent by the stigma of illegitimacy and the overall practice of secrecy. Adoption involved the practice of severing all ties to the child's birth family while seeking to approximate biological parenthood to the extent possible. The following case situations occurring in the practice of one of us in the early 1970s illustrate the nature of adoption during this time.

Stacey, a white 16-year-old high school junior, had been dating Mark, 17, for the past year. Several months after Stacey became pregnant, she confided this fact to her parents, who in turn initiated a meeting with Mark's parents. The parents together planned and executed the solution to this problem. First, they had the two teens marry secretly so that the baby would not be illegitimate. They planned to have the marriage annulled immediately after the baby was born. Second, they sent Stacey away to a maternity home out of state to have the baby and give it up for adoption. The story was that Stacey was spending the summer working at a camp, and Stacey tanned throughout her pregnancy to make this story more credible upon her return home. Fortunately, the timing of her pregnancy enabled her to finish most of the school term, deliver her baby in August, and return home the following week. She gave her son up for adoption and went on with her life as if nothing had happened.

Sarah was a young African American woman in her early 20s who became pregnant as the result of a date rape. She kept her pregnancy a secret from her mother, whom she anticipated would never allow her to give the baby up for adoption. While pregnant, she stayed in a maternity home in the same town in which her mother lived. She told her mother that she was living in England, and during this time, she mailed letters to her mother via a friend in England. She gave birth to a son, gave him up for adoption, and went on with her life as if nothing had happened.

In both situations above, the babies were placed within their first month of life with adoptive families whom workers had selected as the best match for this child. The adoptive families were given brief descriptions of the birth parents' situations, physical characteristics, education level, and talents. These histories were sanitized to remove anything that might be upsetting. There was the obligatory supervisory period of monthly home visits, and then the families were on their own. Any continued agency involvement was viewed by parents and workers alike as interference that might compromise the family's becoming as much like a normal (biological) family as possible. The parents were encouraged to explain adoption to their children as soon as they were old enough to understand. Most stories involved birth parents who loved the children so much that they gave them up and adoptive parents who "chose" them. The children's birth certificates were altered to bear the names of the adoptive parents, and all records with identifying information about birth parents were sealed.

As depicted in the popular movie, *Secrets and Lies* (Leigh, 1996), the nature of adoption and adoption practice has been predicated on a number of myths, misconceptions, and at times unhealthy practices surrounding secrecy and denial. Society has had a romanticized view of adoption involving infertile parents rescuing a needy child who becomes just like the child they would have had. Reitz and Watson (1992) describe the conditions necessary to preserve this idealized view of adoption. For such a family to live happily ever after, three conditions must prevail:

> An adopted child had to approximate adoptive parents' fantasy of the child they might have had by birth; adoption had to be viewed as a static event with no developmental implications; and the reality of the adopted child's other family had to be denied by both the adoptive parents and the agency. The first condition was met by early placement and careful matching. The second was addressed by ignoring the effect of adoption on the way in which the child and the adoptive family develop. And the third condition was fulfilled by early placement and by developing ways of explaining the child's adoption that "avoided" the trauma. (p. 4)

Parties involved in the traditional form of adoption live with a number of powerful feelings that they often cannot discuss and are encouraged to deny. The perpetuation of secrecy and denial has negative consequences for all adoption triad members throughout their lives (Rosenberg & Groze, 1997). Birth parents are not helped to mourn the loss of their child or gain any real information about their ongoing well-being. Adopted children cannot gain basic information about their origins, know their birth families, find truthful answers to their questions about their adoption, or mourn the loss they experienced. Adoptive parents who were infertile often are not helped to mourn this loss. Traditional adoption practice did not recognize that adoption did not necessarily erase the pain of infertility. In past adoption situations, for the most part, these powerful feelings and doubts went unexpressed and unaddressed, and coping mechanisms such as denial, repression, and fantasy were reinforced.

A number of factors resulted in changes in adoption practice and in a greater awareness of the presence of lifelong issues for all members of the adoption triad. Some of these factors include the reduced stigma of having children outside of marriage, pressures brought about by adult adoptees and birth parents to obtain information and access to each other, and the development of knowledge on the effect of adoption on children and families over their life cycle. Many self-help and advocacy groups of adoptees and birth parents have advocated for changes in adoption policies, and there has been a trend toward more openness in adoption (Grotevant & McRoy, 1998).

As more and more children with special needs have become available for adoption, agencies have broadened their criteria for choosing suitable parents for children. Most of the parents adopting special needs children are not infertile couples but others such as foster parents, single parents, or older parents who have raised their birth children yet still want to raise children. Due to the difficulties in finding newborns to adopt, some infertile couples also have turned to special needs adoption to form their families.

Although the adoption of older children is distinctly different from the adoption of newborns, the same philosophy of secrecy characteristic of infant adoptions was transferred into practices in special needs adoptions. Workers feared that negative information about the child shared with the adoptive parents might become a self-fulfilling prophecy. The belief that once the child had a safe, loving family, he or she would become "normal" continued the perception of adoption as an exit service for the child (Project ENABLE, 1994).

As workers learned more about the realities of ongoing challenges in even the most loving, nurturing adoptive families, some aspects of adoption practice began to change. Among these was the provision of more information to adoptive parents about the child's history. At the time the child is placed for adoption, much may not be known about previous experiences and potential problems that may surface later. Sharing with parents all known, nonidentifying information on the child as well as thorough preparation of adoptive families are now embraced as ideals among leaders in the adoption field. The realities of day-to-day practice frequently fall short of these ideals. Workers in adoption still walk a fine line between educating adoptive parents as to potential problems and overwhelming them with concerns that may never materialize.

ADOPTION AS A LIFELONG PROCESS

Early adoption practice was based on the assumption that adoptive families were most successful when they resembled families formed through birth. Careful attempts to match children and adoptive parents by background and physical characteristics represented attempts of adoption professionals to create a family where adoption was undetectable. Social attitudes about illegitimacy increased the incentives to keep adoption secretive, and reinforced the view that adoptive families are the same as other families.

Beginning largely in the 1960s with the work of the sociologist David Kirk (1964, 1981), the idea of the uniqueness of adoption and the importance of this "acknowledgment of differences" in parent-child communication about adoption was advanced. According to Kirk, the development of trust, good communication, and empathy between adoptive parents and children is hindered by parental insistence that adoption is no different, a stance that he calls "rejection of difference." This approach discourages children from exploring aspects of the adoption or communicating their feelings about it. Although this hypothesis has had very limited empirical investigation, there is some evidence to indicate that there is more of a curvilinear relationship between the acceptance of difference and positive adjustment in adoptive families, with an insistence of difference being associated with problematic adjustment of adopted children and families (Brodzinsky, 1987; Kaye, 1990; Kaye & Warren, 1988). Also, the more problems an adopted child manifests, the greater the likelihood that the child and the parents view aspects of adoption as the cause of problems (Cohen, Coyne, & Duvall, 1993; Kaye, 1990).

The developmental aspects of adjustment to adoption for adopted individuals and their families have been underscored by the works of David Brodzinsky and his colleagues (Brodzinsky, Schechter, & Henig, 1992). Adopted children's understanding of adoption changes with their level of cognitive development, and their "lifelong search for self" continues to evolve throughout their lifetimes. According to Brodzinsky, Schechter, and Henig (1992), a wide range of adaptations falls within the realm of normal, healthy adjustment for adopted individuals. Like many issues in life involving intense emotions, adoption is an issue that "emerges, seems to be settled, and then reemerges at some later point along life's path" (p. 4).

In addition to developmental aspects of individual adjustment to adoption, adoptive families confront adoption-related developmental tasks. Adoptive families undergo stresses and adjustments unique to the adoption experience and lasting throughout the family life cycle, whether the child is adopted in infancy or later (Brodzinsky, Smith, & Brodzinsky, 1984; Hajal & Rosenberg, 1991; LeVine & Sallee, 1990). A primary variable shaping the family over time is the child's and parents' ability to develop a secure attachment relationship. This relationship is influenced by many forces. Of particular importance is the fit between the child's temperament, abilities, and needs and the parents' expectations, style, abilities, and needs. Issues related to past losses, entitlement, belonging, and loyalty are important in shaping attachments, particularly when the child has had attachments to previous caretakers. Cultural beliefs about adoption and the attitudes encountered in the family's social network also serve to shape the family's ability to integrate an adopted child into the family and to adapt expectations to the realities they encounter.

Adjustment to adoption under the best of circumstances is complex; however, a child who has experienced maltreatment and loss of a family is likely to pose greater challenges. In particular, children who have experienced significant trauma and multiple losses may go through periods in which their problematic behaviors escalate. Parental perceptions of the child and the adoption may change at different postplacement phases. Although parents may sustain their patience and hope during the first few years of the placement, ongoing problems may lead to a bleaker perspective, and hope may wane as the years add up. The nature of the bond that parents are able to form with their child is a crucial factor in determining their willingness to persevere and to adjust their expectations to the child's abilities. Some families experience few problems in the early years of placement, however, only to confront serious difficulties later on. In these situations, problems dormant during the early years are later reactivated. It is in the long-term that some of the deepest difficulties emerge (Macaskill, 1985).

RESEARCH ON ADOPTION OUTCOMES AND
PROBLEMS OF ADOPTED CHILDREN AND FAMILIES

Much of what is known about the effect of adoption on children and families comes from research on populations made up solely or predominantly of infant adoptions. A review of more than 20 outcome studies on adoption examining primarily infant placements reveals that the vast majority of adoptions are judged as satisfactory by parents, with about 16% assessed as clearly unsuccessful (Kadushin, 1988). Early research on adoptees in clinical populations began to raise questions about a higher risk for behavioral and emotional problems among adopted children (Jerome, 1986; Offord, Aponte, & Cross, 1969; Simon & Senturia, 1966). In reviewing data from 15 studies, McRoy, Grotevant, and Zurcher (1988) conclude that adopted children may be two to five times more likely to require psychological treatment than nonadopted children.

More recent clinical studies employing comparison groups also have reported a higher rate of psychological problems in adoptees (Cohen et al., 1993; Dickson, Heffron, & Parker, 1990; Rogeness, Hoppe, Macedo, Fischer, & Harris, 1988). In addition, several studies on non-clinical populations provide evidence that adoptees from about age 6 through adolescence demonstrate more behavior problems than nonadopted children (Brodzinsky, Radice, Huffman, & Merkler, 1987; Brodzinsky, Schecter, Braff, & Singer, 1984; Brodzinsky & Steiger, 1991; Rosenthal & Groze, 1991; Ternay, Wilborn, & Day, 1985). The studies on infant adoptees stress that the vast majority of these children are well-adjusted, even though there are higher rates of behavior problems in comparing groups of adoptees to nonadopted children.

This view of adoptee vulnerability is not unanimous. Based on their study of adolescent identity formation, Stein and Hoopes (1985) conclude that adopted adolescents do not have more struggles with identity issues than their nonadopted peers. In a major study conducted by the Search Institute (Benson, Sharma, & Roehlkepartain, 1994), a large sample of adolescent adoptees and their parents was surveyed. This study concludes that adoption does not appear to have a negative effect on identity formation, mental health, or parent-child relationships. The vast majority of respondents were satisfied with the adoption. One interesting finding is that 65% of adolescent adoptees reported that they would like to meet their birth parents, which suggests that adoption is not unimportant to them. The results of both of these studies were drawn from data on children placed as infants. Although these results are encouraging about the positive outcomes of adoption, they may not predict adjustment for children placed following trauma or disrupted attachments to previous caregivers.

Although a higher rate of problems in adoptees has been substantiated by the body of research, explanations for their overrepresentation in clinical populations have been evidenced in recent studies. Warren (1992) reports that there is a lower threshold for referral among adopted adolescents. Even after controlling for extent of problems, adopted adolescents are referred to treatment more readily than nonadopted adolescents. Also, adoptive families are more likely to consider placement of the child as a solution to problems (Cohen et al., 1993). Among the clinical families studied, adoptive parents were more likely than nonadoptive parents to seek solutions that excluded the child from the home, even though the adoptive families demonstrated greater psychosocial resources and better functioning overall than biological clinical families.

Some researchers may construe the research on problems and differences in adoptive families to mean that families formed by adoption are fundamentally more problematic than families formed by birth. In reality, adoptive and birth families are much more similar than different. The point is, adoption adds a layer of complexity to family life, one that should be acknowledged and supported.

INCREASED VULNERABILITY OF
CHILDREN WITH SPECIAL NEEDS

Most adoptive families are able to negotiate their lives on their own without the need for mental health services. Some families require therapeutic counseling and specialized supportive services, however, particularly families adopting children with special needs. Many of these children have experienced physical and emotional traumas as well as disrupted attachments that continue to place special demands on them and their families. To a large extent, our understanding of the needs of families adopting special needs children has been a "learn as we go" proposition. Over the past 15 years, adoption research on special needs populations has focused primarily on the risk factors associated with disruption. Efforts of adoption workers have been focused heavily toward recruiting and preparing families as well as facilitating their adjustment during the immediate postplacement period. Only now are we recognizing that legal finalization of the adoption is not the only hurdle for achieving adoption stability.

Only a handful of follow-up studies inform our knowledge of outcomes in special needs adoptions. These studies indicate that a large majority of adoptive parents view the adoption as positive, even though many of the children demonstrate significant behavior problems (Nelson, 1985; Rosenthal & Groze, 1991, 1994). The extreme behavioral and emotional problems of some adoptees jeopardize the stability of their adoption, however (Barth & Berry, 1988; Festinger, 1986; Nelson, 1985).

Two major outcome studies of special needs adoptive families in the postlegal period have been conducted by Rosenthal and Groze (1991, 1992, 1994). They evaluated 757 adoptive families, who were receiving adoption subsidies, in three states using an extensive questionnaire and the Achenbach Child Behavior Checklist (CBC). They report elevated behavior problem scores for the adopted children, particularly on the externalizing CBC scale. A follow-up study completed 3 to 4 years later reports some increase in child behavior problems and a decrease in parental satisfaction. The authors conclude that behavioral problems for many special needs adoptees do not subside over time in their adoptive families.

A recent 1- and 2-year follow-up study by Groze (1996) yields similar findings, showing a persistence of behavioral problems and some decline in family adaptability and cohesion. Also, a 3-year follow-up study of intercountry adoptees reveals increases in problem behaviors and a decrease in competencies on the CBC. The increases were greatest on the scales for delinquent and withdrawn behaviors (Verhulst & Versluis-den Bieman, 1995). This study compares adoptees to nonadopted age mates who did not experience increased problems with age. These researchers were unable to attribute the increase in maladaptive functioning to early adverse experiences such as age at placement, neglect or abuse, and medical conditions, or to a difference in ethnicity between the parent and child. They conclude that adoption-specific factors interact negatively with factors related to adolescent development, resulting in the intensification of problems.

Nelson (1985) studied 177 special needs adoptive families with 257 adopted children. Her sample was made up of families adopting children with pronounced special needs characteristics—sibling groups of 3 or more, children age 8 or older at placement, or children with impairments. Nelson found that 62% of the children were reported to have moderate to severe behavior problems. Despite these problems, a large majority of parents evaluated their adoptions as satisfying. Twenty-seven percent of these adoptions were reported to have a pronounced negative aspect, however, that Nelson perceives as placing them at risk of dissolution. In analyzing seven dissolutions occurring in these families, Nelson reports that parents were inadequately prepared in almost all these situations, and most did not receive adequate information about their child. Also, none of the families experiencing dissolution had been connected to an adoption support group.

Erich and Leung (1998) evaluated the family functioning of 28 families adopting 69 special needs children from a single agency. They report that the majority of families had moderate to high scores on measures of family functioning. Some families reported having difficulties for which they had sought services, with the most frequently used service being family therapy. Those families who had participated in family therapy (39%) had significantly lower family functioning scores, which the authors view as an indication that they had adopted children with greater behavioral or psychological difficulties.

The primary body of research examining problems in special needs families where adoptive placement has occurred is studies examining the causes of adoption disruption. The factors contributing to adoption disruption (prior to legal finalization) have been empirically investigated with increased sophistication in studies using large sample sizes and comparison groups (Barth & Berry, 1988; Festinger, 1986; Partridge, Hornby, & McDonald, 1986; Smith & Howard, 1991). Some of the child-related factors associated with disruption include older age at adoptive placement and at removal from birth home, longer time in foster placement, a history of maltreatment, more previous placements, and multiple behavioral and emotional problems with greater severity.

In a previous study on disruption (Smith & Howard, 1991, 1994), which controlled for the child's age, we found that a past history of sexual abuse is highly associated with disruption. The child's sexual abuse experience poses particular adjustment difficulties in relation to attachment/trust issues and power/control issues (Smith & Howard, 1994). For adoptees who have experienced early childhood trauma and separations, a feeling of powerlessness and lack of control in their lives may lead to a strong need to control. Many behaviors such as lying, stealing, and defiance may result from the adoptee's efforts to maintain a sense of mastery by controlling and manipulating others. Other significant factors associated with disruption in this study include strong attachment to the birth mother and specific behavior problems. Sexual acting out is the only behavior problem that, prior to adoptive placement, was greater among the children who later disrupted. A number of behavior problems were greater among the disrupted children during the adoptive placement, particularly lying, vandalism, and sexual acting out.

In addition to the disruption of a placement prior to legal finalization of the adoption, the breakup of adoptive parent-child relationships can occur both formally and informally at a later point in time. The rates of disruption of children placed through state child welfare agencies have been documented through a number of studies and are generally reported to be around 9% to 15% (Barth & Berry, 1988; Barth, Berry, Carson, Goodfield, & Feinberg, 1986; Festinger, 1986; Urban Systems, 1985). There are few statistics on rates of dissolution, however. A recent analysis of children placed for adoption in Illinois from 1976 to 1987 reports a disruption rate of 13% and a 6.5% rate of return of adopted children to the child welfare system (Goerge, Howard, & Yu, 1996).

Policies and laws related to adoption dissolution vary from state to state, although in most states legal dissolution of an adoption is difficult to accomplish. For example, in Illinois, parents can petition the court to vacate the adoption during the first year after finalization. This will be granted only if circumstances present at the time of adoption were not brought to the court's attention. After the first year, the legal parent-child relationship becomes the same as that of birth families—parental rights are terminated only in connection with charges of abuse, neglect, or dependency. This policy is a recent change. Previously, the child welfare department could accept surrenders on adopted children when it thought surrender was in the child's best interest.

There is a national trend to discourage the annulment of final adoption decrees, known as *set-asides,* based on a consideration of the child's best interests (Bennison, 1992). Courts are more likely to grant "wrongful adoption," which carries a monetary award for damages to the adoptive parents without dissolving the family unit. Even though formal adoption dissolution is relatively rare, the adoptive parent-child relationship can break down in other ways. The parent-child relationship may fail when older teens are legally emancipated or through informal occurrences such as the child's running away, the child being sent to live elsewhere, or emotional estrangement within the family. Needless to say, these outcomes carry a high cost to all individuals involved. The emotional cost of ongoing problems is high for adoptive families even when their adoption commitment remains strong.

THE NEED FOR POST-ADOPTION SERVICES

In earlier adoption practice, workers would assist families through the adoption process to the point of legal finalization, and then the families were left to themselves. Continued involvement between the family and the agency was viewed as unhealthy interference. In the past, when adopted individuals, birth parents, or adoptive parents struggling to assist their children with adjustment problems returned to adoption agencies for help, they were referred to community services such as mental health agencies or child guidance clinics. The professionals in these community agencies often had very little awareness of adoption issues and frequently did not address the realities of their situations. Typically, any effect of adoption in leading to adjustment difficulties of children or parents was overlooked or minimized. Families who wanted to deny or not talk about adoption issues were supported in this need by professionals. Even families adopting special needs children with long histories of loss and trauma have reported that when they tried to focus on these experiences as causing problems for the child, counselors have perceived this as blaming the child for family-centered problems.

Special needs adoptive families also have found that after the adoption is legally final, they are largely on their own. Although adoption subsidies provide limited financial help, many parents find themselves with very troubled children for whom their repertoire of parenting techniques and the usual configuration of community services are inadequate. Counseling professionals seeing these children and families often do not understand many issues related to adoption, trauma, and loss. For example, one adoptive couple served by the Illinois Adoption Preservation Project reported that after seeking help from seven psychiatrists, psychologists, and social workers, this was the first time they heard the term *grief* mentioned or were helped to understand the link between their daughter's behaviors and her past loss and trauma.

The problems faced by many of these families result in ongoing crises and often a desperate search for solutions from counseling professionals. An adoptive parent served through the project expressed this experience poignantly in her written evaluation of services:

> I had gone everywhere I could think of for help. No one had proper help for us until the adoption support services. Our whole family had become dysfunctional. Our marriage was coming apart. We did not know how to cope with our daughter. No one had ever told us about any of what she was going through. We had this fantasy that adoption was the same as forming a family biologically. We were not prepared to help our children, especially our daughter, with the grieving process, the guilt, the anger.
>
> We have all grown to understand adoption and ourselves better. We've learned it's okay that we can't always take away our children's pain—but we can help them cope with it. We have become more open with our inner thoughts. We've learned to share as a family—to be supportive. It saved our family from totally splitting up. Our family has come a long way. We still need improvement. These programs give us hope that one day our family will be coping and functioning "normally." Hope that we will learn how to get through some of those barriers the trauma of the past life has formed in our daughter . . . [and helped us] get through the anger our son has. We need the adoption services!

Post-adoption services are only beginning to develop in response to adoptive families' demands for services. Among groups advocating for change in adoption practice are adoptive parents of special needs children who have sought more services to meet the needs of their families. The needs of this population have led to the creation of most postlegal adoption programs providing intensive counseling services. Also, many public and private adoption agencies have developed rather limited services to accommodate the needs of those involved in search and reunions, particularly individuals involved in adoptions arranged by the agencies.

Postlegal services are a very recent phenomenon, and they remain underdeveloped, fragmented, and in need of leadership. The knowledge and skill needed to work effectively with special needs adoptees and their parents who are coping with the complexities of grief and trauma issues is underdeveloped and not a part of the repertoire of many mental health practitioners. Those who work with adoptive families have learned much about what doesn't work in past practices, but they are still struggling to learn what does work. Much more research is needed to achieve an understanding of the sequelae of child maltreatment within a life-span perspective. Also, interventions to help children and their families in the work of healing from grief and trauma experiences are only beginning to be researched. We need a range of interventions targeted to the particular capacities of children and their developmental levels. Many of the relevant interventions that have been developed, such as attachment therapies, are very specialized and practiced in a select number of treatment centers. Partly due to the lack of research on many of these interventions, they typically have not been incorporated into professional education programs. Also, much of what we do know about the effect of adoption on children and families is not a part of professional education. Much work needs to be done to serve these families effectively.

AN OVERVIEW OF THE ILLINOIS
ADOPTION PRESERVATION PROJECT

Throughout this volume, insights gained from our evaluation of Illinois's adoption preservation program are used to illustrate the needs of troubled adoptive families and the nature of services to meet these needs. This program evaluation was the first large-scale study of families receiving post-adoption services. Illinois began the development of statewide postlegal adoption preservation services in 1991. Services to adoptive families at risk of child placement or adoption dissolution are mandated by the Illinois Family Preservation Act of 1988. These services were originated through a purchase of service contract with two private agencies, and were expanded to 11 sites over the first 3 years of its operation. Through an exploratory study, we evaluated this project, gathering data on the families referred to this program from its inception in June 1991 through November 1994. Data collection and analysis were concluded in the summer of 1995, which allowed for most new cases to complete services.

Because little was known about the needs of adoptive families after finalization and the services that were most effective, the Illinois project was characterized by slow, deliberate expansion and change in response to evaluation findings. There was close collaboration among researchers, state agency adoption coordinators, adoption preservation workers from the private agencies, and state policymakers throughout the 4 years of the evaluation. There were regular statewide meetings of all project administrators, personnel, and researchers to discuss the many facets of the needs of families and the development of services.

The Service Model of Adoption Preservation in Illinois

In Illinois, as in many states, adoption preservation services grew out of the family preservation movement. Family preservation programs seek to prevent foster care placement or to reunify children in foster care with their birth families as expeditiously as possible. These efforts, particularly the prevention of foster placement, are based on a crisis intervention model of services. The family's disequilibrium is viewed as an opportunity for effecting positive change through the provision of immediate, intensive services. The idea of the Illinois project was that services would be timely and short-term. Once the situation was stabilized, the family could be connected with community resources that would help them continue to address needs and problems for the long haul.

From its initiation, adoption preservation in Illinois had three major components: short-term, intensive services; longer-term support groups for children and parents; and linkage to community services. Other service components included 24-hour worker availability and limited use of cash assistance. Over the first year of the project, the nature and length of intensive services evolved to address the needs of the adoptive families seeking help more effectively. The original conceptual model, similar to the Homebuilders' model of services, specified 6 weeks of home-based, intense services during which families would be linked to existing community resources. About two thirds of adoptive families coming to the project had received some form of counseling previously with limited success, however. The time limit, which was extended twice during the first year of the project, was seen by workers and families alike as problematic, imposing an artificial ending in families with many long-standing problems. On follow-up forms, families overwhelmingly recommended a longer period of services.

Also, the majority of families did not require the intensity of services anticipated, and in some sites, services were moved from home to office-based for many families. This led to the development of a service model prescribing up to 6 months of intensive services with the opportunity for rereferral of families with severe needs. Thus, early research results as well as feedback from therapists led policymakers to modify the program and to design parameters and types of services more responsive to family needs. Time limits were extended, after-care services were developed, and some respite services were funded. Adoption preservation services were to be targeted to adoptive families that were at risk of dissolution or placement of the child outside the home. Most early referrals were initiated by adoptive families calling their state adoption assistance worker with a problem and consequently being referred to the private agency adoption preservation program. As the program developed, referrals also came from mental health agencies, schools, and families themselves. Former wards of the Illinois Department of Children and Family Services were the highest priority for services, but any adoptive family experiencing significant difficulties could receive services.

Design of the Evaluation Study

As a result of the collaboration described above, the research model evolved much like the service model evolved. The original research plan sought to develop a comparison group of adoptive families not receiving services from an overflow of project referrals and to compare dissolution and placement rates occurring in these two groups. This plan had to be abandoned for several reasons. The programs did not reach capacity until near the end of the first year. Also, the first two sites were very different in the types of families served. One served inner-city families, most of whom were African American and had adopted foster children. The other served a suburban population with fewer minority or foster-adoptive families. Finding equivalent groups for comparison seemed improbable. It also became obvious that, due to the difficulty of dissolving an adoption in Illinois, very few legal dissolutions were likely to occur, so comparison of dissolution rates was not a useful measure. It became evident that an exploratory, descriptive study of the nature of problems in referred families and the nature of outcomes of services was most relevant to the early stage of knowledge development in adoption preservation. Consequently, this evaluation focused on the following objectives:

1. To describe the nature of problems and needs in the families who seek adoption preservation services
2. To determine the factors associated with severity of child and family problems as well as with parents' desire to end the adoption

3. To analyze the nature of emotional and behavioral problems of adopted children served by the project and to examine the connection between child behavior problems and trauma, separation, grief, attachment, and adoption identity issues

4. To describe the characteristics and goals of interventions developed through the project

5. To evaluate the outcomes of adoption preservation services both at the conclusion of services and after a follow-up period

6. To include, to the extent possible, the perspectives of adoptive parents, children, and workers in this evaluation

Strengths and Limitations of the Research Design

The ongoing development of the service model of this project in response to research findings tailored services to client needs; however, "learning and changing as we go" is also the biggest limitation of this study from a research perspective. The service model that was evaluated during the first year of the project was different from the service model evaluated during the fourth year. The fact that the project existed in only two sites during the first year and that the vast majority of families were served later offsets this limitation somewhat. Also, the original service model was not built on a clear theoretical model or on previous research due to the lack of knowledge on post-adoption services. When there is no true theoretical base, the appropriate questions for research are less clear. Decisions about what to measure and how to measure were modified somewhat during the early stages of the evaluation.

Although this change poses difficulties in dealing with quantitative data, it has been a real aid in interpreting results and learning from qualitative data. In fact, the blending of quantitative and qualitative research methods is one of the greatest strengths of this study. Regular discussion with workers about what works, what doesn't, and with whom, as well as obtaining feedback from many families, has added a richness and depth to this evaluation that is not possible in purely quantitative studies.

Another strength of this evaluation is the collaboration among administrators, workers, and researchers and between the public child welfare agency and private agencies. A feedback loop developed in which workers raised issues based on their practice insights, and we explored these with available data. Workers also assisted in understanding the meaning of certain research findings that seemed to run counter to our current understanding.

Data Sources and Study Variables

Originally, four forms were developed to provide an overview of family needs and services—a referral form, an initial family assessment form, an overview of services form, and family follow-up forms. The first three forms were completed by adoption preservation workers, who were primarily clinical social workers. Early in 1993, at the point the program expanded to five sites, the Achenbach Child Behavior Checklist (CBC) was incorporated, to be completed by both parents at intake and at termination. We also developed a questionnaire to be completed by parents to gain their perspective on the quality of the parent-child relationship and dissolution risk, as well as follow-up forms for the parent and child support groups. Additional sources of data include interviews with project staff, observation of some parent and child support groups, and follow-up phone interviews with some families.

The worker-completed forms survey a range of assessment information on the child and family's history, family composition, identified problems, child behavior problems, attachment issues, family stresses and strengths, previous services received, goals established and level of participation of various family members in identifying each goal, and ratings of parents' views of the problems and children's primary concerns. Data collected on the nature and outcomes of services cover such variables as the level of achievement of goals, child placement information, length and intensity of services, types of services provided, any child maltreatment allegations, and a worker rating of emotional issues present in work with the adopted child.

Data were collected on a total of 401 families with 453 focus children (adopted children seen as needing adoption preservation services) who were referred to the program. Forty-eight families received more than one round of intensive services. Not all referred families became engaged in services. Assessment forms were not completed on families who refused or left services during the 3-week assessment period. Altogether, assessment data were available on 368 children in 331 families and service information was available on 325 families with 357 children. The project staff overall were conscientious about submission of worker-completed forms; however, some sites were inconsistent in administering parent-completed instruments and mailing follow-up forms.

Some measures used for specific variables are summarized below.

Severity of Behavior Problems

Two measures were used for evaluating child behavior problems during the study. A total behavior problem score drawn from a Behavior Problem Rating List on the assessment form was used as a measure of the severity of child behavior problems. (This list of problem behaviors most frequently cited among special needs children in the literature was developed by us and used in a previous study on adoption disruption.) In the initial assessment, workers in collaboration with parents evaluated the list of 22 behavior problems as 0 = not present, 1 = moderate problems, or 2 = severe problem. These values were summed to yield a total behavior problem score. This score is a measure of behavioral difficulty of the child and does not reflect other indicators of emotional disturbance, such as thought disorders or somatic complaints, which are contained on the CBC. The CBC, which was added in 1993, was available on fewer children (n = 223), but provides the advantage of being a standardized instrument, thus enabling comparison to other populations of children.

Dissolution Risk

A question on the service form as to whether parents raised dissolution as an option was used as a measure of dissolution risk.

Underlying Child Issues

The presence of seven specific child issues (separation/attachment conflicts, depression, grief, posttraumatic stress symptoms, problems related to child's need to search, identity issues, and organically based problems) that may have contributed to problems for the child were assessed by workers as present, not present, and unsure. Workers also were asked to describe the child's perceptions of problems in as close to the child's own words as possible. (In the majority of cases, workers worked individually with the adopted children and the parents, as well as seeing the family together. Some workers did not rate these issues on cases where they had limited contact, however.)

Family Strengths

A list of 20 strengths of adoptive parents that the researchers and the initial project staff compiled as relevant to positive adjustment in adoptive families was evaluated by the adoption preservation workers. For example, some of these items include previous parenting experience, knowing and being comfortable with the child's preadoptive history, having contact with other adoptive families, having supportive extended family, having a reasonable degree of flexibility in dealing with children, and having a sustaining religious faith.

Separation and Attachment Issues

In addition to other child and family history characteristics surveyed, 12 specific child conditions theorized to influence separation and attachment issues for children or parents were evaluated as present or not present. These included such items as the child had a strong fantasy or wish to be reunited with birth family, the child received no clear disengagement message from previous attachment figures, the child had an ongoing fear of the birth family, the child rejected overtures of inclusion in the adoptive family, and the child idealized the birth parent or a previous caretaker. Workers also assessed evidence of attachment problems in all family relationships—mother to child, child to mother, and so on.

Family Stresses and Problems

Sixteen specific stressors, including a miscellaneous category, were assessed as not present, moderate, and severe. These variables included financial problems, marital problems and divorce, death of a family member, job loss, and others. Also, the presence of a number of presenting problems was assessed by workers and evaluated as worker identified and/or family identified. These included a range of possible problems from behavior problems of the child to conditions such as substance abuse of parent and a deficit in the parent's emotional care of the child.

*Previous Problem-Solving Attempts and
Degree of Helpfulness*

A list of possible measures for addressing the problems over the past was assessed, as well as the parent's view of the extent of helpfulness of these measures. The measures included formal helping systems such as psychiatric hospitalization and various types of counseling, as well as informal methods such as stricter discipline and increased parental or child absence from the home.

Service Variables

Data on a number of aspects of the services provided were gathered, including the length and hours of service, the types of supportive and concrete services provided, the worker's assessment of the degree of helpfulness of various services, referral services provided, the five strategies and practice techniques relied on most often, plans for aftercare services, reason for case termination, assessment of the family's response to service and level of involvement of various family members, the worker's assessment of needed resources that were not available, any child maltreatment allegations in the case, and the adopted child's perceptions of problems.

Outcomes

Case outcomes examined include family status at the conclusion of services (including whether a child was out of the home at the conclusion of services, actual dissolutions, and worker assessment of dissolution risk); change in children's scores on the CBC; workers' rating of overall success; level of goal attainment of established goals; and parent evaluation of services.

A comprehensive report of this study is contained in the monograph, *Adoption Preservation in Illinois: Results of a Four-Year Study* (Howard & Smith, 1995).

**Description of Population Served in
Adoption Preservation**

The majority of adoptees served by this project were children designated as special needs. Overall, 73% of the referred children were former wards of the Illinois Department of Children and Family Services, and 57% were receiving adoption assistance payments from Illinois. Of the 27% who were not former Illinois wards, approximately two thirds were infant adoptions, followed by children who were adoptees with special needs from other states, as well as a small number of intercountry adoptees.

The most common type of adoption in referred families was stranger adoption (49%), with foster parent adoptions making up 36%, and relative adoptions making up 15%. Most families were two-parent families (72%), with single-parent families headed by mothers making up 25% and father-only families making up 2%.

The majority of children in referred families were Caucasian (55%), followed by minority children, of whom 34% were African American, 9% Hispanic, and 2% of other racial origin. Most children were placed with families of the same race, although 14.5% were placed trans-racially.

Families receiving adoption preservation services typically had had their children in their homes for a considerable length of time (mean = 8.9 years). Workers often described the parents as "at the end of their rope," having grappled with family problems for a number of years, with repeated attempts to receive help. Forty-five percent of the families whose cases had closed raised dissolution as an option at some point during services. Although this percentage is large, it is important to note that the majority of parents do not enter services articulating a desire to end the adoption. Further, even when dissolution is raised, families are not necessarily desiring it but may feel that they have run out of alternatives. For example, even among those who raised dissolution as an option, 50% were rated by workers as committed to keeping their child.

The age of the children at the time of referral for services is presented in Table 1.1. The data indicate that 61% of children served were 12 or older, with the modal age being 15. The gender of children served was 53% male and 47% female.

The placement history of the children served indicates that the majority were very young when they were initially removed from their birth families, as well as when they were placed into the homes of their adoptive families. The mean age for initial removal was 1.8 years; for placement into the adoptive home, the mean age was 3.4 years. The mean age for legal adoption was 5.6 years. For all children served, the mean number of placements prior to their adoptive placement was 1.76. Twenty-four percent of the children experienced no placement moves between their birth families and adoptive families, and 21% experienced more than three moves in care prior to adoptive placement, ranging up to 18 for one child. Also, 9% of these children experienced a disrupted adoptive placement prior to being adopted by their family.

Table 1.1
Age of Adopted Children Served

Age	n	Percent
3-5	19	4.2%
6-7	30	6.6
8-9	63	13.9
10-11	66	14.6
12-13	94	20.8
14-15	104	23.0
16-17	68	15.0
18+	9	1.9
Total	453	100 %

Children served by this project were more likely to have had court-ordered termination of parental rights than voluntary surrenders by birth parents. The court terminated the rights of both parents for 37% and one parent for 34% of children, with 25% being voluntarily surrendered and 4% coming to adoption through parental death or other circumstances.

It is important to recognize that the families served by this project are at the far end of a continuum of all adoptions in relation to the level of problems and adoption instability. It cannot be assumed that this population of families is representative of special needs adoptees in Illinois; rather, it represents special needs adoptive families experiencing serious difficulties who sought services. The nature of the problems they experienced and the types of services designed to address these problems are the focus of the rest of this volume.

Chapter 2

EVERY CLINICIAN IS IN POST-ADOPTION PRACTICE

Adoption is perceived as an unusual social phenomenon. Yet every adopted child has birth and adoptive parents; birth and adoptive grandparents and likely aunts, uncles, and cousins; and often birth and adoptive siblings. Most adopted children grow up to engage in intimate relationships and to have families of their own. Issues related to adoption, loss, trauma, identity, the meaning of parenthood, and the meaning of family may resonate throughout the family and social network of the adopted person, the adopting family, and the birth family. Thus, adoption touches many people.

Further, the phenomenon of adoption includes many of the central topics of the therapeutic endeavor. As Reitz and Watson (1992) note, "Adoption is a powerful experience that touches upon universal human themes of abandonment, parenthood, sexuality, identity and sense of belonging" (p. 3).

Helping professionals of all types will encounter issues related to adoption in their work. Many will fail to understand the significance of adoption in the lives of clients, however, and its connection to other aspects of clients' struggles. They will miss the opportunity to help clients come to terms with this fundamental human issue.

As discussed in Chapter 1, early practice in adoption was predicated on the notion that adoptive families were best served by treating them like families formed through birth. Agencies' careful efforts to match children and parents created families where adoption could be undetectable. The child's status (often a child born out of wedlock) was hidden, as was the adoptive parents' infertility. The birth mother was excluded from knowledge about the family with whom her child was placed, a strategy that enhanced the ability of the adoptive family to be just like a birth family. Such separation was presented as a way to help the birth mother understand the loss as permanent, encouraging her to "get on with her life." The needs of birth fathers and extended family members were rarely addressed.

Likewise, adoptive parents received very limited information about their children. The goal was to help the adopting families claim the children as their own. Societal support for the idea that nurture matters more than nature reinforced the idea of the infant as *tabula rasa,* whose history was significant in that it created the child, not that it influenced the child over time.

The adoption worker was a central player in finding available children and placing them with the "right" families. The expansion and professionalization of adoption practice meant that a skilled decision by a trained worker was critical. The middle-class background of most adoption workers as well as prevailing social standards about what constituted a good home meant a preference for infertile, financially stable couples. Foster parents, single parents, relatives, and others who might have provided adoptive homes were often excluded from consideration.

Early adoption practice was based on the view that secrecy in adoption promoted the sense of a true family. Later practice, though somewhat more open, relied on secrecy to protect the child and his or her adoptive family from the child's damaging past. Such practice came from the same roots—the view of the worker as expert, the birth family as dangerous or deviant, and the child as best served by treating the adoptive family as a family formed by birth. In this way, our entire society, including child welfare and mental health practitioners, ignored or minimized the effect of adoption on a family.

The adoption field changed in its view of who can be adopted and who can adopt; but services to families, particularly after adoptive placement, did not substantially change. With the exception of subsidy, once the adoption was finalized, adoptive families were left to their own devices, as "real" families were. Even families adopting children with special needs were expected to find support for those needs within the larger community of helping services, just like any other family.

The idea that adoptive families are different from those formed from birth is discussed in Chapter 1. Yet the myth of sameness (that the issues encountered in adoptive families are identical to those in families formed through birth) has been perpetuated by the very experts who have the skills to help families. Time, experience, and the growing openness of birth parents, adopted people, and adoptive parents have led to a new understanding. Forming a family through adoption *is* different, adding auxiliary challenges to those all families must meet. Adoptive placement of older children and children who often have experienced interrupted attachment and trauma has led to even greater challenges for adoptive families. All can compromise the child's ability to join with and be accepted by a family.

Families adopting children with special needs may face particular challenges: interrupted attachments, the effect of trauma and loss, unresolved grief, and emotional and physical disabilities. Adopted children join and alter a family system, as do birth children. Significant accommodations to one another by children and parents must occur. The balance of the system is altered, and the resulting disequilibrium can yield new roles, rules, and accommodations when adoption occurs. Although some families are able to integrate a child after a period of adjustment, others continue struggling for years to develop a comfortable balance in parenting children with complicated histories. Also, as children develop and family situations evolve, new challenges present themselves.

ADOPTIVE FAMILIES AND SOCIAL SERVICES

Many adoptive families use social services beyond the point of adoption finalization. The adoption literature notes the overrepresentation of adopted children in special education, outpatient mental health services, psychiatric hospitals, and residential treatment facilities (Brodzinsky et al., 1987; Brodzinsky et al., 1992; Kirschner & Nagel, 1988; Kotsopolous et al., 1988; McRoy et al., 1988; Warren, 1992). One state's (Massachusetts) study of children in specialized care found that at least 12% of children in its residential and inpatient programs were adopted (Landers, Forsythe, & Nickman, 1996).

There has been debate about whether adopted children and their families actually face greater problems that require the use of services or whether other factors account for their overrepresentation. Some studies have found that adoptees are considerably more likely to have had psychiatric treatment, but not solely because they exhibited more problems (Kotsopolous et al., 1988; Warren, 1992). They suggest that the family system and the larger community may see adoption as a particular risk factor so that problems of family life may be wrongly attributed to adoption. Also, issues of identity may pose particular struggles for adopted children, especially given the lingering sense of stigma associated with adoption. Another contributing factor is that adoptive parents, often middle class or systems wise, are more oriented to using services. The fact remains that many adoptive families use mental health and family counseling services after the adoption is finalized.

Both anecdotal and empirical evidence suggest that services for adoptive families are lacking. Frey (1986) surveyed 20 adoption agencies in one state. The most common postplacement need identified by adoption professionals was for qualified, adoption-sensitive mental health professionals. One agency receiving a federal grant for a post-adoption program established a referral network as part of its services. It reported that 75% of its initial calls were from parents seeking a referral to a therapist who had knowledge about adoption and its effect on children and families (Franz, 1993).

When asked directly, families echo this need for therapists and counselors who are more knowledgeable about adoption and skilled in folding adoption issues into individual and family counseling. Needs surveys of adoptive parents have found that mental health counseling is identified by parents as the major unmet need encountered after adoption (Massachusetts Department of Mental Health, 1994; Nelson, 1985; Reitnauer & Grabe, 1985).

The community mental health facility seems a natural source of help for adoptive families. Although such facilities are available and affordable, many adoptive parents report being dissatisfied with the services they received there (Reitnauer & Grabe, 1985). Often the families have to use their own experience and resources to educate the professionals whose job it is to help them.

The experiences of parents in the Illinois Adoption Preservation Project underscore these concerns. Typically, families sought help prior to becoming connected to adoption preservation. Over two thirds of families sought formal assistance. The most common service used was individual counseling for the child (68% of children), followed by family counseling (35%), individual counseling for the parent (31%), parent support groups (15%), and support groups for children (10%). In addition, 26% of children had been hospitalized in a psychiatric setting, and 10% had other types of formal placement outside the home since the adoption. Parents also evaluated the helpfulness of previously used services. For example, individual counseling with the child was rated as not helpful by 45% of parents, and somewhat helpful by 46%, with only 9% rating it very helpful. Although used infrequently, parent support groups and child support groups were the services most likely to be identified as very helpful.

Anecdotal information from parents reveals a number of concerns about the nature of help received. Families report that helping professionals:

- view the family as pathological, sometimes questioning the parents' motives for adoption;
- imply or state that the parent is blaming the child for family problems when the parent raises the need for discussion of adoption issues to be part of treatment;
- lack awareness of the particular needs of children adopted cross-racially, older children, and those adopted in sibling groups;
- frame the child's behavior problems as a means to act out problems in the larger family system without understanding the problems the child brought into the family;
- lack knowledge about adoption and the effect of loss on adopted children, the need for the child to grieve, and the issue of divided loyalty often felt by children;
- advise parents to avoid talking about adoption with the child because it will only "stir things up";
- fail to assess child and family needs thoroughly, including failure to gain information about the child's history, both in the child's birth family and in the child welfare system;
- address child behavior problems through behavioral methods without exploring how these behaviors (such as hoarding food or constant lying) are connected to past deprivation or trauma;
- urge psychiatric hospitalization without understanding the effect of hospitalization on a child with a history of abandonment and rejection;
- ally themselves with the child as the victim in a dysfunctional family and blame the parents for the child's emotional and behavioral problems; and
- suggest the parents return the child to the state, failing to understand that this is not the goal of the parents, nor possible in most situations.

These problems identified by some parents in the Illinois Adoption Preservation Project are representative of those reported by providers of post-adoption services in many states. Concern about the dearth of helping professionals with understanding of adoption issues led to a federal initiative to address this problem. The U.S. Children's Bureau's Adoption Opportunities grants added a postlegal category. Forty-two projects received grants to develop training and support to professionals beyond the traditional adoption practice community. The proposal of one grantee raises issues identified by many:

> The lack of therapeutic resources for adoptive families who seek treatment continues to be a crucial problem, particularly in outlying areas. . . . The significance of adoption issues continues to be ignored or dismissed by many . . . therapists. The mental health focus is most often on visible behaviors rather than on feelings of loss, rejection, and abandonment. (Van Patten, 1992, cited in Howard & Smith, 1997, p. 10)

The experience of one training project provides an illustration of the resistance of some mental health practitioners to the idea that adoption issues are important in treatment. This project used outreach teams of adoptive parents and social workers to provide in-services to mental health centers and residential treatment centers. The attempts met with limited success. Those who were identified as appropriate targets for training seemed distrustful of the expertise of the presenters or "believed adoption issues were of no concern to their clients" (Backhaus, 1989, p. 64). The reaction of the adoptive parents and social workers to this response was instructive:

> Interestingly, it was the social workers who were most discouraged by the mental health community's response to the teams, and it was the adoptive parents who were able to offer the social workers support. The adoptive parents were used to having their information and contributions devalued by professionals they said, and so were not discouraged by the initial response. (Backhaus, 1989, p. 64)

CORE ISSUES OF ADOPTION

What should helping professionals understand to serve adoptive families better? A review of descriptive articles and training materials for mental health and other professionals identifies several basic concepts held as central to effective intervention with adoptive families. Although there has been little empirical testing of some of these premises, they appear so often in the adoption literature as to be articles of faith in adoption practice.

Adoption Is Different Than Birth

Forming families through adoption is different than forming families by birth, introducing additional challenges to child well-being and family functioning (Bourguinon & Watson, 1987; Small, 1987). These challenges are heightened by lack of social support for adoption, absence of ritual or custom, and lingering stigma (Miall, 1987; Rosenberg, 1992). Such differences may diminish a sense of entitlement—that children and parents truly belong to one another (Bourguinon & Watson, 1987). Social attitudes that hold that adoptive parents are not *real* parents can be compounded by helping professionals who unwittingly underscore this by excluding parents from the therapeutic process. Parents need to be involved as allies in the therapeutic process, and their expertise and understanding of their child need to be acknowledged. Adoptive parents may need assurance that information about their child will be shared with them and that they will be partners with the therapist. Even (or perhaps especially) if the child is placed outside of the home, the adopted child is entitled to family relationships, and the family is entitled to ongoing connection and involvement.

Adoption Is a Lifelong Process

Helping professionals must recognize that adoption is a process, not an event. Adoption has salience across the individual and family life span (Brodzinsky et al., 1992), with somewhat predictable points where its importance looms larger. Adolescence, with its challenges of separation and individuation and identity formation, can be a particularly complex time. For adopted children with developmental delays or a history of maltreatment, age and developmental stage may be different.

The Effect of Loss

The effect of loss, and its centrality to the adoption process, cannot be underestimated. Adoption is not possible without loss. Children experience "the loss of relationships with emotionally significant objects, the symbolic loss of roots, genetic identity, and a sense of connectedness" (Small, 1987, p. 36). Although some of these losses are apparent (a child never sees a remembered and loved birth parent again), losses of possibility also can affect children. Having no clear memory of lost birth family members does not mean loss is not felt. Many adopted children have additional losses. They may have lost relationships with foster parents and other caretakers, birth or foster siblings, friends, schoolmates, and neighborhoods.

Many adoptive parents have lost the ability to form a family through birth. Losses include those related to continuation of self, the joining of parental selves through a biological child, the continuation of biological lineage, and control over one's destiny. The process of adoption may heighten awareness of loss. Those who have problems with fertility may have to account for how they have come to terms with this great loss. Those adopting children with special needs are subject to the approval of professionals who must deem them worthy. Further, both parents and children may have *unmatched expectations* about what adoption may bring. The hopes for closeness, mutuality, and warm and sustaining family times may be unrealized, representing yet another loss.

Families face additional losses once a child has joined them. Death, divorce, and even moving can have more serious ramifications for struggling adopted children than for other children. Also, parents may be reluctant to discuss losses in the family. They desire to protect children from the pain of loss. They may wish to avoid revisiting the pain of their own losses. Examination of losses is essential to helping children grieve, however (Silverstein & Kaplan, 1988). When such examination is superficial and when children are given simplistic and unchanging stories about the loss of a family, parents convey that learning the truth is not okay (Small, 1987).

Loss is healed through grief. The adoptive family and those working with them need to be familiar with grief as a process that will be revisited over time. Developmental changes or tasks (such as adolescence, marriage, or childbirth) as well as new losses will trigger grief, and its natural expression will enhance the family's ability to recover.

Brodzinsky and colleagues (1992) suggest that some behavior seen as pathological in adopted children is actually maladaptive grieving. When children have not been able to grieve their losses, their attempts to grieve can look like serious emotional disturbance, behavior problems, or attachment problems. In an attempt to make sense of their unusual status (being raised by a family they were not born to), adopted children may interpret this loss as rejection, that they were not wanted by their families because they were flawed or worthless (Reitz & Watson, 1992; Silverstein & Kaplan, 1988). One child explained her adoption this way: "My [birth] mother took one look at me and said 'YUK!' " Other children served by the Illinois project mentioned their difficulties in understanding why their birth mothers (mentioned far more often than birth fathers) rejected them, and offered this as an explanation for why it was hard to feel accepted by adoptive parents. As Small (1987) states, "If we rate rejection from 1-10, being given up by your mother rates a 10" (p. 38). Children may respond to feelings of rejection by rejecting others before they have a chance to be rejected. Others become overly eager to please, anxious to prove their worth and be accepted (Silverstein & Kaplan, 1988).

The Effect of Previous Maltreatment on Family Functioning

Struggling adoptive families are often not dealing with adoption per se, but with the factors responsible for the child's becoming available for adoption. Maltreatment, trauma, prenatal exposure to substances, deprivation, lack of stimulation, and a host of other complicating factors can impair children and affect their adjustment in their adoptive families. Trauma can impede normal development and reduce a child's ability to trust. Maltreatment that impedes attachment can delay or prevent the formation of a conscience and the capacity for empathy. Sexual abuse can impede capacity for intimacy or can lead to behaviors that disturb parents and make the child seem dangerous or damaged. Parents should receive a full accounting of the experiences of their children before adoptive placement. In particular, they must be helped to understand the current and anticipated effects of maltreatment on their child. Because the effect of maltreatment may not manifest itself until years after the adoption, helping professionals must retrieve the child's history and help the family make sense of the child's behavior in light of his or her past.

It also is important for children to have a sense of their past in ways that allow them to feel proud and confident. People adopting special needs children must walk a fine line, honoring aspects of the child's past while helping children understand the experience of maltreatment. One adoptive mother found this to be a complicated psychological task:

> This is my dilemma. When I think of the abuses heaped on my child by her birth parents, and all the struggles she has had as a result, it is hard

for me not to hate them for the harm they caused. On the other hand, if they hadn't hurt her, she wouldn't have been taken away, and she wouldn't be my daughter. And if it weren't for them, she wouldn't look the way she does, have many of the talents that she does. It's complicated.

Problems in Attachment

Attachment is developed though a cycle of child need and caretaker response. When the infant or young child's basic needs are met, children learn to depend on the caretaker and modify their behavior to keep the caretaker close. Further, the caretaker becomes attached to the child as the child responds to the caretaker's ministrations. In attachment relationships, both parties gain, learning that they have the capacity to influence the behavior of another to meet emotional and physical needs. Some adopted children received basic nurturing and little maltreatment. These children may develop attachments more readily, particularly if they are helped to grieve the losses they have experienced. Children with serious organically based problems (such as fetal alcohol syndrome) and/or a history of severe maltreatment may demonstrate significant problems in attachment. Adopted children with special needs will fall along a continuum of attachment. What the child has learned to expect about trust, intimacy, and caretaker dependability may be quite different from what the adoptive parent wishes to provide. Adoptive parents may experience great frustration as their attempts to comfort or nurture their children are thwarted because the child rejects closeness. Sometimes the child's dependency needs are so great as to appear to be a black hole of need that can never be filled. Attachment is a two-way street. The child may have the capacity to attach, but parents may find that their ability to attach to a child is complicated by other factors, such as physical or temperamental differences. Parents may believe that such a mismatch would not have occurred with a child born to them.

Identity

Both adoptive parents and the adopted child must incorporate "being adopted" into their sense of self. Kirk (1984) and others have spoken to the importance of accepting adoption as a central facet of the family, rather than denying or overemphasizing its importance. But how does this occur when there are so few models for how to "become" an adoptive family? Role theory holds that roles are problematic when the person has not developed a preliminary definition of role, the appropriate role is unknown, or there is lack of consensus between the individual and others about the definition of the role, all of which can apply in adoptive families (DiGiuilo, 1987). Adoptive parenthood diverges from the norm, and there are few examples on which to base one's role assumption. Exploring the meaning of adoption to all parties can help families achieve an identity as an adoptive family beyond stereotypical identities that stigmatize or overidealize adoption.

For the adopted child, integrating adoption into personal identity can be particularly complex. Brodzinsky and colleagues (1992) adapted Erikson's developmental framework as a basis for understanding identity formation in childhood. In this view, adoption interacts with identity formation at two major points in childhood—early latency (when a child comes to understand the difference of his or her family life and begins to consider loss) and adolescence (when physical changes coupled with the tasks of individuation and separation lead to a resurgence of questions about past and future). The adopted child must consider the classic question of "Who am I?" from the perspective of both adoptive and original family. When information about the birth family is limited, distorted, hidden, or primarily negative, the task of incorporating the past into the self is more difficult. Families often seek intervention at the point when the pushes and pulls of adolescence lead children into the expression of feelings or the display of behaviors that disturb their parents.

Mastery and Control

It is a basic human desire to feel a sense of competence and personal power in one's life. Adoptive families often encounter obstacles to the fulfillment of this desire. A lack of power over how a family will be formed (the case with infertility) is present for some parents. Further, adoptive parents are investigated and judged as part of the adoption process. Thus, their ability to form a family through adoption also is in the control of someone else. Adopted children may have no power to realize their desire to be raised in the family that created them. Although older children may be consulted about decisions to place them for adoption, the final decision about if to place them and with whom is typically in the control of others. Likewise, children had no control over the maltreatment that led them into the child welfare system (Prew, Suter, & Carrington, 1990).

Reactions to powerlessness are evident in struggling adoptive families (Silverstein & Kaplan, 1988). Children who have little opportunity for mastery (as is the case with many neglected children) may be unable to develop self-control. They may engage in behavior that elicits strong parental response in an effort to reestablish a familiar pattern or simply to have an adult take charge. Children who strive to gain or regain a sense of control may seek to control all aspects of their environment, rejecting parental affection and guidance or struggling against limits set by parents. Control battles are common in struggling adoptive families as each party seeks to gain power.

The issues listed above support the idea of adoption as a process rather than an event. As the family experiences changes, issues will reemerge. Helping professionals must be skilled in exploring the role adoption plays in family issues and the interaction between adoption issues and family experiences.

RANGE OF PROFESSIONALS INVOLVED
WITH ADOPTIVE FAMILIES

Ann Hartman (1991) states that every clinician is in post-adoption practice. This statement is recognition of the fact that adoption is an important aspect of a family system and that all practitioners will serve families whose lives are influenced by adoption. An example of one family's interaction with the helping system illustrates how many types of professionals have the opportunity to work with adoptive families.

Shannon, an African American child of 13, was adopted at the age of 4 by the Baileys. The Baileys had one older child by birth, and had raised two grandchildren. They had been foster parents for the public child welfare department for about 5 years when Shannon was placed in their home as a foster child. Shannon had had no other foster placements, but had moved often prior to her mother's being indicated for neglect. Sometimes she was in the company of her mother, Chanel, as the mother moved in with male partners. On at least three occasions, Chanel left Shannon with acquaintances with no clear plan for Chanel's return. There is a suggestion in the case records that Shannon may have been sexually abused in one of these arrangements. Shannon was placed in foster care when a caretaker contacted police after Shannon had been left

with her for a week and Chanel had not returned. After her placement at age 3, Shannon had intermittent contact with Chanel, who
was presumed to be using drugs. Chanel voluntarily relinquished
her parental rights, on the condition that the Baileys would adopt.
The Baileys have heard through the grapevine that Chanel has had
several more children, all of whom are now in the child welfare
system. The Baileys do not talk about Chanel with Shannon, nor
have they explored her feelings about adoption. Family members
have advised them to treat Shannon like a child born to them. They
fear that bringing up adoption will make Shannon feel "second
class." Further, they don't want her to identify with her troubled
birth mother.

Despite her chaotic early life, Shannon had a fairly calm and
comfortable childhood. But at about age 8, Shannon became
withdrawn and very quiet, something remarked on by her teachers
and a church group leader. Shannon reported feeling "sad and
alone" and wondering why she couldn't be with her birth mother.
The Baileys, on the advice of their pastor, took Shannon to a
family counselor. The Baileys felt the counselor was a nice person
but didn't have much to offer them. She seemed more interested
in their marriage than in Shannon. Shannon began to spend more
time with friends and be a bit more outgoing, and after a few
meetings, sessions were stopped. Things were quiet for about
3 years. Then Shannon embarked on a stormy adolescence. Her
parents reported that around age 11, her grades began to drop and
she began skipping school. By the age of 12, she was associating
with children the Baileys were concerned about, including girls
who exhibited some signs of gang affiliation or interest. She
stopped her involvement in the church's youth choir, an activity
she had long enjoyed. She began dressing provocatively despite
Mr. and Mrs. Bailey's protests. She became increasingly disre-
spectful to Mrs. Bailey, to the point of swearing at her and using
obscenity when Mrs. Bailey set limits. On two occasions, she
stormed out of the house and was gone overnight, leaving the
Baileys frantically worried for her safety. She told the Baileys she
no longer wanted to live with them because they were too old and
strict and not her real parents.

As experienced parents and foster parents, the Baileys thought
they had the skills to raise a child with a complicated past. They
received little preparation for adoption, agreeing with their case-
worker that their relationship with Shannon was strong and that
the adoption was merely a legal formalization of an already strong
emotional bond. Shannon's behavior caused them embarrassment
in their neighborhood and church community. Their inability to
control her behavior led them to question their abilities as parents
and wonder if they were too old to take on this responsibility. Their
grown son and grandchildren, who lived in the neighborhood and
were an active part of the Bailey family, grew disgusted with
Shannon's behavior and were very angry at her treatment of the
Baileys.

Over the next 6 months, Mr. and Mrs. Bailey became increasingly
strict with Shannon. Mr. Bailey enforced a strict curfew, with privileges earned only if Shannon attended school each day, did her
chores, and abided by house rules. Shannon grew more resentful and
angry. As her behavior worsened, the Baileys became more intrusive, searching Shannon's room and belongings when she was
gone. The Baileys discovered that Shannon had received birth
control information from a local family planning clinic and feared
she was sexually active. Mrs. Bailey expressed fears that Shannon
would turn out "just like her mother." When the Baileys insisted
Shannon no longer see the 17-year-old she identified as her boy-
friend, she superficially cut her wrists and was hospitalized in an
adolescent psychiatric unit. After her discharge, her behaviors
continued unabated. She failed several eighth grade classes and
skipped most of her summer school classes and tutoring sessions.
With a referral from the hospital, the Baileys attended counseling
at the office of a community-based mental health provider.
Shannon was reluctant to participate in these sessions, calling
them a waste of time. She stated that everybody was blaming her
for everything, when all she wanted to do was be a normal teenager.
The therapist worked with Mr. and Mrs. Bailey to establish a system of rewards and punishments meant to alter Shannon's behavior and increase her freedom, if she earned it. After three sessions,
Shannon ignored all the rules and refused to return to the therapist.

Shannon angrily stated to Mrs. Bailey, "You're not my real mother!" a statement that Mrs. Bailey found particularly hurtful. Also, Shannon began insisting that she wanted to find her birth family.

In this case scenario, the family interacted with a number of systems. In none of them was Shannon's past explored or her questions, concerns, or feelings about adoption addressed. Nor were her parents' concerns about adoption examined. Despite repeated opportunities, the helping system ignored the effect of adoption on this family.

The Placing Agency

Foster care and adoption are different, and children and families may not move smoothly from one status to the other. Adoption requires the child to give up aspects of his or her original family (including surname and often contact with birth family members) and formally to become a part of a different family. Children can experience conflicted loyalty and guilt about abandoning siblings and troubled birth parents. Even when there is a close emotional connection between foster parent and child, adoption, particularly coupled with the normal challenges of adolescence, can alter the balance. Foster parents need careful preparation and support. Group preparation for adoption, including the opportunity for foster parents to interact with experienced adoptive parents, can help foster parents understand the differences between adoption and foster care from their child's perspective. Part of preparation for adoption should include helping parents understand adoption as a lifelong process, and to prepare for developmental challenges. The child's need to talk about being adopted and his or her questions or concerns about birth family members should be part of the preparation. Workers could help the family prepare or review a *lifebook*, stressing the importance of providing the child with age-appropriate information. The adoptive parents need direction in honoring the positive aspects of the birth family while helping the child understand his or her limitations. The family could be connected with a support group for children and parents in the early phases of adoption. Further, information on resources available to help adoptive families should problems arise in the future should be provided.

The School

Schools have great potential for early intervention with troubled adopted children. Virtually all adopted children will attend school. Selective information sharing of the child's history with teachers, support personnel, and administrators could alert them to issues with which an adopted child may struggle. In Shannon's case, a teacher noted she was noticeably more difficult following an assignment in which the children had to carry an egg around for a week pretending it was a baby. Collaboration between the school and the family can help the school interpret children's needs in light of adoption and help parents use the school as an "early warning system." For example, Shannon's decline in academic performance could signal increasing preoccupation with adoption issues.

The Family Counselor

Those counseling adoptive families need to include adoption in their understanding of family dynamics. What does it mean to the Baileys that Shannon's behavior is so different from that of the other children they have raised? How can their sense of competence as parents be strengthened? How can the entire family be helped to understand that Shannon's desire to know more about her birth family is normal? How can they be helped to examine Shannon's feelings and behavior in light of her experiences and her developmental stage? Connection to a support group and providing information about adopted child development could provide a context for the Baileys to see their child's needs as normal and common.

The Psychiatric Unit

Adopted children are significantly overrepresented in psychiatric facilities. Shannon's adoption history, including significant losses, lack of continuity in care, and possible sexual abuse, needs to be explored. Shannon may be at a developmental stage where she can be helped to make connections between her past, her feelings, and her behavior. Shannon may have benefited from placement in a facility with expertise in serving adopted children, which could provide adoption-sensitive services to her family as well. The decision to place adopted children outside the home should be weighed with great care, however. For children like Shannon who have had a chaotic early life and lost their birth family, placement may feel like another rejection. Upon discharge, she and her family need to be referred to a therapist with this expertise.

The Mental Health Practitioner

The mental health practitioner enters the system when mistrust and frustration are high. Much of the work not done at earlier points of intervention needs to occur at this point. Shannon's resistance to involvement in treatment complicates this. Meeting with the family in the home rather than the office may increase the likelihood that Shannon will be available. By focusing on Shannon's behavior as the primary family problem, the therapist has accepted the Baileys' view of the problem without considering Shannon's perspective. The therapist also has used a strategy similar to that complained about by several parents in the Illinois adoption project: moving quickly to attempts to address behavior problems without considering underlying issues that may contribute to these behaviors. Although Shannon's parents very much need ideas about how to bring her behavior to a point where she is protected from harm, they and she also need help in making sense of these behaviors.

In a world where helping professionals understand adoption issues and use this knowledge as they intervene with struggling families, exploration of adoption issues would occur in each of the helping systems involved with the Baileys. Further, comprehensive case collaboration where the expertise of a number of helping professionals is brought to bear in helping the family would be the norm. Although there have been strides in offering services to families before, during, and after adoption, many professionals are serving adoptive families without adequate knowledge of issues tied to adoption and maltreatment.

Chapter 3

WE NEVER THOUGHT
IT WOULD BE LIKE THIS

Presenting Problems of
Troubled Adoptive Families

The permanency planning movement and the shift in philosophy that it heralded led to the placement of more troubled children for adoption. The underlying belief is that most children are best raised and sustained through an enduring relationship with a family. Children who have experienced loss, trauma, severed attachments, and the like need the milieu of a committed and nurturing family. Yet the lessons children have learned along the way often lead them to resist the support and protection offered. Further, the preparation for adoption that families receive often fails to include sufficient information about the harm children have suffered, the ways that harm might manifest itself in later years, and the resources that could help the family manage through these difficulties.

Serving families who have finalized their adoptions is a relatively new direction in adoption practice. Because there is limited information on the situations of such families seeking help, this chapter draws heavily on information from families served through adoption preservation services in Illinois. Where possible, other data from postlegal services projects across the country are included.

FAMILY PROBLEMS

Adoptive families seeking help demonstrate a range of problems and attitudes. In the vast majority of families, however, parents frame the presenting problems in terms of behavioral or emotional problems of the adopted child. One or both of these issues were identified problems in 95% of all cases referred to the Illinois Adoption Preservation Project, although other family problems were identified as well. The current problems identified by families and workers during the assessment period are listed below in order of their frequency.

Behavior problems of child	89%
Emotional problems of child	72%
Child-parent relationship	61%
Child's relationship with peers	48%
Financial problems	46%
Child care problems	37%
Emotional problems of parent	26%
Significant unresolved loss/parent	26%
Job problems	25%
Marital problems	24%
Resource deficit	22%
Deficit in parent's emotional care	21%
Death of a family member	21%
Unresolved infertility	21%
Social isolation	20%
Physical illness of parent	19%
Recent disability/family member	19%
Alcohol/drug abuse of child	10%
Alcohol/drug abuse of parent	7%
Deficit of parent's physical care	3%

As might be expected, the adoptive families served often face family-based problems that interact with child-related issues. In some situations, families have coped successfully with chronic behavioral difficulties of the adopted children for years, but due to crisis, family change, or intensification of the problems, they are no longer able to cope. In other families, a complex set of stresses contributes to difficulties in family functioning. These include factors such as divorce, death of a parent, and severe physical illness of a parent. Although reporting the assessed frequency of family stressors or problems does not represent the complexity of the factors involved in problem situations, it does depict a range of the issues involved.

Other than child problems, several specific family problems are significantly associated with dissolution risk, including marital problems, child care problems, job loss, and physical illness of the parent. In addition, many other stressors or problems are unique to particular families. Other factors reported by workers as significant contributors to family problems include conflicts resulting from remarriages, particularly when child-parent attachments are tenuous; conflict with birth family members occurring mainly in relative adoptions; and the family's failure to deal constructively with adoption issues.

An additional problem experienced by some families is a protective services report. In 25% of families, the family had been reported to the Department of Children and Family Services either prior to or during adoption preservation services. Of these reports, two thirds had occurred prior to the beginning of services, and most had not been indicated. In at least three families, false allegations made by the child were directly tied to the family's seeking service. For example, one mother, a teacher whose job would be jeopardized should a report be indicated, called seeking to have her daughter removed when her child falsely reported her for abuse a second time. Of the allegations that were indicated (38%), 12 were physical abuse (1 by a sibling rather than a parent), 5 were for sexual abuse (3 by siblings), and 8 were for neglect, which were cases in which parents refused to pick children up from placement or treatment facilities.

In addition to family problems, workers also assessed family strengths (see Table A.1 in the Appendix). Some specific strengths are significantly associated with reduced risk of dissolution. These are included in Table A.2. Other family strengths that are thought to relate to adoption stability are not significantly associated with a reduced risk of dissolution. These include having supportive friendships, having outside interests, knowing the child's history, having a strong marital relationship, having a supportive extended family, and having a sustaining religious faith.

PARENTAL ATTITUDES
UPON SEEKING HELP

Although a range of perceptions and emotions is present in adoptive parents seeking preservation services, workers in the Illinois project reported a common profile among many of these parents. A few parents would accept services only if the goal was to end the adoption. In a few other families, parents sought the expertise of staff to deal with a developmental challenge or to help the family obtain necessary resources, but ending the adoption was never considered. Most families fell somewhere in between. Parents often came to adoption preservation services feeling inadequate and overwhelmed. Many had struggled for years parenting children whose behaviors grew more challenging with time. It was common for them to have sought services from a variety of sources with little effect. Weary, pessimistic, and burdened with feelings of incompetence, parents often came to services wary about yet another intervention, but desperate enough to make one more try. From follow-up forms completed by parents, descriptions of their situations at the time of referral illustrate this point:

She had severe, recurrent depression. She was expelled from school, truant from home, drugs, gang-wanna-be behavior. We had problems of communication, rule setting, and boundaries. The whole family had low self-esteem.

There were severe emotional problems and severe behavioral problems as well. There were parenting differences between us as parents. It looked like our family could fall apart.

She had lots of behavior problems, and my counselor was advising me to give her back to the state.

Families in crisis may blame one member for the family's distress. In troubled adoptive families, particularly those seeking service, the adopted child is often the identified problem. This view is buttressed by information on a form completed by parents at the initiation of service, the current feelings about relationship with child form. Parents were asked to rate their level of agreement with a series of questions. Their responses are reported in Table A.3. In addition, parents were asked to rate the overall effect of adoption on their family from very positive to very negative.

The complicated nature of special needs adoption is reflected in replies by parents. Parents agreed that the child's emotional or behavioral problems were seen as "the main problem with my family now" in 73% of cases. Serious problems in families are reflected in the following responses: things with the child were "out of control" (47%), parents were hopeless that things could get better (31%), parents were experiencing the "last straw" in the relationship with their child (28%), and parents felt the family was breaking apart (28%). Yet, despite frustration and tension, the majority of parents felt the child belonged to them (77%) and were committed to working through problems with the child no matter what it took (78%).

What emerges is a picture of parents who are committed to their children and feel connected to them, yet feel unable to manage their children's behavior. Parents may feel overwhelmed by the child's needs and their perceived limitations in meeting those needs, yet want to persevere.

Parent responses on the current feelings form were examined to determine which items were associated with raising dissolution. As might be expected, negative parental attitude about the adoption and the child was strongly associated with raising dissolution. The items positively associated with parents' raising dissolution as an option were a desire to end the adoption if possible, the sense that the last straw had been reached with the child, the view that the child needed to be placed outside the home, and feeling hopeless that the situation would improve. Parent disagreement with statements that they were committed to working through the problems, felt confident that they could meet the child's needs, or the child belonged to them also were associated with raising dissolution as an option. As might be expected, those who viewed the overall effect of the adoption on their family as negative were more likely to have raised dissolution.

CHILDREN'S CONCERNS AND PERCEPTIONS OF PROBLEMS

Problems in adoptive families are most often viewed from the perspective of parents or professionals and are framed almost entirely in terms of child problems from an adult perspective. In an effort to overcome this bias, workers were asked to report the adopted child's concerns and perspective on family problems. In analyzing the responses given, two themes overshadow all others: (1) concerns related to adoption or the loss of the birth family, and (2) a variety of complaints about adoptive parents, particularly their expectations and discipline. Children's issues related to adoption include many identity-related concerns such as:

"I want to know more about who I am." (girl, age 15)
"I just want to know about my birth mother." (girl, age 10)
"Since third grade, I was in pain and sad wondering why they gave me up." (girl, age 15)

A 12-year-old girl was struggling with cultural identity issues as well as grieving that she did not know her true birthday and that there was virtually no chance that she could ever find her birth mother. A 14-year-old boy stated that he couldn't figure out what he did wrong to make his birth parents give him up. Confusion about "why" and longing for both contact and information about former parents and siblings were frequently expressed.

The feelings of loss and abandonment were expressed as strong fears by some children. One 6-year-old boy expressed his fear that someone would come and take him away, and talked about his nightmares, which reflected both strong anxiety and grief. Other adoptees had experienced the recent death or critical illness of an adoptive parent and lived with a pervasive fear of being left again. Although some children feared being kidnapped or abandoned again, others voiced their desire, expectation, or hope for a reunion with their birth family.

Although some children expressed their contentment with their adoptive families, they continued to struggle with feelings related to birth families or past abuse. Children expressed emotions of anger, grief, and fear related to abuse at the hands of their birth parents. Some grieved the loss of siblings or worried about how they were fairing. For example, a 10-year-old boy said that he liked being in his adoptive family and wanted to do well in school and make his adoptive mom proud of him. He worried about his 5-year-old sister left with his birth family, however, for whom he felt responsible.

Some children expressed confusion about being adopted or a feeling of stigma related to their adoptive status. An 11-year-old boy said that he didn't know anyone else who was adopted and that other kids made fun of his being adopted.

In addition, children often expressed concerns about their adoptive parents, and their view that the parents were "the problem." Frequent complaints about unrealistic expectations or overly strict discipline were expressed as, "They won't let me do anything"; "My mother wants everything her way and doesn't consider my feelings"; "They're trying to run my life and interfere with my friendships"; and "My parents will love me only if I behave to their expectations." A 10-year-old girl stated, "Everything would be fine at home if I always did what my mother said when she said to do it." Adoptees also expressed concerns that they weren't really wanted. For example, a 14-year-old girl said that sometimes her parents loved her, but they never really understood how she felt and they really didn't want her. Another teenage girl stated that she believed her adoptive parents hated her and that all she could do was survive at home until she graduated from high school.

Although most adopted children seem to place major responsibility for their ongoing problems on parents, some recognize their own behavior as problematic. Many express some insight into the causes of their behavior, such as an 11-year-old girl who said that her behavior was a problem because she was "always mad." Another teenage girl recognized that her inability to love her adoptive family fully had caused her to push them away.

Although some children recognize the source of their problems, they often express feelings of helplessness and desperation in knowing how to change their behavior. For example, one 13-year-old boy reported that he could not control his anger and truly wanted help with it. He had no idea why he had fits of rage. He said he needed to feel safe—that his parents wouldn't give up on him. He knew his rageful outbursts were undermining their trust and his ability to remain in the home, however.

Other concerns that were sometimes expressed by the children include school problems and peer problems, such as not being able to make friends or being ostracized by other children. (Sometimes workers view school failure and peer problems as symptoms of depression triggered in part by adoption issues.) Other children complained of siblings getting preferential treatment. In addition, a few children expressed their desire to leave their adoptive family, usually to return to a previous family situation.

Children were asked open-ended questions about what was the best thing about being adopted and the hardest thing about being adopted. The common themes and samples of their responses are reported next.

In responding to the question, "What is the best thing about being adopted?" children most often reported benefits of having a family, such as being taken care of and loved. Sample responses echoing this theme include the following:

> "That I get loved 'everday.' "
> "My mother and my family."
> "You know your adoption parent loves you and wants you."
> "When you go to a family you know and you feel comfortable in the house and you be so glad you got a roof over your head and food to eat and clothes on your back."
> "Being special—having someone care about you and love you."
> "Having a parent."
> "Your parents are nicer."
> "I have a family."
> "I have more than 1 'pear' of mom and dad."

Other children commented on a variety of residual benefits of being adopted, such as having more money or toys and not having to move around a lot. Some others appreciated achieving the status of being adopted, writing, "I'm not a foster kid," or "You have the same privileges as other kids in Chicago."

In responding to the hardest thing about being adopted, the most frequent theme related to the loss of birth family. Sample responses include:

> "Missing my birth mom."
> "Not knowing my real birth parents."
> "Not seeing my dad a lot."
> "Curious about my biological family."

A second common theme reflects struggling with the "different" status of adoption or a sense of not fitting in with peers or family. Being made fun of by friends was mentioned by several children. Some of their comments include:

> "Worrying about fitting in."
> "Not looking the same as my mom and dad."
> "I'm sometimes afraid that if someone finds out you are adopted, they will make fun of you and treat you different from the others."

A few children wrote about their confusion and ambivalence in coming to terms with adoption, such as, "Not knowing whether it would be better with my birth parents," and "Being confused." Other children commented on particular problems in their lives or families. For them, the hardest thing about being adopted was:

"Getting along."
"Sometimes following the rules."
"My brother beating me up."
"Not feeling like you're being loved enough."
"You have to go for therapy."
"Being with someone I don't know."

On the whole, the adoptees responding were glad to have their adoptive families but struggled in coming to terms with their life circumstances. The strong feelings of pain and confusion that many of them verbalized for the first time to adoption preservation workers or in their support groups validated the need for these adoptees to have some individual time as well as group support to address such central issues effectively.

PREVIOUS COPING ATTEMPTS

Adoptive families seeking help typically have had their children in their homes for an extended period. In the Illinois project, children had been in their adoptive homes an average of 8.9 years. In some families, family crises (such as the death of a parent or divorce) seem to have precipitated the problem. In others, the developmental challenges of adolescence exacerbated problems and led to resurfacing of loss and trauma issues for the child. In most, families had been coping with problematic behavior by children for a long time, finding that their efforts to manage such behavior were unproductive.

Families had engaged in a number of attempts to make things better. Individual counseling for the child was the most commonly used formal resource, followed by family counseling and individual counseling for a parent. Counseling for the child was seldom evaluated by parents as having been very helpful (8%), with their evaluations of the helpfulness of child counseling split between unhelpful (45%) and somewhat helpful (46%). Family counseling fared better, reported as helpful or very helpful in nearly two thirds of cases. Individual counseling for parents was rated even more positively, as helpful or very helpful in over three fourths of cases. Support groups for children and for parents were used much less often, but when families had received this service, the majority found it helpful.

Families also used informal resources to cope. Help from extended family was the most common of these resources, identified by 42% of families, and seen as helpful or very helpful by nearly 75%. Parents relied on emotional support, respite, and guidance from extended family. For some adoptive families, however, the emotional or behavioral problems of their adopted children led to their being estranged from their friends and family.

Perhaps the most challenging cases were those where families had tried a variety of resources and felt no better about their family situation. In the few studies that have asked parents about their experiences in receiving help, common themes emerge. Parents feel that many mental health and other helping professionals know too little about adoption. They often feel excluded from therapy and view the therapist as allying with the child against them. They are troubled that presenting problems are overlooked and remained unresolved. They often feel blamed by the therapist for the child's problems (Frey, 1986; Howard & Smith, 1995; Massachusetts Department of Mental Health, 1994; Reitnauer & Grabe, 1985).

Delaney and Kunstal (1993) write about the failures of many therapists to understand that adopted children often bring very complicated histories with them as they join a family. The authors state:

> These families are routinely overlooked or exiled from treatment. All too often, foster and adoptive parents are passive spectators. These families seldom receive credit for the child's gains, though frequently they take the blame for the child's failures. . . . Children's problems are seen as rooted in presumably disturbed foster or adoptive family dynamics. (p. 8)

Thus, some families seeking postlegal services have found and used services, but are in need of additional help. Others have found professionals to be unhelpful, and even blaming, exacerbating parents' feelings of incompetence and failure.

FAMILY DYNAMICS IN
TROUBLED ADOPTIVE FAMILIES

As is the case in all families, struggling adoptive families develop methods of coping with difficulty. For parents seeking adoption preservation services, the usual parental repertoire of commonly used methods of reward and discipline, nurture, and direction have not yielded the hoped-for results. Parents may become more extreme in their attempts to exert control, and find the child's behavior becomes more extreme in response. Developing a strong will may have been a key to children's surviving trauma and maltreatment. In troubled adoptive families, when there is a battle of wills, the odds are the adopted child wins. Children struggling for power in relationships demonstrate remarkable perseverance. Both direct, confrontive actions and passive tactics are common, as the following case examples illustrate.

Willie Washington, 12, lives with his mother and two younger siblings, also adopted, and a flow of foster brothers and sisters. His has been a fairly calm household. Mrs. Washington is an experienced foster mother who decided to adopt Willie after he had been in her home several years. Willie has always been stubborn, but a year ago his stubbornness turned to defiance. He has begun picking fights with his younger brother, leaving home without permission, and talking back to Mrs. Washington. The more she tries to impose rules, the more defiant he becomes. If she tells him to be home at 9:00, he will return hours later. If it is his turn to do the dishes, he may tell her, "Do your own damn dishes." If she tells him to come straight home from school, he will invariably stop along the way. Mrs. Washington has responded by restricting his activities and, at times, physically restraining him from leaving the house. The last time this happened, he threatened to call the public child welfare agency to report her for abuse, a threat that has potency because Mrs. Washington is a foster parent. It seems to be Willie's mission to oppose every statement his mother makes and to defy every order or request. The household is in an uproar much of the time.

Ten-year-old Samantha is bright and very pretty. She functions
fairly well at school and in the neighborhood. At home, however,
she is locked in a battle of wills with her parents. She never
screams or shouts, is never outwardly defiant. Yet she controls her
family through her constant, relentless lateness. Every school day,
she must be prodded, encouraged, and threatened to get ready. She
takes a long time to get out of bed, takes forever in the bathroom,
can never find shoes, books, or homework. When she misses the
bus and has to be driven to school, one of her parents is late to
work. If they hustle her out the door on time, she doesn't eat
breakfast or goes to school unkempt. Even on weekends, Samantha drags her feet. A trip to the store, doing chores, or any activity
takes forever. The more her parents nag and scold her, the slower
she becomes.

In their efforts to win the power struggle, parents may resort to
extraordinary methods. To the outsider, such methods make the parent
look rigid, angry, and domineering. Sometimes, of course, this is the
personality of the parent. But many times this is the result of raising
very strong-willed children. When familiar techniques fail, parents may
try them again only more harshly, and on and on.

In the Illinois project, parents identified strategies they had tried
prior to coming to adoption preservation services. Sixty-two percent of
the parents reported using stricter discipline, and most found this approach to be unhelpful.

When tried and true techniques fail, parents feel like failures. Continuing or escalating behavior problems prove to the parents that they
are doing something wrong. Disapproval by extended family members,
friends, and the larger social network can intensify the parents' sense of
incompetence. Such disapproval often reflects the view that the child's
behaviors are due to family problems. This is a particular difficulty
when the child's behavior outside the home is more compliant and
normative than it is in the home. Parents appear to be exaggerating
problems or unable to cope with behavior that, to outsiders, looks like
normal behavior. In other cases, the child's behavior causes problems
wherever he or she goes. Parents of children whose negative behavior
is generalized must cope with relentless negative messages about their
child from the larger world. When one's children are constantly in

trouble at school, expelled from organized activities, not welcome in the yards of neighbors, and boycotted by baby-sitters, it is hard to feel like a successful parent.

A new view of struggling adoptive families has emerged that asks us to consider that the troubled child comes to adoption with a set of experiences or characteristics that makes traditional parenting methods ineffective. A history of loss and trauma can lead a child to reject the very nurturing he or she most needs. The child's experience tells him or her intimacy is dangerous. Adults cannot be depended on. He or she is not worth loving. Families are fluid, not stable. Big people consistently overpower the will of little people. Parents hurt kids.

What is the remedy to maltreatment? For most adoptive parents, it is good treatment—love, nurture, consistency, stability, guidance, affection. Yet as Delaney and Kunstal (1993) note, "A disturbed child . . . bring[s] with him uncanny ways of thwarting [parents'] attempts to help" (p. vi). Indeed, many children in struggling adoptive families are masterful at determining what bothers or hurts parents the most and doing it repeatedly.

In traditional family therapy, a child's disturbed behavior is examined as a symptom of family problems. Delaney and Kunstal (1993) ask us to rethink this model as it applies to foster and adoptive families. In troubled adoptive families, the family can be understood as a repository of the child's present disturbance and previous maltreatment. Rather than being the barometer of family problems, the troubled adopted child is the thermostat—moving the family in unhealthy directions. These authors assert that it is a mistake to view the transformed family as a cause, not an effect, of the child's behavior. It is appropriate to consider whether the family is acting out the symptoms of the child rather than the child acting out the symptoms of the family.

Adoptive parents who present themselves for services can look pathological. As one adoption preservation worker notes, "When you first meet some of these people you wonder, 'How did they ever get approved to adopt a child?' I wouldn't trust them with my dog!" Certainly in some families, parental mental illness, toxic marital relationships, and other parental dysfunction operate. But professionals working with long-term adoptive families are coming to understand that a very disturbed child can make a family look very disturbed (Delaney & Kunstal, 1993; Keck & Kupecky, 1995). Delaney and Kunstal (1993) label this *imported pathology*. That is, children can bring a host of needs and problems into a fairly functional family. Over time, the child's effect on the family leads to a family that comes to resemble the situation the child left. The point is that in some families the child is acting out the difficulties of the family, but in many cases the families are acting out the difficulties of the child.

Understanding the effect of imported pathology is important, but insufficient. To understand why families seek help when they do, we must consider the developmental course of both the child and the family. In the Illinois project, the majority of children were adolescents, with those 14 to 15 making up the largest single category. The developmental challenges of adolescence can interact with adoption to make this stage more complicated for children, an idea we explore more fully in Chapter 7.

Popular culture continues to stigmatize adoption. In addition to the idea that adoption is an inferior way to create a family, attitudes about deviance among adopted children persist (Hartman & Laird, 1989; Miall, 1987). The character Rachel in the classic children's novel *Anne of Green Gables* (Montgomery, 1935) provides an illustration. In response to an angry outburst by a young adopted adolescent, Rachel warns the prospective adoptive mother, "Them's the kind that puts poison down the well!" Her statement is in reference to an earlier litany of the dangers a family faces when bringing a child of unknown heritage into the family.

Lingering negative perceptions in the larger society may wield the most power as the child moves through adolescence. Residual concerns about the sexuality of adopted children can complicate family development. The bad seed myth holds that because the child was conceived out of wedlock or because his or her birth parents were flawed, an adopted child is at heightened risk for deviance. When parents internalize such beliefs, the normal behavior of adopted adolescents may be interpreted as evidence of deviance. Thus, the young adolescent girl who becomes keenly interested in boys is feared to be heading toward promiscuity, like her birth mother. The 15-year-old boy who experiments with drugs is thought to be turning to the wrong crowd, associating with the "low lifes" who are like his family of origin.

For some adopted children, behavior in adolescence does worsen considerably. For children who act out violently, are threatening or defiant, the age and size of the child can heighten the parent's sense of competence. As one mother put it, "It's one thing when a child of 6 or 8 has tantrums, tears things up, hits, bites, and screams. It's quite another when he's 6′2″, outweighs his dad, and is punching walls, screaming out dirty words, and threatening us and his sister and brothers." Some parents fear their children, and sometimes with good reason. Mothers often bear the brunt of the child's rage. Physical attacks by children or threats of such attacks can leave families feeling as if they are living in a war zone.

An additional concern of parents is their inability to exert control outside the home. Older children have more opportunities to be away from family, more mobility, and more access to situations that endanger them. Affiliating with children who are in trouble or are without positive goals is common among troubled adopted children. This may stand, in part, as a rejection of parental values. For children who feel different or unsuccessful, such friends may prove more accepting. For children who have poverty or neglect as part of the family's adoption story, such association may be a link to their past. One mother explains:

> When he was little, we knew his friends and their families. They were people like us, who were basically middle class or working people, who valued education and made lots of opportunities available to their children—soccer, church youth groups, Boy Scouts. When he went to high school everything changed. His friends were kids we'd never met and he didn't want us to know them. They were kids (we later learned) who skipped school and eventually dropped out, shoplifted at the mall, did drugs, never studied, and whose major activity was hanging out. None of them seemed to have parents who were very involved in their lives. It sounds strange to say, but one time when I went to pick him up at a rundown trailer park which is sort of notorious in our town, I looked around and thought "This is the kind of place where his birth parents lived!" And I wondered if he had chosen his friends because this was the kind of life he remembered from when he was a little boy.

Adolescence can heighten the parents' fears for their child's future. The child who was so impulsive as a younger child will now be dating, driving, and experimenting with the possibilities of adulthood. The child who has always played with younger children because of his or her delayed social skills may now realize that he or she doesn't fit in. School difficulties may trigger worries about the child's future. Will he ever be self-supporting or will he be dependent for life? What will happen to her if she quits high school? Impending separation and need for the child to function more effectively in the world may frighten both parent and child.

COMMON THEMES

Struggling adoptive families exhibit a range of functioning levels. Among those who are struggling most, adoption preservation workers have identified central themes. These include a limited emotional range, marital tension, sibling conflicts or difficulties, isolation, and hopelessness.

Limited Emotional Range

Two emotions predominate in struggling adoptive families—anger and sorrow. Anger can be directed inward, as parents blame themselves for their inability to help their child or for their loss of empathy for the child. Anger can be directed at the adoption system. Parents complain about being misled about the nature of their child's problems and unprepared for the difficulties the child's behavior presents. Many struggling adoptive parents wonder if important information was deliberately withheld, and feel manipulated by the child welfare system. Such feelings are intensified when the child welfare system refuses to provide additional information about the child's past. Other parents acknowledge that much important information was shared, but that no one helped them understand the meaning of that information. As one mother comments,

> It's one thing to know your child was sexually abused as a 2-year-old and was in a bunch of foster homes. It's something else to know what that means—how it will affect them and you later. . . . I used to be naive. I thought I could take children who had been seriously hurt and give them unlimited love and fix them. I've learned we can't fix what's happened to them. All we can do is give them love and support and fight for them to get the services they need.

The need to fight for services can lead to anger at the broader system. Parents in struggling adoptive families, by necessity, often become experts on community resources. This expertise does not guarantee that such services exist or are responsive. It is common for parents to feel they must educate mental health providers, physicians, and educators about the importance of adoption, maltreatment, and loss in assessing and helping children. Such information may be dismissed by professionals or used as evidence that the parent is blaming the child for family problems. Further, families face problems in access to resources. In some communities, the highly specialized educational programs needed by some children are not in existence. Adoption subsidies through Medicaid may not reimburse private practitioners sufficiently to allow families to make use of them. In many states, the costs of extended in-patient psychiatric care or residential treatment are not covered. Families may run through insurance benefits quickly, leaving themselves vulnerable should such services be needed again. In the Illinois project, several families came to adoption preservation services because they were refusing to pick up children from psychiatric care. One family with a violent 16-year-old was strongly advised to place the child residentially following a psychiatric hospitalization. The therapists felt the boy posed a serious threat to his mother and siblings. The only way the family could initiate such placement was to relinquish guardianship to the state child welfare department. They were then excluded from basic information about their child's care, including not being notified when he ran away from the facility for several days.

When families feel both unprepared to meet the needs of a troubled child and unsupported by community services, anger is a logical reaction. Anger may also be directed at the child. Making a scapegoat of the child may help parents cope with their sense of incompetence or deep disappointment. Parents may lose their ability to see anything positive about their child.

This growing disenchantment is similar to the stages of adoption disruption described by Partridge, Hornby, and McDonald (1986). They describe a series of stages a family goes through leading to removal of the child. First, there is diminishing pleasure as the negative aspects of the adoption begin to outweigh the positive. Second, acting-out behaviors of the child escalate in response to parental anxiety or doubt. Parents come to view the child as the problem in the family. Third, sharing concerns with others, called "going public," serves to increase alienation. Fourth, a critical incident or crisis takes place, and there is no return to a sense of happiness or optimism. Fifth, the parents set a deadline for improvement (often not communicated directly) or give the child an ultimatum. Finally, when the deadline is passed or the ultimatum is violated, the decision to end the placement comes. For many parents who adopt, the decision to end the adoption cannot be realized. In many states, dissolving an adoption is very difficult. Like a partner in a loveless marriage where divorce is impossible, such parents feel caught and hopeless. As one adoptive mother described, "I'm just counting the days to her 18th birthday."

Feelings of great anger and actions stemming from this anger can startle adoptive parents. Parents who see themselves as loving and patient find themselves screaming hateful things at their children. One mother in a support group described her horror at the way she responded to her child's hate-filled tantrums. "I found myself screaming at her 'I know why your foster parents didn't adopt you! They didn't want you! You're too obnoxious and hateful!' " Another mother confessed, "I am not the mother I always wanted to be."

Deep sorrow is another common emotion. As parents struggle with feelings of inadequacy, reinforced by blame from family, friends, and other systems, they may doubt their abilities to be good parents. Adoptive parents, particularly those who have been well prepared, expect some difficulties to arise when a child enters their home. Many parents can be patient and persistent, trusting that when enough time has passed, when enough love is given, when the child has adjusted to family life, a functional and connected family will be the result. After a few years, if problems do not abate or if they intensify, parents may come to the conclusion that the family they envisioned may never be. Indeed, *mismatched expectations,* the idea that parents and children end up with a different family situation than that which they hoped for and expected, is a common theme in post-adoption literature. Such disappointment can be made worse by a sense that the parent and the child do not fully belong to one another, called a *lack of sense of entitlement* (Watson, 1992). Societal attitudes, for example, that a child's real parents are his or her biological ones, also contribute.

In adoptive families, parents hold the expectation that they will do a better job than those who surrendered or lost their children. The acute disappointment at not being successful at nurturing a child can reinforce doubt. One couple who had been unable to have children through birth struggled greatly as their adolescent daughter ran away, became involved in a gang, and used drugs heavily. How could they make sense of it? Their conclusion? "Maybe God was trying to tell us something when we couldn't have children—maybe we're not able to be good parents."

By the time many families reach post-adoption services, much of normal family life has disappeared. Family time is avoided. There is little humor or kidding. Family members take little comfort from one another. Angry outbursts cycle with periods of estrangement and sadness. No one is happy, and there seems to be no way to change.

Marital Tension

Struggles with an adopted child can increase marital problems, but also can cause them. The mother is typically the primary focus of the child's anger, extreme dependency, or rejection. Mothers are more likely to be in the child's presence, to discipline the child, and to represent the family to school, neighbors, and others in the community. Mothers are subjected to more of the talking back, noncompliance, and control struggles than fathers. Fathers are less likely to be the objects of intense reaction. Their interactions are less emotion laden and more positive. In many two-parent families, the father and mother have experienced a very different child (Delaney & Kunstal, 1993).

Workers have attributed this difference to the need for the child to keep the family off balance and to remain in control. Another perspective is that these differences are the result of splitting. In children who have been seriously maltreated or maltreated at a very young age or who have experienced wrenching losses, an important psychological ability may be absent. Splitting is a psychological defense available to troubled children. The world is separated into the good and the bad. Nuance, ambiguity, and gradation are lacking. The normal ambivalence experienced by children (my mother is good because she feeds me but bad because she punishes me) fails to be managed and integrated. In abusive birth families, such pathological splitting can be exacerbated by the child's inability to display anger toward the caregiver. Mothers are more likely than fathers to be judged as negative by the child who has had to rely on splitting to cope.

Further, unresolved loss focuses on mothers. Many special needs adoptive children have not had relationships of attachment with their fathers or male caregivers. Even when the relationship with both birth parents was brief, adopted children often express their losses in terms of mothers. For example, in a study of adopted young women, participants were asked the question, "If you could ask your birth parents one question, what would it be?" All but three of the participants responded with "I would ask her . . ." Further, when questioned about search efforts, most participants expressed the desire to meet or learn about mothers, but had to be prodded to express what they might like to learn about their fathers. This varied only when participants had already found their mothers or had information about them.

Unmet needs, loss, or rejection can surface in many ways. A common one is intense anger toward the adoptive mother. Children may have generalized their experience with one untrustworthy mother to develop a worldview that no mother can be trusted. The adoptive mother inherits the role of all past maltreating mothers. Younger children may be clinging and overanxious. Again, the adoptive mother fills in for the mother who leaves or responds minimally to the child. One mother reported her frustration with her child's unfillable need for reassurance. This child, adopted at age 5, had experienced significant neglect. The child experienced panic when the mother was out of sight, even in the next room. When the mother would use the bathroom, the child would curl up against the door begging her to let him in. Consistent and very frequent reassurance and affection did nothing to alleviate his neediness. His incessant need to be near her, and her alone, left the mother feeling trapped and smothered.

Other children engage in a push-pull relationship with mothers. Their need for closeness draws them near their mothers for comfort and reassurance, but their distrust or fear of drawing close pulls them away. They demand closeness, then demand distance, in ways that make mothers feel uncertain and manipulated.

The demanding child known by the mother is not the child known by the father. His wife's need to catalogue the child's sins, her need for his sympathy, and her frustration and anger often appear exaggerated to the father. He sees a child pretty much being a child. She describes a monster. Tension in the marital pair emerges or is intensified by this very different understanding of the child. Further, the child's ability to be normal when the father is present supports the mother's suspicion that the child's actions are deliberate and that the husband has been duped.

Sibling Issues

When a child enters a family, shifts must occur in all relationships. In adoptive families, parents may expect the children already in the home to make allowances for the newcomer until the family readjusts. If the readjustment never occurs, the family never "settles in" as a cohesive unit, and resentment can be great.

The literature sheds little light on the relationship between status among siblings and family functioning. Does the presence of birth children complicate the family's adjustment? Does it matter if the birth child comes along after the child is adopted? Does creating sibling groups from among special needs children pose more risk to family stability than adopting biological siblings? What effect does changing place in a family (such as an 8-year-old who was the oldest in the family of origin and is the youngest in the adoptive home) have on the family? These are questions that need to be examined.

In many struggling adoptive families, siblings as well as parents may see one adopted child as the problem. "If only Steven would straighten up" or "If only we hadn't adopted Steven" becomes a refrain that brings other family members closer and turns Steven into the scapegoat. Some adoptive parents see their other adopted children or birth children as problem free.

Even when the adopted child is not blamed for family problems, the energy and time devoted to the child with serious emotional or behavioral problems can breed resentment among siblings. A sister or brother's behavior may mean the family's activities are limited or friends don't want to come over. Mom and Dad may be exhausted from the care of one child. Siblings' attempts to get attention, to be better than perfect, or to sabotage the relationship between the struggling child and parents can take their toll on the family.

Isolation

In struggling adoptive families, normal aspects of family life are often lost. The energy required to manage a troubled child may mean that little is left for spouses, friends, and others. Families who feel criticized by others may withdraw from social contacts. Children with severe behavior problems may lead the family to isolation. Mrs. Smithson, who with her husband adopted six children (five with special needs), found that her children's disruptive, sexualized, and sometimes violent behaviors cut the family off. Other families were reluctant to visit or allow the Smithson children to visit them. No one would baby-sit for the children. Even community activities were off limits because of severe acting-out behavior by two of the children. For one parent to leave the home, the other had to be present. The couple did not go out alone together for 3 or 4 years. The only appreciable length of time Mrs. Smithson spent away from her children was when she was hospitalized for emergency surgery. Because of problems with setting fires, sibling violence, and sexual behavior, Mrs. Smithson never left the children alone, even though two were teenagers. If the husband wasn't home, all the children piled into the family van to go grocery shopping or to conduct any family business.

Extended family and friends can contribute to negative perceptions. In addition to absenting themselves from the lives of the adoptive family, extended family may blame the child for the family's problems or the parents for their failure to care for the child in a way that helps the child get better. Also, adoptive families do not usually have contact with other adoptive families, which can enhance a sense of differentness and isolation.

Exhaustion and Hopelessness

When little progress follows significant investments of effort, families can reach the point of futility. Parents speak of "pouring everything we had into this child" and getting nothing back emotionally. Some hold no hope that things can improve, and strive to get through each day. Family interaction is limited, punctuated by angry exchanges. There is little humor or fun. Few kind words are exchanged. The family may live from crisis to crisis. Such hopelessness seems to preclude successful intervention. This is the case for some families when an emotional point of no return has been reached. Similar to a bad marriage, such families separate emotionally and operate separately. Prolonged and unrelieved stress can lead to emotional numbness.

For many families, post-adoption services can restore hope and help a family toward healthy functioning again. In other families, where severe problems continue, commitment to the child enables parents to do what they can to help with each new crisis. When the child's problems are extreme, they may insist that the child live outside the home. Yet even though the family cannot live together, it can still be a family. Parents remain supportive and connected to their child. In a few families, though, such services are too little, too late. In families where emotional distance is great, ending the adoption or permanent placement for the child may be the only solutions parents want to consider.

RUNNING ON EMPTY

The Whitman family illustrates many of the challenges faced by struggling adoptive families. The family consists of Roger (retired), Ellen, and Katie, now age 15. Katie was placed in the Whitman home at age 5. When Katie was 14, Mr. and Mrs. Whitman (particularly Mrs. Whitman) had had enough. Katie was violent and rageful. She rejected affection, destroyed property, and was verbally abusive. The last straw came in the form of two unfounded allegations of physical abuse. These reports were deeply embarrassing, particularly to Ellen, who might have lost her teaching position. Ellen called the state child welfare department and told the adoption worker, "Come and get this child. I can't take it anymore!"

This was not the family the Whitmans had envisioned when they decided to form a family through adoption many years ago. Roger had already raised children in a previous marriage. Ellen wanted to keep working. They wanted a child of 3 or older, and would accept a child with disabilities. At a monthly informational meeting held by the public child welfare agency, they learned it would be a long time before a child would be available. They were disappointed but still interested. Three weeks later, they received a call informing them a child was available. They had had no training and had attended only one meeting about adoption. But the worker indicated they would be perfect for a 4-year-old girl whose adoptive placement was disrupting. The difficulty was presented as the child's inability to get along with other children in the family. She was aggressive and had learning problems. Because she would be the only child in the Whitman home, and because of their financial stability, they seemed good candidates for this little girl. Ellen's experience as a teacher was another plus. Little else was shared about Katie's background. The Whitmans later learned Katie had been removed from her birth home at age 2 due to physical abuse and neglect.

At the first meeting, Katie was shy and hid behind the social worker. When she saw the bedroom decked out in colorful designs, she asked, "Do you have any kids?" When they answered they did not, she said, "I'll be your little girl."

Weekend visits began as a way to help Katie with the transition. The families would meet halfway to make the transfer. Katie would cry at both ends of the visit—not wanting to leave her former family at the beginning and not wanting to leave the Whitmans at the end. Just after Katie turned 5, during Katie's fifth or sixth visit, the former family called and announced they would not meet the Whitmans to pick Katie up. So, abruptly and without good-byes, Katie became a permanent member of her new family. Years later, Ellen learned from Katie that she had no idea the family she left was not her birth family. She couldn't understand why her family decided to give her away.

Katie's behavior was challenging from early on. A social worker did meet with the family for a while after Katie's placement. The Whitmans' relationship with the worker didn't jell—they felt she didn't have much to offer them. Katie was hyperactive and didn't sleep. She had long tantrums, screaming for hours at a time. She destroyed clothes, curtains, bedspreads, and dolls. She demanded immediate attention. On the advice of a psychiatrist, Ellen and Roger began locking their bedroom door at night so they could sleep. Katie would lie outside the door, screaming and kicking the door so hard they thought it would break. Ignoring her behavior only made it worse.

Over the years, the Whitmans sought help from many quarters, but were frustrated. Roger stated, "Just not that many people in the helping professions understand about adoption." Helping professionals told the Whitmans to avoid the topic of adoption unless Katie raised it, to avoid "stirring her up." Well-meaning family members agreed, believing ignoring the adoption was the best way to make Katie feel part of the family. The Whitmans also were advised to use behavioral approaches with Katie, charting and rewarding good behavior and using time-outs. The source of Katie's rage and fear was left unexamined.

Throughout grade school, Katie's behavior problems continued. She was rageful, destructive, and aggressive. In fourth grade, problems became so severe the Whitmans accepted their therapist's recommendation that Katie be hospitalized. In the hospital, Katie had to earn the right to visit or phone her parents. Katie's feelings about the loss of her birth and previous foster families were not explored. She quickly learned to master the behavioral reward system, but made only superficial progress. She spent 10 weeks in a psychiatric setting, returning "worse than ever." Worst of all, she felt she had been abandoned once again.

As Katie grew, her difficult behaviors continued. She was diagnosed as bipolar with possible borderline personality disorder. She received counseling and a variety of drugs. She was placed in a range of special classrooms: learning disabled, emotionally disturbed, learning disabled again, then behaviorally disordered. Finally, she was placed in a therapeutic day school. Her last teacher belittled her and damaged her already low self-esteem.

Katie became adept at playing her parents against one another, "carrying tales" about one to the other. She was often verbally abusive, particularly toward Ellen. She would shout at her mother, "You're not my real mother! I hate you! I wish you were dead!" When Katie made a second report against her parents for abuse, Roger and Ellen were at the end of their rope. They were burdened with a sense of failure as parents. Ellen states, "We were doing the best that we could, but nothing was working. I know we did damage to Katie in our frustration. We were so angry. We didn't feel we deserved this. We had saved her from a bad situation, so how could she treat us like this?" When the adoption preservation worker arrived for the first interview, Ellen and Roger did not want adoption preservation services. They wanted Katie removed from their home.

We will continue our discussion of the Whitman family in Chapter 8.

CONCLUSION

What are the dynamics that make adoption so complicated? We have examined presenting problems discussed by parents in troubled adoptions as well as the perspective of adopted children. Feelings of incompetence, strains in the marital relationship, disapproval from others, lack of a support system, and the very challenging problems of some adopted children lead parents to seek help but also to doubt its usefulness.

Here we add our usual caveat—adoption may be a central aspect of family problems or merely one aspect of the family's story. In working with troubled adoptive families, we must carefully assess the extent to which adoption is salient to the problems at hand.

Chapter 4

THEY CRY OUT IN MANY DIFFERENT WAYS
Behavior Problems of Special Needs Children

Most adopted children do not exhibit serious behavior problems. The persistence of behavior problems among a small minority of children adopted as infants and many special needs adopted children is supported by research on both clinical and nonclinical populations of children, however. The majority of families served by the Illinois project, as well as those served by many other post-adoption projects throughout the country, report a history of seeking professional help without significant improvement in their situations. Their repertoire of parenting skills is exhausted; as their desperation increases, they may resort to extreme measures to control their children. For example, locking refrigerators, putting motion detectors outside a child's room, locking the parents' bedroom door at night, and other means were reported by some families served by the Illinois project. Control battles may escalate for both parents and children, particularly during adolescence. Conflicts can lead to emotional isolation of an adopted child within a family, increased marital and sibling conflicts, very high levels of stress in the family, and profound feelings of hopelessness and desperation for adoptive parents and children alike.

This chapter addresses the nature of behavior problems in special needs children whose histories include experiences such as maltreatment and interrupted attachments. It is important to note that the types of behavior problems and the emotional dynamics underlying these problems are not unique to special needs adopted children, but are found in other children with similar experiences. Some children who are adopted through the child welfare system may have been helped to cope with their experiences and may function successfully with minimal problems. Others may have one or two behavior problems that can be understood within the context of their past experiences and managed adequately. Other special needs children exhibit multiple, ongoing behavior problems, however, that do not seem to be resolved in spite of therapeutic interventions. The dynamics underlying these behavior problems that need to be addressed in treatment are explored in this chapter and later chapters of this book.

FRAMEWORK FOR UNDERSTANDING CHILDREN'S ADJUSTMENT ISSUES IN SPECIAL NEEDS ADOPTIONS

To understand the emotional issues affecting adopted children, particularly those who have experienced lost attachments and trauma, we developed a framework of four critical areas for adjustment. Although this model is most relevant to special needs adoptees who experience significant challenges in these areas of adjustment, to some extent they are areas of functioning that may be affected by any child's struggles to come to terms with adoption. The themes of this model are not unique, but build on familiar developmental tasks advanced by Erikson (1963), as well as some of the themes advanced by Finkelhor and Browne (1986) for understanding the effect of trauma on children. The model is depicted in Figure 4.1. Each area of functioning is introduced here and expanded further in later chapters.

Capacity for Relationships

The ability to develop close emotional relationships with others, to love and be loved, is the foundation of individual development. Experiencing a secure attachment to a caregiver is a prerequisite to healthy development throughout childhood. This relationship supports the development of trust, positive expectations of others, and positive self-esteem. It also promotes the development of self-control, empathy, and a conscience. Experiencing deprivation and physical and emotional pain in early relationships leads to fear of closeness, anger toward others, and the development of defenses for self-protection, such as numbing feelings and avoidance of intimacy. Tasks for children in overcoming

FOUR AREAS OF FUNCTIONING
CHALLENGED BY THE IMPACT OF ADOPTION, LOSS, OR TRAUMA

CAPACITY FOR RELATIONSHIPS
Intimacy . . . . Isolation

IDENTITY
Self-Integration . . . Identity Confusion

SELF-EFFICACY
Mastery . . . . Powerlessness

SELF-REGULATION
Self-Control . . . . . . Impulsivity

Figure 4.1. Four Areas of Functioning Challenged by the Effect of Adoption, Loss, or Trauma

attachment problems include learning to identify and express their own feelings and needs and to manage their fears related to closeness without pushing others away. Children also must be able to resolve their past losses and build on former attachments. To facilitate this work in their children, adoptive parents need to work through their own losses, help their child express grief, accept the significance of former attachments the child has experienced, promote positive interactions with the child, and respond to the child's needs by comforting, calming, redirecting, and deescalating crises. Also, parents need to determine realistic expectations for their adopted child's attachment capacity, and they may need to accept that their current expectations for closeness are not realistic, given the child's past experiences.

Identity

All children begin to develop their sense of self based on the messages communicated to them from others and their own interpretations of life events. It is common for children who were taken away from their birth families to blame themselves for this event, to believe that they were bad or unlovable. Moves in foster care can reinforce feelings of rejection and self-blame. To come to terms with their history, children need to be able to connect their past, present, and future through reconstructing their life history and coming to terms with these events. Children need to be able to affirm the positives they have gained from others and their own ability to survive difficult experiences. They need to be helped to "normalize" adoption by knowing other adopted children and being able to talk about their feelings and find answers to their questions. Adoptive parents can promote their children's identity work by developing open lines of communication about adoption, respecting their interest in their birth families, and helping them to integrate their heritage into their adoptive family. Adoptive parents need to establish a climate of openness and no secrets, and be able to share information with their children without being overly protective. It is helpful if they can give their child permission to search if he or she should ever desire to do so. Also, knowing other adoptive families helps to normalize adoptive children's experience.

Persons with a strong positive self-identification have a sense of wholeness, connectedness, and positive self-esteem. Their search for meaning has led to answers that do not devalue themselves. One adult adoptee described her perception of her life as being like a jigsaw puzzle with a few pieces missing. She said that when she looked at the puzzle, her eye would go immediately to the missing pieces. After her adoptive mother died, she searched and found her birth relatives, following which she felt a sense of filling in these gaps.

Some aspects of adoption, particularly the secrets and deficits in information, can lead children to feel that they are not like everyone else, but are second-class citizens who were "given away." To achieve an integrated sense of self and positive self-worth, they need to be able to come to terms with the meaning of adoption in their lives as well as the meaning of other life experiences that have had a major effect on them.

Sense of Self-Efficacy

Self-efficacy is best understood in relation to its antithesis—powerlessness. Children who have experienced repeated separations and other traumas have feelings of extreme vulnerability, fear, and rage. Finkelhor and Browne (1985) identify powerlessness as a major theme of traumatic effect and define it as "the process in which the child's will, desires, and sense of efficacy are continually contravened" (pp. 82-83). One adopted child described it aptly: "I feel like a ball in a pinball machine." Children who have been a victim of haphazard, outside forces often feel helpless to influence events in their lives. Children who have been unable to protect themselves from harm may have a constant fear of impending doom and a strong need to control. They develop maladaptive behaviors to achieve a sense of power and mastery through asserting control over others. Their behavior problems reflect this need to control. Lying, defiance, and verbal and physical aggression are common. This theme of need to control is reflected in the following excerpt from a psychological evaluation of one adopted child in our disruption study:

> Suzanne is a bright, verbal, engaging child, eager for attention and skilled at eliciting a strong adult response. However, her behaviors of deliberate enuresis, defecation, and ongoing elaborate dishonesty, covert planned escapades, and passive-aggressive vengeful episodes all indicate serious underlying disturbance. Suzanne appears to have a high need to control others in her intimate environment and is skilled at keeping significant others off balance in order to maintain psychological advantage.

Self-efficacy then is a sense of personal control and mastery, the feeling that one can master and manage events in life. Children who have not achieved a feeling of self-efficacy need to learn positive ways to gain control, to achieve mastery in some areas of their lives, and to have an increased sense of personal choice and power. They need to be helped to identify and express their feelings and to recognize when they are reacting in negative ways out of anger or other strong feelings. By finding positive ways of exercising power and control rather than through negative, oppositional behaviors, they can be helped to manage their feelings more constructively. To accomplish this task, adoptive parents have to be able to manage their own anger and to disengage from the power struggles that they continually find themselves engaged in with their child.

Parents and therapists also need to help the child heal from traumatic experiences. This is hard for parents who must accept that they cannot always take away their child's pain. Children need assistance in understanding the meaning of events in their lives and in processing their feelings related to these events. As with grief work, the work of healing from trauma is never finished, but it can become less of a controlling factor in the child's life as the child gains an increased sense of power and choice.

Capacity for Self-Regulation

The ability to regulate one's own overt behaviors and emotions is an outcome of maturation processes stemming from a healthy parent-child attachment. The mastery of cause and effect thinking, the development of a conscience that depends on internalizing values and rules, and the capacity for empathy and motivation to adjust one's behaviors to the desires of others are all founded on parent-child attachment. Overcoming impulsivity and achieving self-control are abilities that also are compromised by the physical and emotional effect of trauma, which affects the functioning of the autonomic nervous system and psycho neuroendocrine activation.

According to Cicchetti and colleagues (Cicchetti, Ganiban, & Barnett, 1991), maltreated children are at the greatest environmental risk for dysfunctional emotional regulation, particularly in the management of aggressive feelings and impulses. The child's major maturational processes leading to emotional regulation depend on the interaction between the child and the caregiver. In the first few months of life, the caretaker's consistent positive responsiveness to the infant's physiological discomfort helps the infant modulate physiological tension and facilitates the rapid development and organization of neurological systems.

The maturation of neurological inhibitory systems occurs very rapidly throughout infancy and is the foundation for the voluntary control of behavior. Also, cognitive development and parental socialization are strong influences on emotional expression. In early childhood, affect evolves from being reflexive in response to physiological discomfort to being reflective and self-guided. Research on infants and toddlers who have been physically abused reveals that they express an inordinate amount of negative affect and very little positive affect; they demonstrate a higher frequency of aggressive and noncompliant behaviors; and they are immature in their internal-state language, with fewer verbalizations of feelings (Cicchetti & Beeghly, 1987; Egeland & Sroufe, 1981).

Children who have failed to develop self-regulation need help in identifying their feelings and linking their feelings and behavior. Parents can facilitate children's expression of their needs and problem solve with children possible responses for achieving these needs. A variety of techniques and strategies for helping children to control oppositional behaviors and to learn ways of managing overwhelming feelings is discussed further in Chapter 6.

BEHAVIOR PROBLEMS
AS COPING STRATEGIES

Through the use of the model, a number of behavior problems of special needs adopted children can be viewed as coping strategies to defend against feelings of powerlessness, fear of closeness, feelings of low self-worth, and overwhelming feelings of rage stemming from past maltreatment. Adoption experts also have referred to these behaviors as survival behaviors, in that these behaviors have helped children survive in birth homes and in the system—to maintain control in situations where they had no power, to distance caregivers to avoid developing an attachment that would result in additional pain and loss, to elevate the child's poor sense of self-esteem, and other such motivations. Hence, behaviors that do not make sense to parents, such as crazy lying and stealing, serve a protective function for these children. Often these behaviors become pervasive, however, and persist long after the child is in a permanent, safe home.

Lying, which is the most common behavior problem reported for children served through the Illinois project, is a behavior that evokes a strong emotional reaction from parents and is highly associated with adoption risk. It creates mistrust in the parent-child relationship and intensifies the parents' feelings of frustration and powerlessness to determine the truth. Some children who use lying as a chronic, defensive pattern may lie to gain power through controlling others' attitudes or actions with false information. Children who cannot express anger directly may use lying as a means of discharging aggression, seeking revenge for unfair treatment, or out of feelings of anger and jealousy. They may lie to create conflict between others or to get someone else in trouble. They also may lie to maintain secrecy and protect themselves from others becoming interested in their business out of a need to avoid intimacy. Sometimes this kind of pathological lying becomes an automatic response for the child in situations where he or she feels threatened or powerless. Parents refer to this behavior as senseless lying, elaborate dishonesty, and lying when telling the truth would be easier.

Other coping strategies include behaviors such as hoarding food or stealing. Parents describe some children as stealing anything that is not nailed down, such as stealing staples when the child does not have a stapler. This compulsive kind of stealing may be the child's means to achieving a sense of mastery or a retaliation against others. Children also may acquire objects as substitutes for love or to give gifts to others to gain their approval.

Katz (1986, 1990), in describing these negative, self-defeating behavior patterns, emphasizes the need to address the underlying emotional issues to achieve any improvement in the child. Even a behavior that seems relatively mild, such as taking a long time to do a simple activity, may become so ingrained that it exhausts the parents' tolerance. For example, one family served in the Illinois project talked about the daily battle to get their daughter off to school. She would take so long to get ready that she would not have time to eat breakfast. She carried her lunch to school, but would often eat it on the bus and then tell her teacher that her parents would not give her food. Katz developed special techniques for helping the child gain insight into her fears and needs and develop more positive routes to self-protection. In this way, a beginning step in dealing with negative behavior problems is helping the parents and sometimes the child to reframe the behavior in relation to its underlying goals.

INSIGHTS FROM RESEARCH ON ADOPTED CHILDREN

Studies on community samples of children who were primarily adopted as infants are not entirely consistent, although most indicate that from age 6 throughout childhood, adopted children have a higher rate of behavior problems.

A number of studies have employed the Child Behavior Checklist (CBC) to evaluate child behavior problems. This instrument, developed by Achenbach and Edelbrock (1983), is a standardized measure with 118 behavioral items yielding scores on three summary scales and eight subscales. For the total problems, internalizing, and externalizing scales, the clinical range is defined as the top 10% of scores in the total population of nonreferred children. On the individual subscales, the clinical range represents the upper 2% of behavior scores of all nonreferred children on that dimension. The scoring norms and scales vary across six age and gender groups (Achenbach, 1991).

A major study conducted by Brodzinsky and colleagues (Brodzinsky, Singer, & Braff, 1984) matched the adopted and nonadopted samples (130 in each) for age of the child, sex, race, socioeconomic status, and family structure. Some of the adoptive families were recruited through adoption support groups and adoption agencies; thus, it is difficult to know how representative they are of all adoptive families. This study reports that adopted children of both genders scored significantly higher on the externalizing problem scale of the CBC than the nonadopted children, as well as on the hyperactivity, aggressive, and delinquent subscales. Adopted boys had higher scores on uncommunicative behavior, and adopted girls had higher scores on depression, withdrawal, cruelty, and the internalizing scales. The differences between adopted and nonadopted children on the subscales were greatest in the area of hyperactivity.

A follow-up study (Brodzinsky et al., 1987) yielded similar findings, with a higher percentage of adopted children (36%) being rated as manifesting clinically significant symptomatology than their nonadopted peers (14%). In a subsequent review of research on psychological risk associated with adoption, Brodzinsky (1987) attributes the increased vulnerability of adopted children to complications in development presented by a unique set of psychosocial tasks associated with the adoption experience.

Two recent studies using epidemiological data are noteworthy. A Canadian study based on data from the Ontario Child Health Study contrasted 104 adopted children with 3,294 nonadopted children (Lipman, Offord, Racine, & Boyle, 1992). Adoption was significantly associated with psychological disorder and poor school performance for boys, but not for girls, although there was an increased risk of substance abuse for adopted adolescent girls. A similar study in the U.S. using 1981 Health Interview Survey data gathered by the Census Bureau contrasted 145 adopted with 3,553 nonadopted adolescents (Warren, 1992). It found that adoptees are significantly more likely to display behavior problems and more than twice as likely to display two or three problems. Also, adoptees are more likely to be referred for treatment even after controlling for the higher rate of problems and higher level of education of their families. Warren (1992) concludes that the higher representation of adoptees in clinical populations is not attributable solely to their being more troubled.

Studies contrasting adopted and nonadopted children in clinical settings yield some interesting insights. In general, these studies report a higher rate of conduct disorder and hyperactivity diagnoses among adopted children (Cohen et al., 1993; Dickson et al., 1990; Jerome, 1993; Kotsopoulos et al., 1988). In addition, adopted children are more likely to have had previous treatment and have problems of longer duration than nonadopted children (Cohen et al., 1993). Research on adoptees with special needs indicates that a substantial number of them demonstrate ongoing behavior problems. A majority (62%) of the special needs adopted children in families surveyed by Nelson (1985) were described by parents as having moderate or severe behavior problems. Special needs children evidence elevated scores on studies using the CBC (Barth & Berry, 1988; Rosenthal & Groze, 1991, 1994). In Rosenthal and Groze's (1992) study, 41% of children scored in the clinical range of behavior problems on the CBC. In the CBC samples for clinical and nonclinical groups of children, mean scores on the internalizing and externalizing scales are very similar. For all adoption samples studied, the mean externalizing scale scores are higher, usually by several points, than the mean internalizing scale scores.

BEHAVIOR PROBLEMS OF CHILDREN SERVED BY THE ADOPTION PRESERVATION PROJECT

Because child behavior problems were the presenting problem of the vast majority of adoptive families seeking adoption preservation services in Illinois, gaining an understanding of the nature and dynamics involved in these issues was critical to helping these families. The specific behavior problems of the adopted children receiving services in the project were assessed jointly by workers and parents. The total behavior problem score constructed by summing the values on this behavior rating list was used as a measure of behavioral severity for most of the analyses reported in this chapter. Table 4.1 depicts the frequency of 22 behavior problems among the 368 children who were assessed during the service period.

A standardized measure assessing the behavior problems of the children served by this project, the CBC, was incorporated into the evaluation in its second year. Parents' ratings on this instrument were obtained on 223 children. Overall, on the total problem score, 86% of the 204 children evaluated at intake in the adoption preservation project fell in the clinical range, and 91% scored in the clinical range on at least one of the three summary scales. This may be compared to Rosenthal

Table 4.1

Behavior Problems of Children

Behavior	% Present	Behavior	% Present
Lying/manipulation	80	Rejects affection	37
Defiance	79	Curfew violations	34
Verbal aggression	77	Running away	33
Violation of family norms	70	Sexual acting out	28
Peer problems	63	Other/miscellaneous	23
Tantrums	60	Arrests/legal difficulties	21
Physical aggression	60	Suicidal behavior	19
Destruction of property	52	Overcompliance	19
Withdrawal	47	Firesetting	16
Stealing	46	Enuresis	15
Hyperactivity	43	Sexual aggression	12

NOTE: Percentages given are valid percentages, based on number of cases reported and excluding missing data and rereferred cases.

and Groze's (1992) sample of special needs children in which 41% scored in the clinical range for total problems. The mean scores on total problems, internalizing, and externalizing are depicted in Table A.4 in the Appendix.

In comparing scores for the adoption preservation children and for the clinical and nonreferred groups on which the test was normed, the children served by the project were above the mean scores of the clinical population on all three summary scores in each age and gender group, with one exception—younger girls' scores on the internalizing scale. Overall, the margin of difference between adoption preservation children and clinically referred children was greatest on the externalizing scales, indicating that anger, defiance, and acting-out behaviors are major issues for these children.

Observation of the profiles of individual children on the CBC indicates that most children scored in the clinical range on some subscales and in the normal range on others. It might be helpful to reiterate that to be in the clinical range on the syndrome subscales, a child must score in the upper 2% of behavior scores for all nonreferred children. The majority of children served by this project scored in the clinical range on several subscales—attention problems, aggressive behavior, and delinquent behavior. The percentage scoring in the clinical range on each of the subscales and summary scores is reported in Table A.5. As is the case in earlier studies of adopted children, the adoptees served by this project scored higher on the externalizing scale in all age and gender groups, although their scores on the internalizing scale were quite elevated also. Of the studies using the CBC on samples of special needs children, the scores of the children experiencing adoption disruption in Barth and Berry's study (1988) are most similar to the children in this project. On most measures, the children served by the project scored somewhat higher than those in the disruption study. These results underscore the severity of the behavioral and emotional problems of these children years after their adoptions were finalized.

BEHAVIOR PROBLEMS AND PLACEMENT INSTABILITY

Overall, greater severity of behavior problems is associated with parents raising dissolution of the adoption. In addition, research indicates that parents are more tolerant of some types of behavior problems than others, and that certain types of behavior problems place children at higher risk of adoption disruption. In previous research, we found that lying, sexual acting out, and vandalism were the behaviors that had the most significant association with adoption disruption (Smith & Howard, 1991).

Little is known about the relationship between specific behavior problems and risk of adoption dissolution. In an attempt to explore this relationship, each specific behavior problem was analyzed in relation to whether parents raised dissolution as an option. Behaviors significantly associated with parents raising dissolution are listed in order of the strength of their association: violation of family norms, sexual acting out, lying/manipulation, running away, defiance, curfew violations, verbal aggression, stealing, sexual aggression, arrests/legal difficulties, rejects affection, and setting fires. Interestingly, the behavior problem that has the strongest association with dissolution risk is violation of family norms. Parent descriptions of these behaviors go beyond a simple breaking of rules. These behaviors often resemble a rebellion against what the parents value most, such as overt racist expression in a family that strongly values nondiscrimination.

This research indicates that, for the most part, behaviors found to be significantly associated with risk of dissolution are hostile, acting-out, and rebellious behaviors often associated with the diagnostic category of conduct disorder, as well as sexual problems and setting fires, which are less frequent but very difficult to tolerate. Generally, these specific behaviors are associated with children who are "out of control." This is the sense expressed by most parents desiring dissolution—a sense of powerlessness and continued failure to help their children modify their problem behaviors.

It may seem surprising that behaviors such as suicidal behavior and withdrawal are not significantly associated with dissolution risk. These findings coincide with other research on problem adoptions, however, in which behaviors associated with internalizing problems such as withdrawal and anxiety-related behaviors are not significantly associated with adoption instability (Barth & Berry, 1988). More needs to be determined about the differences between factors contributing to adoption disruption versus adoption dissolution. It is likely that some severe and pervasive behaviors contribute to disruption before legalization of the adoption, and that behaviors associated with failure of a long-term adoptive placement are somewhat different.

LINKS BETWEEN BEHAVIOR PROBLEMS
AND CHILD'S HISTORY

Demographic Characteristics

Possible associations between age, race, and gender and severity of behavior problems were explored using the total behavior problem score. As might be expected, severity of behavior problems varies significantly with the age of the child. Behavior problem scores were highest among children in early and late adolescence. The task of separating from parents for adopted teens is often more difficult than for nonadopted children due to the complexity of attachment and separation issues operating in these relationships. These conflicts around launching older teens from their families likely contribute to the increase in behavior problems at age 18.

In earlier research on the behavior problems of special needs adoptees, minority and biracial children were found to have fewer behavior
problems than white children (Rosenthal & Groze, 1991). Among children served by this project, ethnicity was not associated with the level
of behavior problems.

History of Maltreatment

A history of maltreatment and experiencing multiple moves in care
are two factors frequently cited as underlying behavior problems of
special needs adopted children. The majority of adoptees served by this
project had had both of these experiences. Seventy-one percent were
reported as experiencing some form of maltreatment, and 76% had one
or more placements in care between their birth family and their adoptive
placement.

The most common form of maltreatment experienced by these children was serious neglect, reported for 65% of children. Physical abuse
was identified for 38% of children, and sexual abuse for 31%. The
association between each of these abuse types and the severity of
behavior problems was explored. Children who were sexually abused
had significantly higher behavior problem scores than those who were
not known to have been sexually abused, and their parents were more
likely to raise dissolution as an option. This finding coincides with our
previous research on adoption disruption, in which a history of sexual
abuse was strongly associated with disruption (Smith & Howard, 1991).

To explore the range of children's experiences of maltreatment across
the population of adopted children served, a combined maltreatment
scale was constructed ranging from 0 (no abuse or neglect identified)
to 3 (child experienced all three forms of maltreatment). Experiencing
multiple types of abuse and neglect was associated with greater behavior problems; it was not associated with parents raising dissolution,
however.

Placement History

Separation from birth families and multiple moves in care are sources
of trauma for children who have developed attachments to birth parents
or other caregivers. All the children served by this project had experienced some separation events; however, most had few moves in care.
The majority (61%) either were placed directly into their adoptive

homes from their birth families or experienced one foster placement prior to placement into their current homes. There was not a significant relationship between number of moves in care and the severity of behavior problems. The number of placement moves was significantly associated with parents raising dissolution, however. The mean number of placements for children whose parents raised dissolution was 2.14, as compared with 1.19 for those whose parents did not raise dissolution as an option.

An analysis of variance indicates a significant association between age at placement in adoptive home and severity of behavior problems. The mean behavior problem scores by age at this adoptive home placement are depicted in Table A.6. Surprisingly, the highest behavior problem scores are found among children placed prior to age 1. Despite the severe level of behavior problems among these children placed in infancy, their parents were less likely to raise dissolution.

In seeking to explain the high level of behavior problems among these children, a number of possible explanations were explored. Differences between those placed as infants and those placed later were analyzed in relation to age at case opening and the presence of organic problems, attention deficit hyperactivity disorder (ADHD)/attention deficit disorder (ADD), and identity issues. There was a significant difference between the two groups in the presence of ADHD or ADD, with children placed in infancy having a higher percentage of ADHD/ADD. Some authors have theorized a link between the high incidence of ADHD among adoptees and identity conflicts related to adoption. In other words, adoptees who are conflicted in relation to identity issues often fantasize and daydream in class and seem distracted to teachers, leading at times to mislabeling them as having attention deficit problems (Lifton, 1988).

The data do indicate a significantly higher prevalence of identity issues among adoptees placed in infancy as opposed to those placed later. Of the infant placements being rated on this item, 82% were rated as having identity issues, as compared to 57% of those placed after age 1. Those adoptive parents who would prefer to suppress discussion of adoption issues may be able do this more easily with children placed as infants. It also is likely that these children who have no memory of a preplacement history may have little information available to them related to their history.

BEHAVIOR PROBLEMS AND
UNDERLYING EMOTIONAL ISSUES

The adoption literature recognizes that many special needs adopted children exhibit self-defeating, negative behaviors that do not respond to traditional interventions, such as behavior modification programs. These behavioral patterns are often defensive patterns for coping with underlying emotional conflicts. These conflicts include attachment difficulties stemming from painful losses and maltreatment; anxiety and fear of repeated trauma or losses; control issues related to powerlessness to protect themselves from trauma and unwanted changes; low self-esteem and identity conflicts; anger and rage issues; and issues stemming from children's experiences surrounding placement and adoption. Workers were asked to identify the involvement of specific emotional issues with the children, and the relationships between these issues and behavior problems were explored statistically. The associations between these issues and behavior problems are discussed briefly here. In addition, the primary issues are examined individually in separate chapters, and interventions useful in addressing these issues in parenting or counseling these children and families are explored.

The presence of specific emotional issues that may contribute to behavior problems was evaluated by workers at case closing. These issues are reported in Table 4.2. Workers did not rate these issues on cases where they felt they could not judge, particularly for cases with limited contact.

Attachment, Separation, and Grief

Separation and attachment conflicts are the most commonly identified emotional issue attributed to these children (74%), and a related issue, grief, is the second most commonly identified (72%). These adopted children's stories include many complications arising from loss, grief, and attachment conflicts. Children related fantasies of being reunited with birth parents, confusion about a former foster family's failure to adopt them, sadness and worry related to a birth sibling whom the child thought was still at home, fear of losing the adoptive family, and many other feelings involving loss.

Table 4.2

Issues Related to Child Problems

Issue	% Yes	% No	% Unsure
Separation/attachment conflicts	74	16	10
Grief	72	16	12
Identity	63	17	20
Depression	54	26	20
PTSD symptoms	36	40	23
Need to search	33	51	16

The presence of separation and attachment conflicts is significantly associated with parents' raising dissolution as an option and with the severity of behavior problems. Likewise, children experiencing grief have significantly higher behavior problem scores than those who are not so identified.

Children who have experienced traumatic separations often have strong fears and confusion related to these events that subside and resurface over time. Workers reported that children's birthdays are often occasions that revive grief issues or unanswered questions in their minds. Children experiencing a recent loss, such as the death of a family member or a divorce (either of which occurred in 29% of all families served), often demonstrated severe reactions and resurfacing of past issues. These children had significantly higher behavior problem scores than children not experiencing a recent loss.

Brodzinsky and colleagues (1992) contrast the loss felt by adopted children with children's experiences with divorce or death, concluding that a number of factors make the loss of adoption pervasive and difficult to resolve. The authors note that some adoptees mask their sense of loss with intense anger, argumentative or defiant behavior, and emotional distance, and frequently deny that they have been affected much by being adopted. Sometimes they become physically threatening to others, which had occurred with many acting-out teens served by the project.

For adoptees who have experienced repeated separations and maltreatment, closeness is often connected with pain and loss in their past experience. They have an ongoing desire and need for closeness, yet this need is coupled with strong fears of intimacy. Their behaviors in relation to attachment are often described by parents as characterized by a push-pull dynamic. One adoptive mother described her teenage daughter's behavior in this way:

> Part of what she has cried out for is not her need; that's part of her push-pull. She wants to push you away from her, and part of it is to prove that you will not stick around. . . . I think she's still testing, and I think one of the major tests is about, "Will you leave me?" "Will I be abandoned again?" . . . She's really afraid for me to leave at any time, and even though she's 18-years-old, and technically she should be able to be left with someone, or even by herself, she's not able to do that. (Spaulding for Children, 1989)

Some children recognize and even articulate their need to test out their parents' commitment. For example, one 12-year-old child expressed his feelings in the following way,

> I'm so happy that I'm not going to move anymore, but I had to test my mom and my dad out to see if they were going to give me up. I would like run around and behave my baddest to see if they were going to give me up. And sometimes I still do try, and they haven't given me up yet . . . since I was 6-years-old. (Spaulding for Children, 1989)

Attachment issues are discussed further in Chapter 5.

Identity Issues and the Need to Search

One dynamic that Brodzinsky et al. (1992) advances as underlying behavioral difficulties is the ongoing adjustment concerning identity issues coupled with coming to terms with the loss of birth family connections. Identity issues, which were noted in 64% of cases rated on this dimension, vary in frequency with the age of the child. For younger children, identity issues were most common among 7- to 8-year-olds (54%), and they increased again for 11- to 12-year-olds (63%), continuing to intensify through age 16. The percentage of children identified as having identity issues for each age group is as follows: 4 to 6 years, 20%; 7 to 8 years, 54%; 9 to 10 years, 41%; 11 to 12 years, 63%; 13 to 14 years, 77%; 15 to 16 years, 85%; 17-plus years, 54%. These results correspond to Brodzinsky et al.'s (1992) conclusion that around age 7 or 8, children's understanding of adoption changes to incorporate more of the loss aspects of their origins and that identity issues typically peak in adolescence.

Children expressing identity-related issues have significantly higher behavior problem scores than those evaluated as not having identity issues. Children express their frustration and desperation to resolve these issues both verbally and behaviorally. Anxieties and confusion surrounding identity and adoption were experienced by a majority of the children served.

Some children struggling with identity issues express a need to search for their birth family or information about them. Most adoptees have search ideation throughout their lives, but do not actively search for their birth parents (Schechter & Bertocci, 1990). Active searches are more common among females, as was the case with this population of adoptees—59% of those identified as needing to search were girls. Also, the need to search was most common among older adolescents.

Interest in searching is not necessarily associated with problems, although at times it may be. Problems created by children's need to search are reported for 33% of children rated on this dimension. This issue is not associated with the severity of behavior problems, but it is associated with parents' raising dissolution. Some of the adoptive parents served have been resistant to their children's need to reconnect with the birth family. One adoptive mother felt angry that her 13-year-old daughter wanted to see her birth parents, especially when they had mistreated her. Identity and search issues are explored further in Chapter 7.

Depression

Depression, which may result from unresolved grief, ongoing feelings of anger and rejection, low self-esteem, lack of acceptance by peers, feelings of powerlessness, and other emotional conflicts, is identified as present in 55% of adoptees rated on this dimension. It is expressed behaviorally through hostile, aggressive behaviors as well as self-destructive behaviors. For example, one 16-year-old boy expressed that he thought his adoptive parents had been forced to put up with him and that he would be doing them a favor by killing himself. The presence of depression is significantly related to severity of behavior problems. Those identified as having depression had a mean behavior score of

15.6, as compared with a mean of 9.2 for those identified as not having depression. This issue also is associated with parents' raising dissolution as an option.

Although depression is an important emotion underlying behavior problems in many troubled adoptive children, it is a complicated phenomenon to identify and to understand. Although the *DSM-IV* (American Psychiatric Association, 1994) recognizes that the manifestations of depression vary with age, there is no consensus in the literature or diagnostic classification systems on the criteria for identifying depression among children at different developmental levels and with different overlapping conditions. Also, the identification of depression in children is related in part to their ability to identify and communicate their emotions accurately. This ability is limited in children generally, especially in many special needs adoptees, who use numbing and other means to defend themselves against a range of feelings.

Research has identified a number of risk factors for depression in children, including loss of a parent or other attachment figure, a history of maltreatment, family histories of psychiatric disorders, low self-esteem, negative body image, learning problems, low peer popularity, repeated experiences of rejection, stressful life events, family conflict, and emotional unavailability of parents (Kaufman, 1991; Peterson, Compas, Brooks-Gunn, Stemmler, Ey, & Grant, 1993). Most of the children served through the project experienced several of these conditions, placing them at risk of depression.

In addition, some conditions such as neuroendocrine dysregulation or cognitive distortions may be seen as both cause and effect factors in depression. It has been estimated that only a small minority of depressed children are diagnosed or treated (Keller, Lavori, Beardslee, Wunder, & Ryan, 1991). This condition is likely underdiagnosed among adoptees, and many of their depressive symptoms may be masked as conduct-disorder-related diagnoses.

Research among clinical and nonclinical populations of adoptees has recognized that adopted children, especially girls, are more vulnerable to depression than their nonadopted peers (Brodzinsky et al., 1987; Fullerton, Goodrich, & Berman, 1986; Senior & Himadi, 1985). In their analysis of hospitalized adoptees, Fullerton and colleagues (1986) describe the impulsive acting-out behaviors of these children as defenses against a "depressive core." They report that many adoptees resist treatment attempts to address their emotional issues, sometimes running away in reaction.

Studies of special needs adoptees that administered the CBC report high percentages of children scoring in the clinical range on the anxious/depressed subscale (Barth & Berry, 1988; Rosenthal & Groze, 1991, 1994). Barth and Berry's (1988) study reports 68% of girls ages 6 to 11 and 44% of all 3- to 5-year-olds are in the clinical range for depression. Rosenthal and Groze's (1994) follow-up study indicates that depression is one problem that increased for these children since the original study.

For adoptees served in the Illinois project who had been evaluated on the CBC, 35% scored in the clinical range on the anxious/depressed scale. There has been some criticism of this instrument's coverage of depressive symptoms (Harrington, 1993), and it is dependent on parents' familiarity with their children's feelings. Workers' evaluations of children reflect a higher presence of depression (55%). Workers reported that these children expressed depression behaviorally both through hostile, aggressive behaviors, as well as in more internalized ways such as withdrawal, anxiety, and self-destructive behaviors. Children as young as age 6 expressed suicidal ideation. For example, one mother reported that she found her 6-year-old daughter throwing herself against the wall in her bedroom. When stopped and given holding time, the child said, "Mommy, I want to throw myself out the window and kill myself."

Some children express very negative self-images approaching self-hatred that contribute to their depressive feelings. For example, a child with a physical anomaly who was in gifted classes was struggling with feelings of anger and rejection by his birth mother and by his peers. He viewed his birth as a mistake, saying he should never have been born. Another girl described herself as follows: "I'm a bad girl . . . all bad." A few children whose parents were seeking to dissolve their adoptions expressed extreme feelings of despair and hopelessness. One teenage boy wrote, "If only I could change my past to what I wanted it to be, then I could be 'normal.' The biggest loss in my life has been not living with my real family like normal people."

Posttraumatic Stress Disorder

Posttraumatic stress symptoms are reported for a number of adolescents and preadolescents who have past histories of trauma. Thirty-six percent of children rated on this dimension were identified as having posttraumatic stress symptoms. These children have more severe behavior problems and greater risk of dissolution than children not identified as having posttraumatic stress symptoms.

Some children have reported intrusive thoughts or nightmares about events that they did not remember previously. They often expressed feeling that they were crazy, and wondered if these things really happened to them. Several children served by the project began experiencing anxiety and flashbacks related to early abuse experiences. Some children reported feeling flooded by waves of emotion over which they felt they had no control. The posttraumatic stress symptoms of many of the children served by the Illinois project seemed to be triggered by a variety of factors, such as disclosure of previous abuse in therapy, experiencing a new trauma or loss, the reemergence of birth family issues in adolescence, and the onset of puberty. The prevalence of PTSD symptoms was highest for children at age 12. Fifty-nine percent of 12-year-olds were identified as having PTSD symptoms, as compared with 35% of all other children served by the project.

The resurfacing of trauma-related issues often was interwoven with loss-related experiences. We observed this interaction of loss and trauma experiences and delayed surfacing or resurfacing of these issues in a study of adoption disruption (Smith & Howard, 1991, 1994). The effect of trauma on children and strategies for helping them to heal are discussed in Chapter 6.

The findings of the evaluation of the Illinois project demonstrate the persistence of severe behavior problems in these children and the interrelationships between ongoing emotional issues and behavior problems. The primary dimensions for emotional adjustment and intervention in parenting and other therapeutic work with special needs children are explored throughout the remainder of this volume.

Chapter 5

ADOPTION MEANS SOMEBODY LOVES YOU AND SOMEBODY DOESN'T

Separation, Grief, and Attachment Issues in Work With Families

An adoption worker reported that when she asked a young client what adoption meant to him, he responded, "Adoption means somebody loves you and somebody doesn't love you." This statement captures the struggles of many adopted children in coming to terms with their separation from birth family members. For some children, their mistreatment in birth families and their separation experiences have led to feeling unloved by anyone. Their greatest need and their greatest fear intertwine in relation to loving, trusting, and risking another overwhelming loss.

Attachment is the process central to adjustment within adoptive families—adopted children's attachment to all family members, and other family members' attachment to adopted children. It is an affectionate bond that develops through positive, need-satisfying, and pleasurable interactions. For most of us, our earliest attachments are to parents, and these relationships establish a pattern for emotional connections to people and defining one's sense of self. A close, satisfying infant-caregiver bond is the foundation for child development in all areas. The failure to develop healthy attachment or the interruption of an established parent-child attachment poses major challenges to a developing child. In adoptive families, creating attachments and the grief that comes from lost attachments are primary areas for adjustment.

The concept of secondary losses is important in understanding the loss experiences of adopted children and their families. Children coming to adoption through the child welfare system not only lose relationships with birth parents, siblings, and extended family members, they lose almost every other aspect of their lives. Most children entering foster care must part with favorite toys, friends, teachers or other positive adult relationships, a school and neighborhood, pets, familiar foods and customs, and many other familiar things. They also lose access to information about themselves and a sense of continuity in their lives. Likewise, adoptive parents often may experience secondary losses such as the loss of an earlier relationship with their child, a loss of status in the eyes of some people, and the loss of biological continuity.

OVERVIEW OF ATTACHMENT THEORY AS IT RELATES TO ADOPTION

The process by which adopted children resolve the loss of fantasized or actual attachments to a birth family and develop attachments to adoptive family members is unclear. Although there is a considerable body of theoretical literature on this subject, empirical examination of this process is limited.

Children placed in adoptive homes soon after birth develop attachments to caregivers in the same way birth children do; however, eventually they must come to terms with the fact that another family created them. Research indicates that infant adoptees do not perceive the loss aspects of adoption until around age 8 or older (Brodzinsky et al., 1992). Between ages 8 and 11, children's understanding of adoption broadens markedly, and adoptees at this stage of cognitive development often experience confusion and ambivalence. Also, the normal process of adaptive grieving usually begins during this period for children adopted as infants (Brodzinsky, 1987). Unlike adults, who can process loss at many different levels, children repeat the grief process for a major loss each time they achieve a new level of cognitive development (van Gulden & Bartels-Rabb, 1994). Therefore, issues that seemed settled and successfully resolved often resurface at a later age, accompanied by intense emotions.

Adoption literature presents two models for understanding the attachment struggles of adoptees, particularly those removed from birth homes through the child welfare system. Both of these models stem from the classic works of Ainsworth (1969, 1985, 1989) and Bowlby (1960, 1973, 1980). These two models are the negative working model and the grief and mourning model.

Disturbed Attachments and the Negative Working Model

The negative working model focuses on the long-term effect on children of unhealthy attachment relationships in early childhood (Cicchetti, 1989; Cline, 1992; Delaney, 1991; Egeland, Sroufe, & Erickson, 1983). Children develop internal representations of themselves and other attachment figures based on their early interactions with the primary caregiver. When the caregiver is inaccessible, unresponsive to the child's needs, or punitive, the child develops a cynical, pessimistic negative working model of himself or herself and caregivers that results in habitually disturbed patterns of interaction in future attachment relationships. Safety is a primary function of bonding or attachment, and attachment relationships are linked to feelings of security. Attachment relationships develop as a result of need satisfaction and stress reduction. For a child who is separated from the primary caregiver, inability to gain access to the attachment figure under threatening conditions produces ongoing separation distress. Weiss (1988) describes some of the characteristics of attachment relationships, including the fact that they endure over time and are never wholly interchangeable or replaceable by another. Once a young child has developed an attachment to a primary caregiver, this attachment persists despite poor parenting and long separations. Theoretically, children who have experienced a strong attachment have greater capacity to develop future attachments. Children must be helped to resolve the loss, however, to make a commitment to a new attachment relationship.

In humans, attachment serves a number of functions beyond safety. These include learning to modulate arousal; learning basic cause and effect thinking; cognitive development; learning to trust others and to develop reciprocity in relationships; development of social emotions such as shame, guilt, empathy, and pride; development of a conscience; and development of a sense of self-worth and boundaries for self and others (Fahlberg, 1991). Attachments develop not only through the arousal-relaxation cycle initiated by a child's needs, but also through a positive interaction cycle whereby the parent initiates positive interactions with the child and the child responds positively to these. These two cycles of interaction between the infant and primary caregivers lead to a relationship pattern and an internalized map of what the world is like (the working model). The quality of a child's earliest attachment relationship has lasting importance for his or her development, and children experiencing poor nurturance and maltreatment develop unusual patterns in relating to others. For example, the child may avoid any physical and emotional closeness altogether or may seek and accept closeness, become fearful, and then behave in ways to push people away. These patterns serve some coping function for a child in a maltreating family, but become counterproductive in a nurturing family that is seeking to meet the child's needs.

Children who have a secure attachment relationship with their caregivers have a positive working model of their world—an internalized representation related to expectations of the accessibility and responsiveness of others and the value of self. Children who have experienced pain in relation to closeness develop a negative working model, however, based on their accumulated experiences with primary caregivers. The maltreated child views his or her situation as unsafe and sees himself or herself as worthless and impotent to influence others. For the child who has ambivalence and fear connected to attachment, conduct problems serve three functions—to increase caregiver interactions, to keep the caregiver at a distance, and to vent the child's anger (Delaney, 1991).

Landmark studies on attachment identify three types of attachment relationships: insecure-avoidant (type A), secure (type B), and insecure-anxious or ambivalent (type C; Ainsworth, Blehar, Waters, & Wall, 1978). Children whose needs are consistently met develop secure attachments to caregivers. Two types of patterns resulting from maltreatment have been identified. The insecure-avoidant children may seek attention from strangers but do not look to caregivers for comfort. These children express mostly negative emotions, are sullen and oppositional, and tend to be socially isolated from peers and adults. The insecure-anxious or ambivalent pattern is characterized by the child's alternating between seeking proximity and resisting contact. These children are very anxious, whiny and demanding, intrusive with adults, and immature. They may use manipulation to engage others in interaction. Research studies have demonstrated that the vast majority (70% to 90%) of maltreated infants form insecure attachments to their caregivers (Carlson, Cicchetti, Barnett, & Braunwald, 1989; Egeland & Sroufe, 1981). These studies also report that these children show greater instability over time in the quality of their attachments. They often mix approach and avoidance behaviors, and are prone to noncontextual aggression.

A fourth pattern of attachment common in maltreated children has been identified in recent years—a type D attachment pattern called "disorganized-disoriented" (Main & Solomon, 1990). Rather than maintaining a single pattern of interaction with caregivers such as the A, B, and C types, maltreated children often are characterized by disorganization of their behaviors. One study found that 82% of maltreated 12-month-olds demonstrated type D attachments, reflecting pronounced forms of insecurity, fearfulness, and difficulties related to expression and modulation of affect (Carlson et al., 1989).

At later ages, children with disorganized attachment styles demonstrate a range of externalized behavior problems and disturbed patterns of relating. For example, one 9-year-old was described in a psychological evaluation as having "a core of detached, cold distrust that is subtle and alarming especially as it is masked with winning and engaging social interaction." Some of these children alternate between periods of responsiveness and periods of active hostility or passive-aggressive expressions of aggression. One foster parent who was struggling with a child in her home described this pattern in these words:

> She spent the first 3 months being perfect. She made us all feel very close to her, trust her, and bond to her. Then she systematically and deliberately tore down by behavior and attitude all our trust. She laughed at our hurt and bewilderment and said: "You thought I cared about you. You were wrong. It was just an act you were stupid enough to fall for!" Then she insisted on leaving.

Of course, this young girl's behavior may not have been as cold and calculating as the foster parent perceived. Often children experience honeymoons at the beginning of new placements. But as they begin to feel close, they become afraid of the pain of another loss and push people away. They may devalue the developing relationship and in effect reject others before they have a chance to be rejected once again.

Most research studies related to attachment patterns in maltreated children have focused primarily on infants and toddlers. A recent study analyzing attachment patterns among special needs adoptees reports that an abuse history is a predictor of low scores on trust and an anxious-avoidant pattern of relating (Groze & Rosenthal, 1993). Children with multiple abuse histories have the most attachment difficulties. Although the mental blueprint that children have developed from early interactions can be modified, some children who are attachment avoidant may be very resistant to change. Such children have developed survival or coping mechanisms for self-protection that are deeply entrenched. Keck and Kupecky (1995) describe the child's response in these words:

> The child who has experienced abuse, neglect, sexualization, and chaos has a limited range of emotional responses. He frequently attempts to disconnect from his most uncomfortable feelings—specifically, sadness and fearfulness—because they make him feel vulnerable and weak. In trying to escape these feelings, he often heightens his arousal with anger. Anger for him feels strong . . . and people respond to it. (p. 51)

Despite the overflow of anger in these children, many of them have difficulty expressing anger directly, and are more likely to express it indirectly through negative behaviors.

Beech Brook, a residential treatment center in Ohio, specializes in the assessment and treatment of children with attachment disorders. It has developed an attachment disorder diagnostic questionnaire, which it administers in addition to a battery of standardized measures. Behaviors that are most often associated with attachment problems include the following:

- The child lies even when the truth is obvious.
- The child seeks negative attention over positive.
- The child steals from home or from household members.
- The child seriously hurts or kills animals.
- The caregiver finds that things that work with other children don't work with this child.
- The family becomes worried when things are going well with the child, knowing it is the "calm before the storm."
- The child goes from one extreme to another in his or her view of others.
- The child distances himself or herself from others in relationships where closeness is expected.
- After a negative interaction, a period of emotional distance occurs (Beech Brook, 1995).

Another interesting tool used at Beech Brook for assessing attachment problems is the "Draw a Nest" exercise. Children are asked to draw
a nest and tell a story about it. The children with the most severe
attachment problems draw empty nests with no mother bird and recount
stories related to loss or abandonment.

According to professionals who specialize in helping children with
severe attachment problems, it takes more than normal parenting or the
usual repertoire of therapeutic techniques to reach these children (Cline,
1992; Delaney & Kunstal, 1993; James, 1994; Keck & Kupecky, 1995).
Specialized techniques must be used to change cyclical power struggles
between child and parent, to facilitate direct expression of emotion from
the child, and to increase the child's acceptance of nurturance. Some of
the attachment therapies use intrusive techniques and holding to provoke the child into emotional expression, articulation of needs, and
acceptance of control and nurturance. Goals and strategies for working
on attachment issues are discussed further at the end of this chapter.

The Grief and Mourning Model

A second model for understanding the effect of interrupted attachments on children is the grief and mourning model (Fahlberg, 1991;
Jewett, 1982; Kubler-Ross, 1969), which theorizes that lost attachments
must be mourned successfully so as not to interfere with the development of new attachments. Most children removed from birth homes due
to abuse or neglect do not have strong, secure attachments to their
caregivers (Smith & Howard, 1991), but many have at least moderate
attachments to parents, and a few are strongly attached. Theoretically,
children who have experienced a strong attachment have greater capacity for developing future attachments. In our study of adoption disruption (Smith & Howard, 1991), however, children strongly attached to
birth parents were particularly vulnerable to disruption; 83% of those
children evaluated as strongly attached to a birth parent disrupted in
their first adoptive placement. One example is the case reported below.

Sherry was a 7-year-old who was placed for adoption with her two
younger siblings after spending 3 years in foster homes. She began
acting out a great deal in the adoptive home. The adoptive mother
reported that Sherry would come up on her lap and attempt to
cuddle, but there was not a warmth or genuineness to the actions.
When the adoptive parents tried to discipline Sherry, she would

often become hysterical, repeatedly calling out for her birth mother, Kathy. At times Sherry would withdraw into her own little world of rocking and humming. The social worker came to talk with Sherry after a period of very high conflict, and she explained to Sherry that this was a permanent placement from which she would not be moved. Sherry told the worker that if she loved Kathy, she would not be able to love anyone else. She said that she liked it at this home because she liked school, but she said that it was important that she be able to love Kathy. Sherry asked when she would be old enough to go back looking for Kathy; she asked if there were pictures of Kathy or of the house she grew up in, because she was afraid she would forget them. She also explained to the worker that when she was being mean to her brother and sister, she was angry at them because they were not thinking about Kathy. The next month, this placement disrupted and all three siblings were removed. A psychologist evaluated Sherry and concluded that her struggles with issues related to permanence and separation from her birth mother were feelings that were not available to her until they were unsettled by the crisis of adoptive placement.

In this case, Sherry had not been able to mourn the loss of her mother. Many children in the foster care system are focusing on survival. The work of grieving does not really begin as long as the child is denying the permanence of separation and maintaining the expectation of returning home. Many children have a natural tendency to shut out memories and feelings related to lost relationships because the pain associated with them is too overwhelming. In fact, some argue that mourning by children in care really does not begin until after some degree of trust and relationship has developed with new caregivers (Eagle, 1993).

Children frequently are not helped to grieve the loss of their birth family. Too often, caregivers are threatened by children's idealized images of past attachment figures. Caregivers may not understand the process children go through in grieving, or may fail to give children permission to express these feelings. Children's ability to resolve their grief is further limited by their placement experiences. For example, in a survey of adoption workers in Illinois that we conducted to identify barriers to adoption for special needs children, one worker wrote about the failure of workers to allow for a time of grieving after the termination of parental rights. As this worker wrote, "children are rushed from the termination proceeding to a photo shoot for an adoption matching service. No time is given to grieve the biological family" (Smith & Howard, 1995).

Even for children who have begun coming to terms with the reality of a permanent separation from birth families, the demands of making a permanent parental attachment in an adoptive home may trigger resurfacing of both separation trauma and other traumas experienced earlier in their lives. Achieving a higher level of cognitive development changes a child's perceptions related to losses and initiates a resurfacing. Likewise, confronting new developmental tasks, such as the identity conflicts of adolescence, requires a reworking of major losses and traumas.

Adoption practice literature emphasizes preparing children and families for adoption. Part of the preparation of both the child and the adoptive family involves addressing unresolved grief issues. A piece of this grief work with the child involves helping the child disengage from the birth parents so that he or she is free to invest in a new parent-child relationship. The grief literature varies in its assertion of the necessity of breaking bonds with a lost attachment figure to develop a new attachment relationship. Most scholars on grief, from Freud (1957) and Bowlby to more modern authors such as Parkes and Weiss (1983), recognize that through mourning, the lost relationship is put into a different perspective, but remains a part of the person's identity. For example, in Bowlby's (1980) description of the loss of a spouse, he writes that widows and widowers "retain a strong sense of the continuing presence of their partner without the turmoil of hope and disappointment, search and frustration, anger and blame that are present earlier" (p. 96). Some theorists assert the necessity of successful mourning to develop new attachments (Kates, Johnson, Kader, & Grieder, 1991; Steinhauer, 1979). Others assert that when their parents are still alive (the case in divorce and most adoption situations), these attachments continue but children can make new attachments without mourning (Rosenberg, 1992; Silverman, Nickman, & Worden, 1992).

It is likely, however, that coming to terms with abuse and neglect and long-term separation from one's birth family involves a somewhat different process than mourning a parent's death or a divorce. Research needs to address the process by which children in the child welfare system come to terms with their losses and develop new parental attachments. Experts who have specialized in working with these children emphasize the necessity for children to understand and come to terms with significant losses (Fahlberg, 1991; James, 1994; Jewett, 1982). Bowlby (1980) perceives the necessity of working through one's rage related to the separation to move on. If this is not done, a "defensive detachment" persists in which emotions are not felt or expressed, the need for the lost object continues, and a person is not able to develop new attachments. Frequently, children in the child welfare system lack the capacity to grieve and demonstrate denial of feelings, emotional withdrawal, and ongoing rage that is not directly expressed (Eagle, 1994). These children need special help and support to facilitate processing significant losses.

Sometimes parents have information that would be helpful to their child in understanding loss, but they never share this with the adopted child. Reasons for holding back usually relate to waiting for the child to ask or trying to protect the child from pain. One family served by the Illinois project was encouraged to share a letter from the birth mother with their daughter. When the daughter had read it, the worker asked her what she had learned that she didn't already know. The girl replied, "That she loved me!"

A part of the necessary work in helping children with the grieving process is disengagement work. The goal is not detachment per se. Rather, this part of the grieving process leads to a reorganization of the self in relation to the lost attachment figure and a new perspective that frees the child to establish new attachment relationships. A pioneer in the development of adoption practice, Kay Donley (1984) articulates four disengagement messages that a child needs to receive from birth parents or other caregivers to whom he or she is attached to be able to move on to an attachment to an adoptive family. The messages children need to receive are:

I am loved . . . I'm an okay person.
It's not my fault that I cannot stay with you.
I will always be remembered.
I am wished well, and it is okay to love someone else.

In addition, the child needs to accept that he or she cannot return home, and overcome feelings of self-blame and badness. Ideally, child welfare workers will help children say good-bye either in reality or symbolically. Creative workers have gone to great lengths to facilitate this disengagement work. Donley (1984) recounts a worker taking a young boy to visit his grandmother's grave and talking with him about how much his grandmother had loved him and that she wanted him to be happy with a family. A worker in Illinois visited a child's birth mother in a mental institution and videotaped her explaining to the child why she could not care for him. The adoptive father reported that his son and he watched this video over and over. In the best case, birth parents, adoptive parents, and children are brought together for a formal good-bye visit. Before the visit, the worker carefully prepares all parties separately, explaining the purpose of the visit. The worker is closely involved with birth parents to assess whether they can participate in a way that will be helpful to the child. The goal is that the birth parents will express love for the child, acknowledge their inability to care for the child, and make clear the wish that the child be happy in the new home. The child is given the direct message that the separation is not his or her fault. The adoptive parent is able to see the pain felt by the child and the birth parent. The birth parents are assured that they are an important player in helping the child have a better life. Birth parents also can be reassured that the adoptive parents are committed to their child. Gifts often are exchanged. The visit is videotaped, and the child is given a copy to keep.

BARRIERS TO RESOLUTION OF
LOSS FOR ADOPTEES

Weiss (1988) discusses the processes necessary to recover from loss as well as the barriers that interfere with recovery. All the barriers that he identifies as interfering with resolution of losses are present in the situations of most adopted children with special needs. First of all, recovery from loss requires cognitive acceptance or developing a satisfactory account of the causes of the loss. If the loss makes no sense, there is an ongoing search for a satisfactory explanation of the event. Children struggle in developing an account of why they were separated from their birth families. They need to be helped to understand the reality of their situations.

It takes children much longer than adults to grasp the permanence of loss. Also, children who have been removed from their families because of maltreatment frequently blame themselves for this loss. Even teen-agers will say that they were removed because they were misbehaving or that their parent did not want them because they were bad or in some way unlovable. One adoption preservation worker reported going to great lengths to help an 8-year-old girl understand that it was not her fault that her birth family had abused her. The worker went so far as to show the child X-rays of the broken bones she sustained at the age of 9 months, and helped the girl think of what a 9-month-old was like, questioning her about what a baby could possibly have done to deserve that kind of treatment.

Helping children understand the reality of their birth parents' situation is often a very complicated task. Difficult information needs to be reframed so that children can better understand it. For example, a parent's mental illness may be explained as a problem that leads to confusion about what is real and what isn't, which makes it hard to take care of someone else. In fact, the parent needs someone to take care of him or her. In addition to an understanding of the loss of birth family, children's need for letting go and moving on also requires an understanding of all families that they have lived with—why they went there and why they left, and what if anything they might have done to make things work out differently. It is important that children be helped to say goodbye, directly or symbolically, to past caregivers (Jewett, 1982).

In addition to cognitive understanding of the loss, a second step in the process of recovery from loss is emotional acceptance. This requires confronting emotion-laden memories and associations and fully expe-riencing or expressing the feelings related to them. The child needs to explore in detail significant relationships in his or her past, including pleasant, ambivalent, and painful aspects. Although full emotional ac-ceptance may rarely occur to the extent that sad feelings are never evoked, the feelings become less intense and of shorter duration. Some conditions that Weiss (1988) describes as creating barriers in this process include ambivalence toward the attachment figure, low self-esteem together with a feeling of having been dependent on the attachment figure, and feelings of responsibility and loyalty toward the attachment figure. All these conditions are common to children coming through the child welfare system. They often struggle with ambivalent feelings toward birth parents—feelings of love, anger, guilt, fear, and rejection. A child may idealize a birth mother yet express fears of returning home. He or she may be attached to an adoptive family and want to stay there, while at the same time projecting anger on the adoptive mother to the degree that he or she is physically abusive toward her.

Sometimes children defend against their rage and ambivalent feelings toward birth parents by idealizing them. Thus, they can stay connected to birth parents. There are conflicting views on the role of idealization in the mourning process. One psychologist (Eagle, 1993), in discussing mourning for children in care, emphasizes that caregivers need to allow the child to come to a more realistic assessment of birth parents in his or her own time. The permission, respect, and encouragement of new caregivers to acknowledge the importance of past attachments (whether idealized or not) helps the child move beyond denial and mourn his or her losses, while, at the same time, supporting new attachments.

The final aspect of recovery from loss is an identity change. Weiss (1988) describes this step as a reorientation whereby the connection to the lost attachment figure is part of a past self rather than a present self. Of course, most of our knowledge about grief work relates to loss of a relationship due to death. When attachment figures are still alive and, to some extent, attainable, this process is complicated further.

By integrating the child's past with the present, the child can be helped to maintain an internal connection to past attachment figures and incorporate them into a sense of identity and continuity. Sometimes children idealize lost parents to extreme degrees, and in turn denigrate the new (adoptive) parent (Parkes, 1988). It is often hard for adoptive parents to understand children's loyalty to birth parents who mistreated them. Adoptive parents need to be helped to understand and accept their child's need for a connection to past caregivers in achieving a positive sense of identity. Also, the tendency of some workers to cast the biological parents as bad and incompetent and the substitute parents as all good can contribute to splitting for the child (Minuchin & Elizur, 1990). As a result, the child may need to defend his or her birth family by taking the reverse position.

Preserving children's access to significant birth family members or other caregivers is often constructive for them in coming to terms with their life circumstances (Eagle, 1993). Of the children served by the Illinois project, 29% continued to have contact with birth family members. These children were not identified as having any more attachment problems to adoptive parents than children with no contact with birth family members. There has been some reorientation in child welfare practice to maintaining some continuity to past attachment figures, particularly previous foster parents and siblings. Children's needs to maintain healthy connections to past attachment figures are often not appreciated by workers or adoptive parents, however. Policies have been developed to support children's ongoing contact with the birth family before termination of parental rights. Adoption policies generally do not support children's access to past attachment figures after adoption finalization, however. Ongoing access based on the needs and wishes of the child is an area for development in adoption policy and practice.

SIBLING CONNECTIONS

Some of the strongest, most positive attachments that children coming through the child welfare system have experienced are to siblings. Siblings in maltreating families often nurture each other and form strong bonds of dependence and loyalty. For example, in our study of adoption disruption, a brother and sister had been placed together for adoption. The brother adjusted well in his new family; his sister struggled to develop an attachment to these new parents and displayed many acting-out behaviors. When the adoptive parents finally decided that they could not keep the sister, she was removed. The young boy wrote the following letter to try to explain his conflicted feelings:

> I fill (feel) bad when I stay with the people who put my sister out and it make me want to hate but I can't. You was the nices(t) family I ever had . . . I love you with all my heart. But I think I got to leave, because I fill bad about you putting June out . . . we were close from the first. I just don't fill right because . . . I'm just like half of June's heart.

Even many years after adoption, children may sustain feelings of responsibility or longing for siblings. One boy served through the project was worried about his little sister, whom he had helped take care of and who had stayed in the birth home when he left. His worker was able to gain information about the sister, who was then living with another family and doing well. Just knowing this relieved the young boy's fears. Several children served through adoption preservation yearned for visits with siblings whom they may not have seen for 8 years or longer. At least one child ran away trying to locate siblings from whom she had been separated; others ran away to search for birth mothers. Policies protecting children's rights to visit siblings while they are in foster care have been strengthened in recent years; however, other means are needed to support children's relationships with siblings after adoption.

CHILDREN'S FEELINGS OF
ANGER AND FEAR

Each child has a somewhat different experience and different needs in relation to coming to terms with loss. For some children, anger, hatred, and fear are the predominant emotions that they feel toward birth parents. Such reactions are more likely for children who were repeatedly abused in their birth families and for children who have had a sustained relationship in a substitute family that they want to protect. For example, one child, whose case was in the comparison group in our study of adoption disruption, had lived with his foster family for many years and longed to be adopted by them. He had experienced a few returns to his birth family, only to be scapegoated and physically abused by them. After he had been in foster care for many years, his birth family contacted a lawyer and tried to seek custody. The judge ordered visitation to begin again, and the young boy, who was 13 by this time, would get physically ill when he was forced to visit his birth family. He was able to give a disengagement message to his birth parents, having composed letters to them that were handed to them at the beginning of a visit. The letters were addressed to "Old Woman" and "Old Man." They read:

> I told you once I did not ever want to see you again. You must have forgot so I will put it in writing so you can read it over and over. You are not my mother and never will be and as far as I concerned I never never want to see you again. Please stop messing up my life by forcing me to see you. If you really care for me you would let me be happy. Why do you keep upsetting up my life. No one of you are my Family. I hate the name . . . and do not want to be that ever again. You have been mean to me and I will never forget you are not my family and I don't want you. I am happy with my family and want to be left alone. Please don't interfere in my life ever again. I mean every word I wrote in this letter and have not been told. These are my ideas and I mean them. I HATE you and get sick when I see you.

After reading the letters, his birth parents stated that they didn't need this treatment and contacted their attorney to surrender their parental rights, paving the way for the boy to be adopted by his foster parents. Some children express ongoing fears that an abusive parent will find them again and hurt them or take them away from their adoptive family. Because some adoptive parents have lurking fears of losing their children, it is not surprising that the children themselves retain such fears. Several children whose birth parents have died report having nightmares that the parent came come back from the dead and harmed them.

Sometimes the fears of repeated loss do not stem from children's fears of birth parents as much as from repeated experiences of being moved by workers. Some children have a fear of strangers (professionals) coming to see them. For example, one mother reported that when the school psychologist came to take her son from his classroom to be tested, he became hysterical and ran away. Adoption preservation workers report that a few children become very distraught when they first try to talk with them. This ongoing feeling of vulnerability and impending doom is an aspect of the separation trauma experienced by many of these children. One of us observed a support group for latency-age girls in which they expressed their ongoing fears of being kidnapped and being alone. When the worker asked them when or where they felt safe, they all replied, "Nowhere!"

Children's fears related to repeated loss and other grief issues may abate and resurface over time. Workers report that children's birthdays are often stressful times and revive issues related to loss or unanswered questions. Also, new losses experienced in the family often trigger resurfacing of issues.

BARRIERS TO ATTACHMENT
FOR ADOPTIVE PARENTS

It is important to recognize that attachment is an interactional process influenced by aspects of both the child's and the parents' experiences. This is not unique to adoptive families. In birth families, difficulties sometimes arise in bonding with birth children due to temperament differences or a mismatch in personality styles of the child and parent. Developing an attachment to a child entering a family at age 5 or 8, with a lot of emotional baggage and unmet needs, is vastly more complex.

Just as the effect of past losses is a major consideration for the child, resolution of past losses is a need for adoptive parents. Infertility, when present, is a major loss that continues to affect couples over time. It is a loss for which there are very few supports to assist in grieving. The pain of infertility is not erased by adoption, but continues to resurface at predictable and unpredictable times. Sometimes, a spouse feels responsible for the couple's inability to have children, and undercurrents of perceived resentment continue to affect their relationship. One single adoptive mother served by the Illinois project had an abortion as a young woman and later was infertile. During a session when she finally expressed her anger and disappointment with her adopted daughter, she also broke down in tears and began talking of her abortion. For this mother, as for many other parents, the real child fails to measure up to the fantasy biological child, an awareness that sometimes asserts itself when disappointments with the adopted child arise.

Many couples have lost previous children either to death or to failed adoption attempts. Sometimes a family seeking adoption preservation services recounts adopting a child who was the same age as a child of theirs who had died. Also, some families still grieve the loss of a child placed with them whom they had wanted to adopt but were unable to. In addition to grieving for lost children, adoptive parents also grieve for the child their adopted child might have been if he or she had not suffered so many blows before coming into their life. They grieve the damage done to their child and the pain their child still experiences.

Entitlement and claiming also affect parents' development of attachments to adopted children. The sense of being entitled to be parents of this child is compromised by having to answer to an agency worker who supervises the placement before finalization and agency policies such as having to get permission to take the child out of state. Claiming a child as one's own is a feeling and a commitment. Some parents who have been career foster parents and parented many children in the child welfare system may have a tendency to revert to viewing the child as a part of the system when problems arise. They may need encouragement and supports that underscore their unique role as adoptive parents of the child.

In addition to claiming by parents, adopted children need to be claimed as family by extended family members. The attitudes of relatives can affect children's and parents' feelings about belonging. When adopted grandchildren are not included in wills in the same way that birth grandchildren are, or when relatives are quick to disclaim a child because, "No one in our family ever acted like that," such messages are received by the adopted child and parents alike.

Some adoptive parents struggle to accept their child's limitations. In an adoption training video, one professional couple talks about being on a downward spiral in relation to their expectations as their adopted children both had trouble in school and entered the world of special education. Another parent verbalizes her struggles in attaching to an older child. She says when you have a baby, everybody loves the baby, and cuddling with it seems so natural. But with an older child who already has her traits and her ways, it doesn't come naturally. It was especially hard at first when the child would say, "I love you," and the mother felt she should say it back. She wondered if she really meant it, if she was saying it from her head and not from her heart. Many times, at first, it would not be from her heart. The development of a truly loving connection takes time, something she had not fully realized before adopting (National Resource Center, 1995).

When a special needs child continues to have problems for years after the child is placed with a family, many parents begin to feel like failures as parents. They begin to doubt their parenting abilities and to think that perhaps they shouldn't have adopted. They may feel rejected by their child's lack of responsiveness to them and avoid reaching out for fear of experiencing more rejection. Also, ongoing stress with a difficult child takes its toll on the couple's marriage and on other children in the family. Excessive emotional demands grow to be a very heavy burden over a period of years, particularly when parents fear that their child will never be able to make it on his or her own. Their situation may come to feel like a life sentence.

In particular, parents who have never parented before may struggle with accepting an older child with special needs. One mother whose first adoptive placement disrupted reported her difficulties in attaching to a 5-year-old girl placed with her. This mother and her husband had never had children, and applied to adopt an infant. They were persuaded to take a 1-year-old and her 5-year-old sister. The older girl had been sexually abused, was overweight, and was perceived by the mother as unattractive. After months in placement, the mother finally poured out her guilt and disappointment to the worker, saying that she couldn't help seeing her older daughter as "tainted." She felt very badly that she had not been able to give this child what she needed. The placement of both girls was disrupted.

Table 5.1

Level of Parent-Child Attachments

Relationship	Fully Attached 1	2	Ambivalent 3	4	Very Limited 5
Child to mother	31%	23%	26%	14%	7%
Child to father	32	23	21	14	10
Mother to child	46	23	19	7	6
Father to child	42	20	16	12	10

NOTE: Percentages may add up to more than 100% due to rounding.

Sometimes the issues that adopted children struggle with recall unresolved issues in an adoptive parent's own life. For example, one adoptive family had been seeing the adoption preservation worker about their child's problems. The child had been sexually abused and was confronting a number of loss and trauma-related issues in her early teens. The adoptive mom finally disclosed for the first time that she had been sexually abused by her own father, who had died recently. This father was a beloved community leader, and she had felt no one would believe her story. As she began to deal with her own abuse, she was better able to help her daughter.

INSIGHTS RELATED TO
ATTACHMENT PROBLEMS

To explore the kinds of attachment issues that may create problems in special needs adoptive families and may pose a dissolution risk for the family, some of the insights gained from analyzing data gathered through the Illinois project are included. First of all, it is important to recognize that even among troubled adoptive families, attachment relationships fall along a continuum from very attached to minimal attachment. Adoption preservation workers assessed the level of parent-child attachments among the families served. The range of worker ratings for each type of relationship is reported in Table 5.1.

Table 5.1 can be framed in a positive light. Only a small minority of children and parents have very little attachment to each other. Experts who specialize in treating these children emphasize that probably only 1% to 2% are unattached (Delaney, 1991; Fahlberg, 1991). The vast majority of these children have some attachment to someone, but they may experience disturbed patterns of attachment relationships and vacillate between approach and avoidance. There is real potential to change these patterns, but strategic and therapeutic parenting are often required.

As might be expected, the level of parent-child attachment is significantly associated with parents raising dissolution as an option and with severity of child behavior problems. Using the workers' assessment of the existence of attachment problems in specific relationships, we explored possible associations between attachment difficulties and several factors. Factors that are significantly associated with attachment difficulties appear to relate most frequently to the adoptive mother's attachment to her adopted child. Problems in mother-to-adoptee attachment are primary, having a strong association with parents raising dissolution.

Difficulty in the attachment of adoptive mothers to their children is associated with type of adoption. Attachment problems of adoptive mothers to their adopted child are noted in 46% of relative adoptions, 34% of stranger adoptions, and 25% of foster parent adoptions. The association between type of adoption and attachment difficulties is not significant for other family relationships. Likewise, age at adoptive placement and number of previous placements are significantly associated with attachment problems for adoptive mothers to children and children to mothers.

The only specific form of maltreatment associated with any type of attachment problems is the child's history of serious neglect. Such neglect is significantly associated with attachment problems of adoptive mothers to adoptees. Also, having experienced multiple forms of maltreatment is associated with mother-adoptee attachment difficulties. This association is not significant for adoptee-to-mother attachments or father-to-adoptee and adoptee-to-father attachments, however.

A number of adopted children are identified as having separation and attachment issues related to their birth families as well as attachment issues within their adoptive families. The most frequently cited issue is that the child received no clear disengagement message from the birth family or previous caregiver. Eighty-three percent of children are identified as having one or more of the issues in Table 5.2.

Table 5.2

Children's Issues Related to Birth Family

Issue	*% Present*
Child received no clear disengagement message	34
Knows of siblings with birth family	32
Has some contact with birth family	29
Strong fantasy or wish to be reunited with birth family	27
Wishes to search for birth family	23
Idealizes birth parent	19
Has ongoing fear of birth family	10
Wishes to be reunited with previous foster family/caregiver	7

It is likely that the incidence of these issues is greater than what is known by workers at the time the assessment form is completed. Workers report that children's support groups elicit children's expression of conflicts and fears that seem to have never been verbalized previously. For example, many children express fears related to being taken from their adoptive parents.

We explored associations between these separation-attachment issues of adopted children and the existence of attachment problems in parent-child relationships. Only one children's issue is associated with problems in the father-child relationship. Children wishing to search are more likely to have attachment problems in their relationship to their adoptive fathers. Again, factors related to attachment problems are most likely to center on attachment difficulties in the mother-child relationship. Notably, a child's having some contact with birth family members is not associated with attachment problems in these adopted children or parents; however, both the child's desire to reunite with birth family and idealizing birth parents are associated with problems in the attachment of adoptive mothers to their children and children to their adoptive mothers. Adoptees' ongoing idealization of their birth parents and fantasizing return appear to be linked with their own and their adoptive mothers' difficulties in attachment. These issues seem to be indicative of the adoptee's failure to come to terms with past loss, move through the grief process, and freely engage with the adoptive mother. They also seem to impede adoptive mothers' attachment to their children.

An illustration of this pattern was expressed by one adoptive mother in a follow-up phone interview. She reported that her 12-year-old daughter recently had met her birth mother and sister, but had been disappointed after the meeting. In the long run, however, this meeting had a positive effect on the adoptee. Her mother reported, "It has burst that bubble that she had some perfect birth family out there . . . she has actually become more open and friendly towards us since."

CHILDREN'S EXPRESSIONS RELATED
TO SEPARATION AND LOSS

To understand the variety of concerns children affected by loss and adoption may express, we examined some of the issues identified by children served through the Illinois project in the children's own words. The complexities of children's struggles related to separation and attachment issues frequently are minimized because children often do not verbalize their grief, fantasies, and fears. Responses often reflect ambivalence toward both birth and adoptive parents. Of course, the attachments of adopted children as well as nonadopted children fall along a continuum from securely attached to unattached. Many special needs adoptees have had experiences that lead to more difficulties and complexities in their attachment relationships. This does not mean that most of them should be labeled as having attachment disorders. It means that there may be bumps along the road in developing new attachments, and that complicated feelings will surface and resurface periodically. If children are not helped to express and understand these feelings, the feelings can contribute to unhealthy patterns in relationships.

The following statements of children served by the project illustrate some of their conflicts related to separation and attachment:

"I can't see my brother and sister, and if I can't, something is gonna' happen!"
(girl, 17, separated from siblings since age 6)

"I miss my first adoptive family . . . I don't know why they gave me up!"
(girl, 10)

"I'm scared my Mom is going to die and I'll have to move again!" (boy, 12, whose adoptive mom is 74)

"I want to contact my birth mother and sisters, but I'm afraid of hurting my adoptive parents." (girl, 16)

"My mom expects me to be perfect. She does not trust or understand me. There are so many foster kids, she doesn't have time for me." (girl, 14)

"I never thought of my adoptive mother as my mother. I want to go back and live with my real mother." (boy, 13, adopted with his sister by an aunt)

"I love my (adoptive) mother very much, but I cause so many problems, I'm afraid they'll send me away." (girl, 9)

"I'm afraid to talk about adoption because my mom cries. I don't want to hurt her. My mom wants to keep me like a baby." (girl, 12)

"I still see my birth mom . . . she lives 6 blocks away. It makes me kinda uncomfortable because I don't know how to act." (girl, 9)

"My parents love me only if I behave to their expectations." (boy, 14)

"All my brothers and sisters are still in foster care. It makes me so mad that I can't see them." (girl, 10)

"My father always told me that when I turned 18, he would tell me about my birth mother. I am so mad because three weeks before my birthday, he told me he still wouldn't tell me anything." (girl, 18)

"Sometimes my parents love me, but they never really understand how I feel and I don't think they really want me." (girl, 14)

"My parents are nicer to their other kids, and they don't really love me." (boy, 15)

GOALS AND STRATEGIES OF INTERVENTION TO SUPPORT ATTACHMENT

Society offers no intervention that is more comprehensive than a new family. Yet, this is not a complete intervention, especially for very troubled children. Older children adoptions need the support of detailed planning and lasting and empirically derived interventions. (Berry & Barth, 1989, p. 237)

A warm, nurturing relationship with a parent is indeed the most effective intervention possible for overcoming unmet emotional needs or damage inflicted by disturbed attachments with previous caregivers. Yet, the saying, "love is not enough" has become synonymous with special needs adoptions. For some adoptive parents, achieving healthy attachments with children who have complicated emotional histories does not just happen. Conventional strategies for communicating, guiding, and developing emotional bonds with children may not lead them down the right path. Many families need special help to chart their way through this unfamiliar territory. Such help has only begun to be developed, and often has not been empirically tested. The studies of special needs adoptive families do offer some direction for these children and families.

Assessment of the Child's Attachment Experiences

To meet the needs of children in coming to terms with losses and to prepare adoptive families for facilitating this work with children, all children in the child welfare system need to have ongoing assessments related to significant losses and traumas they have experienced. A number of tools have been developed to assist with assessing attachment relationships with children. Historical information on relationships and the kind of interaction existing between the child and a caregiver or other family member are of central importance. Further, direct observation, such as observing the interaction of birth parents and children during visits, also is very valuable. Assessing how responsive the parent is to the child's signals, the frequency with which the child and parent seek each other out, and the nature of the exchanges between them provides much information.

Several psychological interaction scales are available for assessing parent-child relationships. An assessment tool developed by Anthony (1983) and discussed by Fahlberg (1991) is useful for exploring children's perceptions of adult-child interactions they have experienced. A series of cards with line drawings of family members as well as Mr. Nobody (with his back turned) are spread out in front of the child. The child is asked a series of questions about who he or she would go to when he or she is hungry, sick, wants to play a game, wants a hug, wants someone to listen, and so forth. The child points to the person fulfilling that need . . . or Mr. Nobody. Examiners can make up items to explore other areas related to discipline, guidance, protection, and other forms of nurturance.

Resolution of Past Losses

Adoption of an older child requires building on old attachments—the goal is to "add an option" rather than to replace a past relationship. Many workers use the lifebook to facilitate this type of work on the child's part (Fahlberg, 1991; Harrison, 1988). The lifebook is a scrapbook of the child's life that explains his or her entire life history, the important people in his or her life, and his or her feelings about situations and events both good and bad. It facilitates the child's processing of his or her life story throughout childhood. Sometimes workers may write explanations of events as well as how the child felt at the time. Making lifebooks and other rituals of adoption facilitates the child's claiming of positives he or she receives from different caregivers and a sense of continuity in life experiences.

One technique used with older children is called *revisiting*—the parent takes the child on a journey to past families and has each of them share some happy memories and relay messages to the child that they think of the child and want him or her to be happy. For one boy served by the project, revisiting a former foster family was a very positive experience. This boy wondered why the foster family with whom he lived for several years had not adopted him, especially because they had adopted another child. The adoptive parents contacted this foster family and visited them on a vacation. The foster parents were able to tell the boy how they thought of him often and were so glad he was happy with his family. These and other techniques for helping children integrate their history are discussed further in Chapter 7.

In adoptive families, mourning losses may become more difficult because each family member has experienced a different type of loss. Also, the fear of hurting other adoptive family members often interferes with the ability to mourn adequately (Berman & Bufferd, 1986). Some adoption practitioners have developed creative activities for helping family members acknowledge and share their losses. One such intervention is called the Loss History Graph. This activity evokes intense story telling, and should be conducted in an atmosphere of unrushed attention, usually over several hours. A long sheet of paper is taped to the wall, and a horizontal line is drawn to represent a time line beginning with the birth of the oldest family member and extending to the present. Each family member from the oldest to the youngest is asked to recount the losses in his or her life. The events are written on the time line with the year and a vertical line depicting the intensity of the loss. Through this exercise, unresolved losses often are discovered, as are the ways in which family members deal with losses. The opportunity can be used to talk about healthy grieving, and it helps the family members recognize the commonality of losses in their lives (DePelchin Children's Center, 1993).

As discussed earlier in this chapter, much of the work of helping children resolve their past losses must begin at the time that the child enters the child welfare system. Unfortunately, much of what is helpful to children in managing separations in care is not done routinely. Children frequently are moved precipitously, without preparation or termination work. Because they are struggling to survive, they may block feelings and deny the reality or permanency of losses. Even when workers do the best job possible in preparing children for adoption, the child will continue to deal with loss as he or she matures. The most obvious goal for attachment work with children and adoptive parents is to facilitate their resolution of past losses. This requires an open and supportive atmosphere where sad and angry feelings can be expressed. To resolve past losses, the first step is cognitive understanding of the events and their meaning. To facilitate processing these events, we have to help the child and parents reconnect with the child's history by reconstructing these events. The lifebook and other interventive strategies are helpful means to helping children reconstruct and come to terms with the events in their lives. These activities facilitate children's clarifying distorted perceptions about what and why events occurred. They provide opportunities to explore emotions related to these events and the meaning of these events in their lives.

Adults often wait for children to express sadness verbally or appear sad before they discuss painful events in their past. Adoptive parents as well as therapists need to create opportunities to address these issues in addition to responding to openings the children may give. A number of therapeutic interventions that have been developed to assist children in processing past losses include constructing a placement genogram or the child's eco-map or helping the child to write a life story. Therapists sometimes use letter or journal writing to help older children and teens express their feelings. Some of these tools, also known as "Regina's bag of tricks," are described in Keck and Kupecky (1995). Models for constructing lifebooks are available through adoption resource catalogs. One such model is Filling in the Blanks (Gabel, 1988).

Adoptive parents need to provide regular opportunities for children to talk about their thoughts and feelings related to past events or relationships or future fears and fantasies. Keeping the lifebook up to date is recommended. Some families develop rituals around certain dates or holidays that commemorate the adoption, such as placement day (called "gotcha day" by some). For example, candle-lighting ceremonies commemorate the significant attachment figures in a child's life and the positive things they have given the child. At Christmas, the family may have ornaments on the tree representing a former family the child lived with or foods or customs that the child remembers from previous years. For example, one child reported that his favorite food of all time was the macaroni and cheese he had in a former foster family. His adoptive mother wrote and got this recipe and made this dish for him, to encourage his discussion of memories of his life with this family. A goal that often stated in adoption literature as "building on former attachments" embodies the theme of this type of life review. It is important for the child to claim the benefits he or she received from others, as well as to provide a sense of continuity between past, present, and future. One book that the workers in the Illinois project used for achieving this goal was the Dr. Seuss (1990) book, *Oh, the Places You'll Go!*

Therapeutic goals of life review work include helping the child reconnect with important events and people, either symbolically or in reality; finding answers to missing pieces of the puzzle whenever possible; recognizing and resolving emotions related to past events; and gaining a sense of how all these experiences have contributed to who and what the child is today.

Parents' responses to children are central in facilitating their resolution of past losses. Parents need to facilitate open communication and ongoing support for the child to explore feelings. There are many books for children on adoption that adoptive families may read together to stimulate exploration of these issues. There are children's books with stories on many different ways to create families, even donor insemination.

For parents to facilitate their child's processing of these issues, the parents have to accept the significance of past attachments in the child's life and overcome their own feelings of being threatened by previous attachment figures. They have to move toward a sense of shared parenting of this child . . . a sense that he or she is our child, rather than yours or mine. Also, it is important for the adoptive parents to show respect toward past parental figures in the child's life. This does not mean that they justify maltreatment that may have occurred, only that they convey to the child that his or her mother was a person of value, as he or she is a person of value.

Strategies for Parents to Build Attachment

Technically, bonding is a process that occurs immediately after birth between an infant and his or her caregiver. Bonding promotes an attachment relationship, which develops over time as a result of need satisfaction and positive interactions between the parent and child. Many of the strategies for building an attachment relationship with an older child seek to build on knowledge of normal infant-parent attachment processes. For attachment to develop, an adoptive parent must successfully meet the child's needs, particularly during periods of high arousal. Attachment also is facilitated by adoptive parents' initiation of positive interactions with their adopted child, a goal that may take strategic planning when the child is particularly resistant to attachment.

It is important to determine realistic expectations for children in relation to attachment and to encourage parents not to push too far, too fast. In this way, they will be more accepting and patient, and will not blame themselves or their child for slow progress. It takes a myriad of small acts of kindness and affection to modify the child's negative expectations from previous painful experiences. The child's periodic responses of rejection and hostility may be very hurtful to the adoptive parents. They need to be helped not to personalize the child's behaviors, to take care of themselves, and to recognize positive gains the child has made. Parents may need support from other adoptive parents or professionals to sustain their patience and acceptance of their child.

In addition, experts specializing in work with maltreated children who have attachment problems emphasize the need for strategies beyond traditional therapeutic approaches to "jump start" the child's frozen emotional development and change his or her cognitive map of the world (Katz, 1991; Keck & Kupecky, 1995; Magid & McKelvey, 1987). The parent or therapist seeking to engage the child who lacks trust needs to use active, intense means for engaging the child. Suggested ingredients in a corrective, therapeutic experience include the following: high energy, close physical proximity, much eye contact, experiential activities, intensely positive sensory stimulation, frequent touch, movement, fast-paced verbal exchanges, confrontation, and warm nurturance.

Helping Children Identify and Express Feelings and Needs

Relationship building is promoted by sharing intensely positive and negative experiences with the child. A nurturing response to the child during periods when he or she is very aroused, whether through positive stimulation or upset feelings, goes a long way toward building attachment. A primary aspect of helping children who have experienced disturbed attachment relationships is to facilitate their getting in touch with their feelings. For many of these children, denial of feelings is a common way of dealing with tension and anger. They need to learn to express feelings more directly rather than blunting their emotions or defending against them indirectly through negative behaviors. Encouraging children to verbalize their thoughts, feelings, needs, and wants is an ongoing process. In addition to identifying and expressing feelings, parents need to help their children consider constructive ways for acting on these feelings. This process requires parents to respond to the child in a direct, nurturing manner that elicits and accepts honest expression of feelings while confronting and limiting unacceptable behaviors. For some children who are particularly resistant to attaching, special therapy may be needed to help them connect to their feelings and overcome their fears.

There are a number of techniques for helping children label feelings and communicate them. For example, many therapeutic games for children elicit expression of feelings. Telling stories or reading books can focus on talking about a range of feelings occurring in the characters. Parents can verbalize their own feelings at times when they are not confronting the child, as well as sometimes when they are involved in negotiating a conflict with the child. They also need to listen to their child's feelings and to express verbal empathy to their child. Often this requires parents to decode what their children are telling them through their behaviors. Therapists may assist both parents and children in reframing negative behaviors as coping mechanisms for emotional problems not yet resolved. This understanding helps parents move beyond their anger toward the child for behaviors they perceive as willful defiance and rejection.

Also, children need to become aware of their own fears related to closeness. Intimacy may provoke feelings of vulnerability and loss of control. Michael Katz (1986, 1990), a psychologist who has developed many creative techniques for working with foster and adopted children, emphasizes the need to give the child permission to express his or her fears of closeness and to help the child develop more constructive ways of regulating closeness. Katz attempts to help children understand how they act in ways that irritate others to keep people at a distance due to fear and distrust from things that have happened in the past. He seeks to help them determine what level of closeness they feel comfortable with and to reassess periodically if they want to stay at the present level or have more closeness. Children are taught that there is a difference between being nice to someone and getting close to them; even if they don't feel comfortable with more closeness, they can still be kind to others. Parents are included in this awareness of children's comfort zone with closeness, and encouraged not to pressure children. In this way, children are taught that they can control closeness without negative, distancing behaviors.

Responding to Children's Needs

Responding to the arousal-relaxation cycle in infants is a primary foundation for developing attachment. In older children, it is important for parents to come through when their children are really hurting or needy, a time when their defenses are usually lowered and they may be more accepting of nurturance. For example, Kay Donley (1984) humorously states that she prays that a child will get sick soon after adoptive placement, because this gives the adoptive parents an opportunity to meet their child's needs at a very basic level. By calming a hurt or fearful child in a nurturing manner, parents help both children and themselves develop attachment. Also, by accepting a child's expression of fear, verbalizing his or her need for safety, and providing supports to promote the child's sense of security, parents help lessen the child's sense of vulnerability. For example, such simple acts of expressing understanding of a child's fears when he or she awakens from a nightmare and sitting with the child for a time so that he or she feels safe promotes the development of attachment.

Some children may be particularly resistant to physical nurturance from parents and resist being touched or held. Sometimes parents can use "reparenting techniques" to expand on the child's comfort level with physical closeness. For example, a 7-year-old child may not feel comfortable being held and bottle fed as an infant would, but may allow the parents to hold him or her on their lap and suck on a Popsicle for comfort when sick. Foster and adoptive parents are often creative in developing ways to reach out to a child and expand the child's acceptance of love. Delaney (1991) recounts one foster mother's helping a 10-year-old foster son accept touch through her treatments of his head lice. When shampoos were initiated, they were the only form of touch that this boy had accepted from the foster parents. The foster mother gradually increased the frequency and duration of the shampoos, which were later expanded to include brushings, facial massages, and neck rubs, and were accepted by this young boy.

Other activities that promote positive acceptance of touch among older children include nesting behaviors. These are times when family members bunch together, such as piling in the parent's bed to tell a story, sharing a tent while camping, or staying in a single hotel room (James, 1994). Interactive games requiring physical contact may be helpful, even mild tussling such as foot wrestling.

One technique developed by an Illinois adoption preservation worker in attempting to meet the needs of her young adopted son has been shared with other adoptive parents and used by many. This technique, called "Fill Me Up," was begun by the adoptive mother when her son was a toddler, and used for many years through his early childhood. This young boy had been slow to attach, and his mom had carried him in a pouch as much as possible during his infancy to promote his comfort with physical closeness. As a preschool child, he was extremely active and difficult to control. On one occasion when the child was agitated and upset, his mom tried this technique, which became a ritual. She told the little boy that whenever he was upset, he could come to her and she would stop whatever she was doing and fill him up with love. (She would pick him up, hold him, and pretend to be pouring love into the top of his head.) This little ritual gave many positive messages to the child. It conveyed his mother's view that he was important, her acceptance of his feelings, and her willingness to respond immediately to his needs.

Of course, needs other than safety and affection are important to children as well, including their need for a sense of self-worth and mastery. Parents' praise of positives about their child is very important in building attachment and a sense of self-worth in their child. One speaker on treating attachment disorders in children emphasizes the need for five times more positive interactions with the child than negative, saying "Kids won't bond with a bitch!" (Watkins, 1992). Unfortunately, the negative behaviors of the child and ongoing power struggles between child and parent too often result in the parents' overlooking positives and focusing entirely on the negative with their child. Learning new discipline strategies that allow the parent to disengage from power struggles and to discipline the child out of love more than anger are important. Often, these children escalate their negative behaviors after periods of closeness, seemingly due to their discomfort with closeness and fears of repeated rejection. In spite of this, parents need to be able to continue to give them messages that they are safe and loved and that the adoptive parents will be there for them.

Helping a child cope with feelings of anger and frustration or feelings of grief and ambivalence related to birth family members is a way to encourage attachment. Also important is sharing a child's excitement over positive experiences. In addition, Fahlberg (1991) emphasizes the need for adoptive parents to assist children in coping with feelings related to change, such as a move, and to other upsetting situations, such as doctor's visits, as ways to encourage attachment.

Promoting Claiming and Family Identity

Ongoing but subtle messages including the child in the adoptive family enhance the child's sense of belonging and support attachment. For example, concrete evidence of belonging, such as displaying pictures of the child or work that he or she has done, is important. Developing ways to connect the adopted child to extended family members promotes family identity. Also, rituals of inclusion are helpful, such as ceremonies that confirm the child as a part of the family. An agency serving adoptive families in Minnesota has developed an anthology of adoption rituals that contains many religious and secular rituals (Mason, 1995). It is also helpful to incorporate some of the child's past in family customs and family claiming of the child so that the child's heritage becomes a part of family heritage.

Initiating Positive Interactions with the Child

Spending positive time with the child, whether it is helping with homework, playing a game together, or a trip to the zoo, is essential to developing an attachment relationship. With young children, one-on-one activities that are fun but require the child to internalize and model the parent's behavior are especially helpful—such as nonsensical rhymes and songs or teaching the child to bake a cake. Reading to children and other activities that allow touching or physical proximity are also particularly helpful in encouraging attachment. With older children, supporting the child's outside interests may be particularly important. The emphasis should be on parents finding ways of spending time with the child that the child views as positive, not on the parents' insistence that the child do what the parent wants them to do together.

Several experts who specialize in working with children with attachment problems emphasize playful interactions and the use of humor for engaging these children. For example, Delaney, the coauthor of *Troubled Transplants* (Delaney & Kunstal, 1993) and a popular trainer on parenting children with "extraordinary" needs, has compiled a number of creative strategies for dealing with problem behaviors. He recounts story after story of adoptive parents' playful, unexpected stimulation and arousal of the children to engage them or to confront a problem behavior. One mother reported her frustration with her son's creating chaos at dinner. His behaviors included getting under the table and acting like a dog and harassing family members as they ate. She had tried time-outs and a variety of other disciplinary measures to end this behavior. Finally one night she jumped down on the floor on all fours, chased her son around the table like a dog, and playfully nipped him on his rear end, ultimately leading to a change in his behavioral pattern. In another family, a single mother and 9-year-old son who rarely interacted at home, Delaney worked with the mom to develop playful ways to engage her son—he instructed her to come home from work early, hide when her son came home from school, and jump out and surprise him. This interaction was repeated by mother and son and later escalated to a water pistol fight and other practical jokes.

Theraplay Techniques

The type of playful interactions described above have been developed into a model of therapy for children and their parents known as *Theraplay* (Jernberg, 1979, 1990, 1993). Theraplay is an intensive, short-term treatment method modeled on the healthy interaction of parents with infants and young children that promotes engagement, enhanced self-esteem, and joyful learning. Through Theraplay activities, the therapist assists the parent to create with a child the early engaged responsiveness that is seen naturally in healthy families. These activities replicate four crucial dimensions of the early parent-child relationship: structuring, challenging, stimulating, and nurturing (Jernberg, 1993). Theraplay uses the Marschak Interaction method (Marschak, 1980) to assess the attachment relationship between child and parent and to determine what each may need in the way of help to improve their relationship. Parents are given feedback and helped during the treatment phase to learn to structure, challenge, stimulate, and nurture their child in a manner that engages the child and promotes attachment. Parents also are prepared to anticipate a negative phase during which the child may become resistant to pleasurable interactions. Holding techniques may be used to get through the child's resistance, but they are not used to provoke the child, nor is there pushing to identify an earlier source of the child's anger. For example, a parent may straddle a tantrumming child and reassure him or her in verbal or nonverbal ways until he or she is calm.

Theraplay activities include tasks such as putting lotion on each other's hands and arms, feeding each other pretzels, trying on many different hats together, cradling and rocking a child in a blanket, counting freckles, thumb wrestling, or hiding notes on the child for the parent to find and respond to. The emphasis is on playful touch, verbal feedback that builds self-esteem, and promoting engagement and responsiveness in the relationship. Although Theraplay has been used primarily as an intervention with families having problems, it also would be a very useful tool for prevention or early intervention in relation to attachment problems.

Holding Therapies

Several varieties of *holding therapy* stem from a technique of forced holding developed for the treatment of autistic children (Tinbergen & Tinbergen, 1983; Zaslow & Menta, 1975). Others have further developed holding techniques and used them in treating children with behavior or attachment problems. Welch (1988) advocates using regular holding times as helpful in treating a wide range of parent-child problems, and even suggests their use in general mother-child relationships. She describes "holding time" as having the mother sit with the child facing her and straddling her lap. (With older children, they may be on the floor.) The child is held and talked to for an extended time period. When the child ultimately resists and struggles to get away, the mother persists in holding and prevents the child from withdrawing. The child's frustration and anger are aroused, but protests ultimately are resolved as the child relaxes and submits to his or her mother's control. This calming period of tender caressing, holding, and gentle conversation is viewed as highly effective in promoting a strong attachment bond. It is also during this period that the child is able to express his or her feelings more freely and accept intense physical and emotional contact.

Foster Cline (1979, 1992) is perhaps the most well-known proponent of holding therapy in adoption circles. His development of holding therapy, also known as rage reduction therapy, uses intrusive techniques to provoke the child's rage and to break through the child's strong defenses. The child's safe, cathartic expression of rage and relinquishment of control are seen as essential to developing trust, submission, and attachment. Cline advocates using as little intrusiveness as possible to achieve the desired holding and release of emotions. The end relaxation phase is described as being like the nurturing holding mentioned above.

Some attachment therapists have used modified forms of holding therapy. For example, Keck and Kupecky (1995) propose that holding results in an intensity that cannot be achieved in any other type of therapy. It leads to cognitive restructuring by providing the level of intense relationship needed to access the child's feelings and prior experiences and unfreeze the child's arrested development. They use holding with children only with their permission. It is usually in the form of having the child or adolescent lie across the laps of two adults—usually the therapist and a parent or two parents. Sometimes the style is modified, but physical proximity and close eye contact are important to maintain. Another attachment therapist who uses holding (Boeding, 1998) has rejected the use of intrusive techniques to induce rage in the child but uses a range of psychological techniques to help the child revisit traumatic experiences in the context of a nurturing, emotionally corrective experience. He wraps a blanket around the child during holding to provide this tactile stimulation and to contain the child in a safe manner.

Some therapists use other techniques directed toward the body to provide positive stimulation and promote tension reduction, including fun tickling, swinging, jumping and bouncing together, and spontaneous, imitative play (Allan, 1986). All these techniques focus on helping the child identify, express, and release feelings in the context of a safe, nurturing relationship.

Several of the families served through the Illinois project have received intensive attachment holding therapy, most with very positive outcomes. For some children, this therapy has produced dramatic changes in their negative behaviors and in their acceptance of closeness. One example is a 10-year-old boy who was described as having no conscience, urinating in the heat vents, wetting the bed nightly, and rejecting any physical affection. During the course of his 10 sessions of holding therapy, he ceased all wetting and began seeking and accepting physical closeness.

Some professionals who specialize in work with attachment-trauma problems in children object to intrusive, coercive holding methods such as immobilizing, tickling, poking, and intimidating the child. This treatment is perceived as cruel, unethical, and potentially retraumatizing to the child (James, 1994). Systematic research is needed to determine the effective parameters of holding techniques, as well as the effectiveness of other strategies for promoting attachment.

Ideally, attachment work occurs for children both before and after adoptive placement to assist them in processing their losses and developing new attachments. This work needs to be considered even when children are adopted by foster parents or kin. Also, parents adopting children with any attachment difficulties need to be taught a range of strategies for building attachments that could be incorporated into their parenting repertoire soon after adoptive placement. For children evidencing characteristics of reactive attachment disorder as defined in the *DSM-IV* (American Psychiatric Association, 1994), specialized interventions need to be provided at the earliest possible age. Addressing these needs early on in the parent-child relationship will likely prevent or reduce much of the chronic distress characterizing adoptive families with attachment disordered children.

Chapter 6

INVISIBLE WOUNDS
Trauma and Its Wake

> You can't forget the bad things that are done to you by telling
> yourself that the world isn't all bad. We really can know only the
> people and things that touch us. Everything else is like words in a
> dictionary. We can learn them but they don't live deep inside us.
>
> Potok, 1985, p. 269

Children's traumatic experiences touch the core of their being, living
on inside their minds and bodies. These experiences profoundly affect
the way children view themselves and others, their emotions, and their
behaviors. Spontaneous healing does not occur when children are
adopted. Healing from childhood trauma is a complex, difficult process
that requires understanding, assistance, and support from others. Integration of trauma experiences must occur for children to be able to
assimilate fully the positive experiences in their lives. Only then can
loving trust, confidence, and mastery live deep inside.

TRAUMAS EXPERIENCED BY
SPECIAL NEEDS CHILDREN

Children who are removed from their homes by the child welfare
system experience separation trauma, a blow that is devastating to
most and lingering in its effects. In addition to the emotional aspects of
grief associated with a loss, other characteristics of trauma experiences

stem from the separation. Children who are abruptly separated from family often have feelings of extreme vulnerability, rage, mistrust, and numbing of feelings. It is hard for adults to understand the overwhelming devastation that being removed from family creates in a young child. In the animal world, young offspring cling to their mother for safety and security, and they usually die when they are separated from their mother. The security of young children also is centered in closeness to their caregiver, even among children who have had their needs met only inconsistently. As discussed in Chapter 5, ongoing loss of access to one's parent is an overwhelming blow to a young child that resonates long after his or her return home or placement in a substitute family.

In addition to separation trauma, most children entering the child welfare system have experienced other traumas, such as serious neglect, physical or sexual abuse, or witnessing violence to siblings or parents. Often the adaptations that children make to cope with repeated traumas, such as hypervigilance or disassociating from feelings, help them defend against these experiences and survive. Over a period of time, however, these adaptations enabling children's survival may mold their personalities in damaging ways.

The effect of traumatic experiences is a topic that has undergone only brief periods of study until recent decades. The diagnostic category of posttraumatic stress disorder (PTSD) was not officially recognized until its inclusion in the *DSM-III* (American Psychiatric Association, 1980). Most study has examined the effect of trauma on adults. Research-based knowledge about the initial and ongoing effect of trauma on children is developing, but it is still rather fragmentary. There are traumatized children who meet the criteria for a diagnosis of PTSD. Other traumatized children, who are equally if not more disturbed overall than those with a PTSD diagnosis, do not exhibit the same pattern of symptoms (Kiser, Heston, Millsap, & Pruitt, 1991). Thus, many children who have experienced serious trauma may not receive treatment that helps them heal from these experiences. This chapter examines the variety of responses that children may have to traumatic experiences and explores strategies for helping children in adoptive families heal from these experiences.

THE PHYSIOLOGICAL EFFECT OF TRAUMA

The physiological effect of trauma underlies many psychological trauma symptoms. The structural and functional aspects of the mature brain are affected by childhood experiences, particularly during the critical period of brain development during infancy and early childhood. The brain mediates all cognitive, emotional, behavioral, and physiological functions. The neurotransmitters and hormones involved in the stress response are important influences on the process of differentiation of neurons during the early years of brain development. Traumatic experiences produce neurophysiological changes that are normally reversible; however, the more frequent a certain pattern of neural activation occurs, the more indelible it becomes. Therefore, the more trauma a child experiences, the more likely he or she is to have neuropsychiatric symptoms following trauma (Osofsky, 1995; Perry, Pollard, Blakley, Baker, & Vigilante, 1995). In other words, the stress response becomes a template for brain organization among children who have chronic trauma experiences.

According to Perry and colleagues (1995), the human brain is organized into systems that sense, process, store, perceive, and act on information from the external and internal environment. Different systems in the brain mediate different functions, but all neurons are designed to change in response to external signals to promote survival. Some of the biochemical changes associated with stress include increased levels of norepinephrine, which affects arousal level, cardiovascular, and respiratory functioning; cortisol, which ultimately affects the immune system; and dopamine and testosterone, which enhance aggression and hypervigilance. In addition, there are reduced concentrations of brain serotonin, which helps modulate the emotions. Because traumatic experiences result in profound sensitization of neural response patterns, minor stressors may then result in major response patterns.

Different parts of the brain are activated by different arousal states, varying from terror to vigilance. Different kinds of memory are regulated by different parts of the brain so that cognitive and emotional functions are affected by the type and intensity of response. The more threatened an individual is, the more primitive his or her style of thinking and behaving will be. An example of moderate arousal is a child who is in a state of alarm such as when he or she is thinking about the trauma. This level of arousal affects the midbrain, which results in the child having difficulty concentrating, feeling more anxiety, and being more attuned to nonverbal cues than verbal messages. It is only when a child is calm that he or she can make maximum use of cortical functioning for learning and complex thought processes (Perry et al.,

1995). At the extreme, terror activates the brainstem functions associated with the autonomic nervous system and reflexive cognitions. Early life traumas may have a more long-term effect on self-regulation and self-identity because memories at this stage are encoded on a sensory-motor level rather than on a verbal level. Young children who display somatic or behavioral sensations or perceptions related to trauma rather than explicit, conscious verbal memories have less capacity for integrating and processing their experiences (van der Kolk, 1996). Two primary response patterns to stress are hyperarousal (fight) and dissociation (flight). The hyperarousal response is triggered by an increased release of norepinephrine. The brain regions producing the hyperarousal response are involved in regulating arousal, vigilance, affect, behavioral irritability, locomotion, attention, sleep, and the startle response (Bhaskaran & Freed, 1988). Hence, a child who functions in a state of increased arousal may have motor hyperactivity, impulsivity, sleep problems, and hypertension; be overly sensitive; and exhibit other such symptoms.

The dissociative response is associated with freezing, surrender, or escaping the reality of the situation. The neurobiology of dissociation is like the "defeat" response in animals—decreased blood pressure and heart rate and modulation of opiod and dopamine systems. The latter affect emotions and mediate pain and sensory processing so that perception of pain and time, place, and reality are modified. For young children, this response results in numbing of feelings, avoidance, and passive compliance. Children's reports of such experiences include descriptions such as going to a different place, just floating, watching themselves from afar, or not being there. Sometimes when children feel out of control, they react with a "freezing" response in which they cognitively and physically freeze. This self-protective and often automatic response frequently is misinterpreted by others as noncompliance to a directive or willfully ignoring someone.

According to Perry (Perry et al., 1985), the part of the brain involved in dissociation is the limbic system, which is associated with attachment and affiliation. The limbic system differs between males and females, being more prominent in females, so that they tolerate more pain and dissociate more easily. This pattern of adaptation is related to the severity of the trauma. The more pain or torture involved and the more powerless individuals feel, the more likely they are to dissociate.

It is important to recognize that these physiological changes do not disappear when traumatized children are no longer in a threatening situation. Many of the children served through adoption preservation programs demonstrate physiological and psychological symptoms of their experiences many years after they have moved into secure adoptive families.

TRAUMAGENIC STATES

There are several conceptual frameworks for understanding the psychological effect of trauma. One of these frameworks stems from the work of Finkelhor and Browne (1985, 1986), who developed four themes for understanding the traumatic effect of sexual abuse. These themes are linked with specific dynamics, emotional and psychological reactions, and behavioral patterns. Others have expanded on Finkelhor and Browne's work to identify additional emotional conditions arising from traumatic experiences. For example, James (1989) proposes nine traumagenic states for assessing the emotional effect of trauma.

Individual children perceive and react differently to similar experiences so that the psychological effect of trauma varies from one child to another. The concept of traumagenic states emphasizes the need to assess the involvement of each of these areas to understand an individual child's response to trauma. The framework for understanding adjustment issues of special needs adoptees that was introduced in Chapter 4 will be used for organizing and explaining traumatic response patterns.

Capacity for Relationships

Children who experience maltreatment at the hands of a family member or other caregiver experience a sense of betrayal when the child realizes that a trusted person has harmed them or failed to protect them from harm. Children experiencing a traumatic separation from family have similar emotional responses—rejection, betrayal, and failure of trusted adults to protect them. For many children who have been deeply hurt, closeness is something to be avoided because it makes them feel vulnerable to pain and a loss of control. Their emotional responses include grief, depression, extreme dependency, mistrust, and anger. Behavioral manifestations range from attachment disturbances such as clinging or withdrawal to aggressive behaviors (Finkelhor & Browne,

1986). Other symptoms connected to this theme include hoarding, lack of empathy and emotional reciprocity, and explosive rage or vengeful episodes.

Identity

Negative messages about the self result from traumatic experiences. Children receive negative messages from others, *stigmatization,* as well as from themselves, *self-blame.* Stigmatization as an aspect of sexual abuse is described by Finkelhor and Browne (1986) as messages about the child's "badness" communicated directly by others or construed by the child because of the emphasis on secrecy. The resulting psychological effect is manifested in low self-esteem, self-destructive behavior, feelings of guilt and shame, isolation, and body image problems. Self-blame, shame, and guilt are common dynamics of traumatic experiences beyond those involving sexual abuse. Children who have experienced maltreatment and are removed from family frequently see themselves as responsible. Even a teenager will verbalize that he or she was taken away from parents because he or she was misbehaving. Adults as well often react to traumatic events with the belief that somehow they were responsible and could have done something to prevent or avoid the event.

Understanding the involvement of shame in trauma responses is essential to helping these individuals. Shame can be defined as "a painful awareness of oneself as defeated, deficient, exposed, a failure, inadequate, wanting, worthless, and wounded . . . The very essence of the self feels wrong" (Lazare, 1987, p. 1653). Shame is concerned with what one is, as compared with guilt, which relates to what one has done. Traumatic experiences shatter individuals' basic assumptions about the world and themselves. Hence, shame is like a rupture of trust in oneself, one's sense of competence, connectedness, and control (Stone, 1992). A pervasive sense of shame blocks a child's accurate assessment of his or her own accomplishments and self-worth, as well as interrupting positive experiences of interest and enjoyment. A sense of differentness sets children apart from others in their own minds and contributes to their behavioral isolation. Adopted and foster children often retain a sense of differentness, which for some children is akin to shame. Chronic trauma experiences serve only to intensify the child's negative self-identification.

Self-Efficacy

The destruction of an individual's feeling of self-efficacy or mastery resulting in a feeling of powerlessness is an immediate and long-term effect of traumatic experiences. When a child is unable to protect himself or herself against harm and repeated painful experiences, he or she feels trapped, afraid, and vulnerable. This strong sense of personal vulnerability and belief that the world is a dangerous place produce ongoing feelings of anxiety and strong fears. The dissociative symptoms and other avoidance phenomena frequently connected to abuse victimization are responses to feelings of powerlessness to defend against trauma. Also, some children attempt to defend against their lack of mastery by achieving power and control through other means. This high need to control leads to behaviors such as defiance, lying, and excessive aggression.

A primary emotion associated with powerlessness is intense feelings of anger or rage. Research indicates that anger is a predominant long-term emotion for males and females who have been sexually abused, stronger than guilt, anxiety, or other emotions (Stein, Golding, Siegel, Bunam, & Sorenson, 1988). If the child has not been able to resolve traumas that he or she has experienced, the anger is only intensified. Many children's anxiety is increased by this residual anger because they experience conflict between discharging aggressive impulses and fear of loss of affection or punishment. Their rage may be demonstrated in explosive tantrums, profanity, destructiveness, and cruelty to others, including animals. Some children have adapted an overall coping style labeled *identification with the aggressor,* whereby they escape feeling like a victim; they almost always seem angry, defiant, and aggressive. Others act in an acceptable fashion most of the time but flare into rages when frustrated.

Expressions related to powerlessness were common among the children served through the Illinois project. Some reported feeling flooded by waves of emotion over which they felt they had no control. They reported intrusive thoughts and nightmares about events that they had not remembered previously. Some children also described themselves as "always mad." For example, one 13-year-old boy reported that he could not control his rageful outbursts and truly wanted help with it.

It is important to note that these dimensions of traumatic effect are all interwoven. The behaviors stemming from feelings of powerlessness are also fueled by children's low abilities for self-regulation of emotions and behaviors discussed below. Although many of the children served through post-adoption services express a desire to change negative behaviors or to escape overwhelming thoughts and feelings, they had been unable to exercise self-control in these areas. For example, one teenage girl who was extremely lacking in this capacity stated, "I can't control lying and stealing. They (adoptive parents) have to control me, but I don't like it!" Her feelings reflect both a need for the safety of being protected by parents and her strong ambivalence about relinquishing any power and control to them.

Self-Regulation

As discussed earlier in this chapter, the physiological effect of trauma results in chronic hyperarousal symptoms that compromise the physiological systems that regulate responses. In addition, many children experience ongoing blows with which they do not have the internal or external resources to cope. Often the disruptions in attachment they have experienced have compromised their development as well. All these factors contribute to inadequate development of impulse control. This impulsivity relates to a low level of self-control of cognitions, emotions, and behaviors. Reexperiencing symptoms such as intrusive thoughts and nightmares as well as avoidance symptoms such as numbing of feelings and blocked memories evidence difficulties in self-regulation. Likewise, sudden mood changes, concentration problems, and even the inability to modulate sexual feelings and impulses resulting from sexual victimization fall within the domain of self-regulation.

In addition, some children may engage in ongoing behaviors stemming from their traumatic experiences that are secret and dysfunctional. These behaviors may include deviant sexualized behaviors, dissociative behaviors, or ritualistic behaviors associated with their past victimization. For example, one child who had been sexually abused hid feces in a box under his bed. Unless discovered by caregivers, these behaviors are not likely to be disclosed by the child unless a therapist seeks to discover them through active, accepting therapeutic efforts.

A lack of awareness of feelings is common among maltreated children. As children develop language, they use cognitions to gain control over their emotional responses. Maltreated children are less likely to articulate physical needs as well as positive or negative emotions, however (Toth & Cicchetti, 1993). Also, the numbing of feelings resulting from overwhelming trauma makes it more difficult for children to access their emotional experiences, which in turn makes verbal expression of emotions difficult. This lack of awareness also interferes with the child's modulation of feelings and behaviors. Conversely, the expansion of a child's internal-state language use may facilitate control over nonverbal emotional expressions (Cicchetti et al., 1991).

POSTTRAUMATIC STRESS DISORDER

Another conceptual framework for understanding the psychological effect of trauma is the classification of symptoms characterized by the diagnosis of PTSD. The classic posttraumatic stress symptoms may be grouped under three categories: increased arousal, reexperiencing the trauma, and constriction mechanisms to protect against or avoid pain. To meet the official diagnosis of PTSD, an individual must display symptoms in each of these categories.

Hyperarousal

Arousal is a natural, biological response to trauma that prepares animals, humans included, to defend against threat. The ongoing symptoms of increased arousal resulting from chronic traumatic experiences go beyond an acute adrenaline surge, however. Traumatized children may function in an ongoing state of hypervigilance, in which they are constantly monitoring the environment and on the lookout for threats. Ongoing irritability with escalated responses to small provocation is another common symptom of hyperarousal. Those who are hyperaroused may have difficulty sleeping and startle easily. Hyperactivity, anxiety, mood swings, impulsivity, and hypertension stem from the physiological changes accompanying chronic trauma experiences. The increased levels of dopamine and testosterone enhance competitive and retaliatory aggression and contribute to hypervigilance and paranoia (Lewis, 1992).

Reexperiencing the Trauma

Intrusive thoughts and feelings are hallmark symptoms of trauma. Children relive traumatic experiences through flashbacks and nightmares. They also may experience bodily responses to certain stimuli associated with their traumatic experiences or demonstrate repetitive behaviors in play that stem from these experiences. Traumatic memories have unusual qualities in that they involve very vivid sensations and images. This reality may stem from physiological alterations in the central nervous system.

Children are most likely to reexperience trauma visually. Terr (1991) relates the case of a 5-year-old who had been sexually abused between 15 and 18 months of age. This child drew pictures with strongly visualized elements from the abusive experiences even though the only aspect of the experience that she could verbalize was the word *danger* in relation to the day care building. Play and behavioral reenactments of aspects of traumatic experiences are also common in traumatized children. For example, one young girl who had been sexually abused drew pubic hair on her dolls and acted out sexual intercourse with her Barbie and Ken dolls. Unfortunately, this behavior was viewed as evidence that she was "sick" by her preadoptive mother, who later demanded her removal.

Fears are common posttraumatic symptoms in children, including fears of the dark and of being alone. Sometimes specific stimuli are associated with traumatic experiences that are linked to fears. For example, a child who is kidnapped by someone in a green car may react with fear to green cars. One adoptive mother served by the Illinois project related her son's extreme fear of police officers during his early years in placement. The pervasiveness of this fear prompted her to dig deeper into his early history. She learned that he had been locked in a closet by his father for several days just before his removal from his home. Eventually, the child had an emotional breakdown and was taken to the emergency room. His father had told him that if the boy talked about his experience, the father would force him to drink poison and then would kill himself. The father did commit suicide, and the boy left the hospital to attend his father's funeral. This 5-year-old boy thought he had killed his father and that the police were going to come put him in jail. He also feared that his father would come back from the dead and kill him.

In addition to stimulating fear, specific stimuli associated with traumatic experiences may serve as triggers for recalling painful memories. Senses that are not consciously associated with events, such as tastes, smells, or bodily sensations, serve as powerful triggers. Situations, places, and feelings trigger traumatic memories. For example, a boy served through the Illinois project had memories of his parents coming into his room at night, beating him with wires, and laughing at him. He had difficulty sleeping, and said, "When I go into my room, all I can do is hear them and see them coming."

Theoretically, children who have repressed traumatic memories wait until they are in a safe place in their lives to allow these memories to resurface. Sanford (1990), in her study of survivors of childhood abuse, describes reconnection to traumatic memories as occurring in the presence of a "positive trigger," which provides the safety and structure for the survivor to face the trauma. This positive condition allowing for reconnection may be the child's presence in a nurturing environment, the supports in a particular program of therapy, or other such conditions. For example, it was not uncommon for children whose cases were reviewed in our disruption study to reconnect with their earlier traumatic experiences after they had been placed with an adoptive family or, for some, after their adoption was finalized.

Constriction or Avoidance Mechanisms

Because reliving trauma is so painful, people will go to great lengths to avoid these feelings and will develop defensive mechanisms to ward off intrusive symptoms. These mechanisms may range from consciously avoiding situations that may trigger memories or feelings associated with the trauma to massive denial and numbing of feelings. Dissociation is a defense through which children can wall off their experience from consciousness. They mentally escape the reality of traumatic experiences by leaving their body and going somewhere else in their mind. Avoidance symptoms include feelings of detachment, flat affect, and a sense of a foreshortened future. Older children and adults may use drugs and alcohol to assist in numbing the pain.

These mechanisms are important protections for the child to avoid reliving the trauma. Long-term use of avoidance mechanisms is a barrier to the healing process, however. As Herman (1997) writes,

> Although dissociative alterations in consciousness, or even intoxication, may be adaptive at the moment of total helplessness, they become maladaptive once the danger is past. Because these altered states keep the traumatic experience walled off from ordinary consciousness, they prevent the integration necessary for healing. (p. 45)

Unfortunately, children who have experienced chronic abuse and traumatic separations have difficulty believing and feeling that the danger is past. They have an ongoing sense of vulnerability that maintains chronic traumatic responses. This interferes with adaptation to improved family situations when children move into adoption.

Some children served through adoption preservation programs meet all the criteria for a PTSD diagnosis. Others who are known to have extensive histories of trauma exhibit many maladaptive behaviors but do not meet the criteria for a PTSD diagnosis. Some experts in the field have criticized this diagnostic categorization as being too restrictive. It is seen as biased toward those showing reexperiencing symptoms rather than denial symptoms, and not accurately capturing chronic forms of untreated PTSD that result in ingrained patterns of rage and antisocial behaviors (McCann, Sakheim, & Abrahamson, 1988; Scurfield, 1985).

Recent research on traumatized children is beginning to verify the variations and complexity in chronic traumatic responses. For example, Terr (1991), who has completed several studies of traumatized children, advances two typologies for children's coping patterns following trauma. The type I pattern is related more to single-incident traumas, after which children have detailed, though sometimes distorted, memories of their experience. These children devote considerable mental energy to processing the traumatic experience in their mind and usually meet the criteria of repetition, avoidance, and hyperalertness characteristic of classic PTSD. The type II pattern, associated with long-standing or repeated exposure to trauma, is more likely to lead to massive denial and other attempts to protect the self. Repression, psychic numbing, self-hypnosis, and dissociation are often found among these children. Terr describes the emotions stirred up by type II traumas as an absence of feeling, a sense of rage, and unremitting sadness. These children are often diagnosed as having conduct disorders, attention deficit disorders, or depression. Their intense feelings of rage stemming from repeated abuses often lead to habitual patterns of aggressiveness, sometimes including self-injury.

Some recent studies have supported the prevalence of Terr's (1991) type II symptomatology among children experiencing repeated abuse or having chronic duration of PTSD symptoms. Famularo and his colleagues (Famularo, Kinscherff, & Fenton 1990) studied a group of children diagnosed with PTSD. They found that children with chronic PTSD showed increases in symptoms of detachment, including a restricted range of affect, dissociative episodes, sadness, and a belief that life will be too hard. In another study of 89 patients in a day treatment program who had physical and/or sexual abuse histories, two distinct symptom patterns were identified. A majority developed symptoms characteristic of PTSD; however, children without PTSD symptoms exhibited more anxiety, depression, externalizing behaviors, and more problems overall (Kiser et al., 1988). The victims of ongoing abuse appeared significantly more disturbed and had more delinquent and aggressive behaviors. Kiser et al. (1988) theorize that the development of PTSD serves a protective function for these children.

DIMENSIONS FOR
UNDERSTANDING TRAUMATIC EXPERIENCES
OF SPECIAL NEEDS ADOPTEES

Many factors influence the manner in which children respond to traumatic experiences. Some of the variables that are important in influencing how children experience trauma as well as how they react to it are discussed below.

Access to Memories and Disclosure

Most children who are served through adoption preservation programs have experienced a range of traumatic experiences. The full extent of the traumas they have experienced frequently is not known. Traumatized children may not have clear memories of their past. Even when children do remember their experiences, they often do not disclose them. For example, research indicates that the majority of sexually abused children do not disclose their experiences during their childhood (Russell, 1983; Sorenson & Snow, 1991). Children may disclose traumatic experiences many years after trauma occurred. For example, in one analysis of the effect of sexual abuse among special needs adoptees (Minshew & Hooper, 1990), the authors report that 57% of the sexually abused children placed through their program were not known to be sexually victimized until after adoptive placement. Lack of disclosure may mean that the child does not have conscious memories of these events. It may also mean that he or she feels constrained from talking about them.

Our research on special needs adoptions underscores this pattern of delayed disclosure of traumatic experiences. Many children seem to be in a survival mode during their foster care years, and they either avoid facing traumatic memories or do not have access to these memories.

Traumatic memories often resurface after children are placed for adoption. The demands of making a permanent attachment to adoptive parents or sometimes the event of adoption finalization may trigger resurfacing. For example, one boy had been sexually abused by his mother until he was 5 years old, at which time the mother died. When the boy was being prepared for adoptive placement at age 10, he was having nightmares about his mother coming back from the dead and hurting him. At this point, he finally disclosed his sexual abuse.

In addition to adoptive placement, a variety of stimuli may serve as a trigger to traumatic feelings associated with past experiences. Anniversary dates, people, places, objects, or other reminders may stimulate reexperiencing traumatic responses. Severe stresses that cause children to operate on emotional overload may also contribute to reconnecting to past trauma experiences. As children go through developmental stages, their thinking abilities mature, and they may process their experiences differently. For many of the children served through the Illinois project, later losses or traumas or the onset of puberty seemed to lead to resurfacing. Among these children, posttraumatic stress symptoms were most prevalent in 12-year-olds. It is unclear as to why puberty appears to be related to resurfacing of trauma. Perhaps the physiological changes stimulate resurfacing of memories, or the developmental changes in cognitive functioning may contribute to this association. For some children, these reactions seemed to occur abruptly, as was the case for a 12-year-old boy who began reliving maltreatment by parents from whom he had been removed at age 4. While taking a shower one night, he began screaming hysterically, "I'm locked in the closet and I can't get out."

Children report being overwhelmed by emotions and memories of events that they struggle to understand. Some begin having dreams or flashbacks about experiences that happened at a very young age. One example is a 13-year-old girl who had last been removed from her birth family at age 3. Her history included suffering a fractured skull from abuse. During her participation in a support group, she began to have flashbacks that disturbed her. Her behaviors became more destructive, and she expressed feelings of being out of control. In individual sessions, she became detached if her birth history was raised. Finally, this child was hospitalized due to suicidal behaviors. During her treatment, memories of incidents that happened 10 years ago emerged. She recalled seeing her little sister dipped head-first in scalding water, having the sister die in bed with her after a beating, and being blamed by her parents for not waking up to help the sister. She remembered her sister's funeral and her fears that her sister was being buried alive. Children often report feeling "crazy" when they experience these fragmentary but vivid memories, and they struggle hard to understand them.

Severity and Duration of Trauma

Children's traumatic experiences and the effect of these experiences vary in severity and duration. Sadistic physical and sexual abuse are among the most severe traumas experienced by children. For the children served by the Illinois project, those who had been sexually abused were most likely to have posttraumatic stress symptoms, although physical abuse also was associated with such symptoms.

Repeated incidences of trauma have a more pervasive effect than a single event. The severity of a trauma also is related to a child's perception of the experience. Mediating factors such as the use of force and the extent of physical threat vary with the particular experience and the child's perception of the experience. Research indicates that the child being in a role of responsibility for others, guilt, and exposure to the grotesque are factors that increase the severity of effect (Green et al., 1990). Longitudinal studies of children growing up in maltreating families indicate that the likelihood of sustaining social competence in the face of ongoing traumatic experiences diminishes over the course of the early childhood years (Farber & Egeland, 1987). In other words, the longer a child remains in an abusive and neglectful environment, the more likely the child is to be damaged by traumatic experiences.

Age at Onset

Earlier onset of trauma is associated with greater severity of effect (Famularo, Fenton, Kinscherff, Ayoub, & Barnum, 1994). The physical and psychological resources of a very young child are easily overwhelmed. The child's immature nervous system and cognitive processes limit his or her ability to cope as readily with traumatic experiences as older children. Experiencing physical and emotional deprivation and severe trauma, particularly during the critical period for brain development from birth to age 3, can produce physical changes in the brain, endocrine system, and other physiological functions that may result in permanent physiological changes (Briere, 1992; Reite & Field, 1985; Ver Ellen & van Kammen, 1990).

Children without memories of traumatic events have more difficulty processing and healing from these events. There is some evidence that children as young as age 2 retain memories of traumatic events, but are able to articulate them only when language has developed (Hewitt, 1994). Children who are preverbal or who have repressed their memories of traumatic events may not have conscious memories of trauma, but they may have somatic memories, that is, memories that are anchored in bodily sensations (Droga, 1997; van der Kolk, 1996). Infants and toddlers may not be able to retrieve full verbal memories of traumas, but they may reexperience aspects of their traumas visually and express these through play or drawing (Terr, 1991).

Social Support

For adults and children alike, social support is the most important factor in mediating the effect of traumatic events. Among studies of reactions of men in combat, having close relationships with comrades and commanders is critical in reducing the traumatic effect of these events (Kardiner & Spiegel, 1947). In research on children, a good relationship with at least one parental figure ameliorates the negative effect of family conflict and child abuse (Luthar & Zigler, 1991).

Children who have experienced early and ongoing emotional deprivation are highly susceptible to the effect of trauma. In some families, sibling support helps sustain children. In families where children lack any social support, however, the effect of ongoing trauma is more severe. For example, one child served through the Illinois project was adopted from an Eastern European orphanage at age 6. At this institution, she had been singled out for abuse by a female caregiver due to the child's mixed ethnicity. This woman had sexually, physically, and emotionally abused the young girl, and had influenced other children to do likewise. The child remembered having her head shoved in a toilet, being forced to eat feces, having food taken away, being beaten, and having objects stuck in her body. She was repeatedly told that she was evil and inferior. Her total lack of support within this setting amplified the devastation of the abuse.

Resiliency in Children

The effect of trauma is influenced by the interaction of characteristics of the child and the environment. Although a supportive environment can moderate the effects of trauma, specific aspects of children themselves make them more or less vulnerable to the negative effect of trauma. Some of these aspects are dispositional attributes of the child, which are thought to be largely genetic, constitutional factors (Wertlieb, Weigel, Springer, & Feldstein, 1989). These include three aspects of temperament: distractibility, threshold level of stimulation, and approach (response to novel stimuli). In other words, children who have positive temperaments and adjust more readily to environmental changes are more resilient.

There are inconsistent findings on some variables in relation to their protective functions. Gender and intelligence may act as buffers or vulnerabilities depending on the age and the circumstances. For example, boys are generally viewed as more vulnerable to a number of negative influences in childhood, but recent research indicates that this gender association with vulnerability shifts over the life span. During their second decade, males are less vulnerable than females (Werner, 1989). Intelligence is generally associated with higher levels of social competence; however, some studies indicate that at very high levels of stress, intelligent children may lose their advantage due to heightened sensitivity (Luthar & Zigler, 1991).

A number of qualities associated with better-coping abilities in children are both cause and effect variables. Interpersonal awareness, strong social skills, higher levels of empathy, positive school experiences, and problem-solving skills are themselves indicators of greater social and emotional maturity.

A primary characteristic of children that mediates the effect of trauma is an internal locus of control. Children who have faith in their ability to exert control over their environment and take steps to deal with challenges are less likely to be overwhelmed by challenges (Luthar & Zigler, 1991). Even children who are able to use their intelligence and courage to outwit abusers and find ways to survive horrendous experiences are demonstrating this internal locus of control. In his moving account of his own severe child abuse experience, Dave Pelzer (1995) describes his determination to survive victimization, abuse that included deliberate starvation, torture, and being consigned to sleep in the garage:

> I used my head to survive. . . . Standing alone in that damp, dark garage, I knew, for the first time, that I could survive. I decided that I would use any tactic I could think of to defeat Mother or to delay her from her grizzly obsession. I knew if I wanted to live, I would have to think ahead. I could

no longer cry like a helpless baby. In order to survive, I could never give
in to her. That day I vowed to myself that I would never, ever again give
that bitch the satisfaction of hearing me beg her to stop beating me.
(pp. 42-42)

Knowledge of the qualities that serve protective functions in children
can be helpful in developing interventions for traumatized children. For
example, strategies that promote the development of empathy and an
internal locus of control may ameliorate the negative effect of trauma.
Case studies of individual children who have endured extraordinary
life circumstances and survived to become socially competent adults
underscore their strengths and abilities to cope. Ongoing severe trauma
takes its toll on the physical and emotional health of individuals,
however, even those who survive to become competent, achieving
adults. The former Miss America, Marilyn Van Derber Atler, poignantly
relates her own struggles in coming to terms with childhood sexual
abuse (Terr, 1994). Her life exemplifies the coexistence of psychological pain and dysfunction, social and emotional achievements, personal
triumphs, spiritual strengths, and physical and emotional vulnerabilities
that characterize individuals who have survived severe childhood traumas and worked diligently on their own healing.

It is important to underscore the coexistence of strengths and vulnerabilities in special needs adopted children, as well as their potential for
healing. For example, one young boy was struggling with his feelings
of rage and fear related to being the victim of ritualistic sexual abuse.
At the same time, he demonstrated many creative abilities and received
an award at school for the most improved student. For special needs
children, the need for purposeful interventions that promote healing at
the earliest possible stage of their childhood and ongoing thereafter is
critical to their survival and personal growth.

OVERVIEW OF INTERVENTION
WITH TRAUMATIZED CHILDREN

Ideally, children who have endured traumatizing experiences receive
early intervention that lessens the intensity and severity of their responses. The child's cognitive understanding of traumatic events is
much more malleable within the first few days following a trauma. This
early understanding has been likened to wet cement. Months and years

following an event, the child's understanding may be likened to hardened cement, which must be chipped away in layers (Crimando, 1997). In the absence of intervention, particularly when the child continues to experience traumatic events, the child's sensitized neural systems result in persistent hyperarousal or dissociative symptoms, or both (Perry et al., 1995). The physiological aspects of persistent trauma responses have implications for treatment in that treatment needs to be directed at the areas of the brain that mediate the trauma response. The primary ways to affect these primitive parts of the brain are through nurturance, predictability, providing for feelings of safety, and attachment relationships. Therefore, the development of a truly secure attachment relationship is the first line of defense against the negative effects of trauma. Holding and soothing a child who is in a fearful, aroused state and planning for ways to support the child in situations that arouse feelings of vulnerability assist with reintegration. The child needs to be helped to face pain by acknowledging his or her feelings as he or she is supported and protected. Therefore, one of the primary interventions by adults is effectively meeting the needs of the child when the child is in a highly emotional, needy state.

Interventions by both parents and therapists should be built on an ongoing assessment of the child's history of trauma and responses to these experiences. The specific nature of traumatic experiences as well as the child's perceptions and feelings related to these experiences need to be understood. Ideally, this assessment begins as soon as children enter the child welfare system. Often children may not talk about experiences at a young age, but their play and drawings may reveal clues to their past experiences. Children need to be provided with many opportunities for assessments to take place, and all the traumatic experiences that they disclose need to be documented for future caregivers and counselors. At the point of providing postlegal adoption services, any information contained in the child's case records should be obtained. In addition, the worker needs to engage the child, the adoptive parents, and possibly past caregivers or workers in reconstructing the child's traumatic history and the child's interpretation of this history.

As with other types of interventions with adopted children, treatment efforts to help traumatized children should be collaborative efforts with adoptive parents. Adoptive parents need to be helped to understand the child's needs and the most effective strategies for helping the child. Parents may be included in therapy sessions with some children. Parental involvement is particularly important with children who have not developed attachment relationships with parents. At the very least, parents should be kept abreast of the goals and progress of individual work with the child. Parents can collaborate by working with children on therapy-related homework assignments and adopting strategies for interacting with the child at home that complement therapeutic goals.

A number of experts in child welfare stress the need to do preparatory work with emotionally fragile children before delving directly into traumatic experiences and feelings. Otherwise, treatment efforts may intensify symptoms, anxiety, and defenses. Gallagher and colleagues (Gallagher, Leavitt, & Kimmel, 1995) advocate such careful preparation. Early treatment focuses on supportive techniques to stabilize the child's overall functioning, developing coping strategies, and developing a relationship with the child through nonthreatening activities. During this stage, traumatic play is viewed as premature and is interrupted. Also, symbolic play is not connected to real-life situations. Feeling safe is stressed, and rules and boundaries are established. Activities may focus on strengthening the child's abilities to engage in focused activities and to articulate thoughts and feelings in a non-anxiety-provoking manner. Only after a sense of safety and trust has been developed does treatment begin to delve deeper into very painful experiences.

Treatment of traumatized children needs to be a very intense, active approach characterized by high energy and nurturance to have a significant effect on the child. James (1989) describes the style of therapy that is needed:

> Traumatized children are usually well-defended emotionally, but locked inside them are powerful and terrifying beliefs that they are helpless, bad, and at fault. The messages the child receives from therapy must match the intensity of these negative messages in order to be heard, felt, and believed. It is fun that keeps the child emotionally receptive so that the intense positive messages can slip through her defenses. . . . An intense outreach of positivism is needed to get the message through the child's distorted, and usually negative, self-image. Direct verbal messages should be continually reinforced through therapeutic activities in clinical sessions and (with the therapist's providing guidance to the adults) in home, school, recreational, and church settings. (pp. 13-14)

An effective therapeutic approach also needs to be multidimensional. Talk therapy alone is not as effective as involving activities that reinforce verbal messages as well as those that embrace the body and the spirit. Therapies oriented toward body work such as movement, breathing, and touch therapies are often helpful with these children. Spiritual healing is especially important for children who have had profoundly negative experiences over time. They need to feel that they have value as a human being, that they are intrinsically good, and that their life has meaning. Spiritual healing is facilitated through creative works, rituals, connecting with nature, and the teachings of specific religious groups.

It is important for parents to recognize that healing usually is a long-term process involving periods of improvement and regression. Children may need therapeutic help at different points during their childhood. The goals discussed below represent ongoing themes for working with these special needs adoptees.

GOALS FOR FACILITATING HEALING FROM TRAUMA

The body of research on treatment of PTSD has primarily studied cognitive-behavioral therapies, eye movement desensitization and reprocessing, and pharmacology. All three of these therapies have been shown to have positive outcomes with adults experiencing classic PTSD symptoms. Although aspects of these treatments may be used in working with children with special needs, they generally are more applicable to acute trauma reactions than to the chronic, pervasive effects of trauma affecting many of these children. Much of the thrust of these treatments relates to deconditioning anxiety symptoms. Another major goal of treating trauma victims is altering the way the individual views himself or herself and the world to establish a feeling of personal integrity and control (van der Kolk, McFarlane, & van der Hart, 1996).

Facilitate the Child's Feelings of Safety

A basic foundation for helping children recover from traumatic experiences is the promotion of feeling safe and protected. This is hindered when children hide their fears. Children served through the Illinois project often did not communicate their fears and nightmares or the depth of their anxiety to their parents. In general, research indicates that parents tend to underestimate their children's anxiety and other inner responses to trauma (McFarlane, 1987). Many children reveal the intensity of their fears in children's support groups, an ideal environment for them to explore feelings.

A beginning principle for helping traumatized adoptive children is to understand the child's inner world to adapt the adult's methods of intervening to the child's way of thinking about the world and himself or herself. Telling a child that he is safe does not necessarily make him feel safe. For children in particular, relating to their inner reality is essential before trying to achieve a shift in the meaning they attribute to an event. Hence, many rational arguments alone may not help a young child who is afraid. In using cognitive methods to modify irrational thoughts with children, techniques must be adapted to the individual child's age, developmental stage, and inner reality. For example, the 4-year-old who is afraid of monsters coming in the night might be helped by putting a picture next to the bed of a guardian angel who watches over her or having a stuffed animal that is even scarier but protective for her to sleep with.

This reality is illustrated by a case situation mentioned earlier, the little boy who was locked in a closet for days by his father, followed by the boy's hospitalization and the father's suicide. This boy believed that his father would come back from the dead and kill him. His mother reported that she tried every rational way she could conceive of to teach her son that his father could not come back from the dead. She had a doctor talk with him, took him to visit his father's grave, had a cemetery worker tell him that no one came back out of their grave, and so on. The experience that seemed the most reassuring to her young son was a movie about a kidnapping. In the film, the child's mother never gave up looking for him until he was found. The adoptive mother recounted that her son would look at this video over and over with her and ask her to promise that if he ever disappeared, she would not give up until she found him.

It is important for parents and workers to work with children to identify the situations or other stimuli that provoke their feelings of powerlessness and fear. Identifying triggers related to intrusive thoughts and memories is a part of this. After these situations have been identified, problem solving around ways to support and comfort the child can take place. For example, in the situation of the young boy who was flooded with memories of abuse when he went to bed, his parents began reading him a story at bedtime and sitting with him while he went to sleep. This soothing was effective in stopping the night terrors he was experiencing.

A traumatized child needs reassurance that intrusive memories and intense emotional anxieties make sense, can be coped with, and will lessen in time. Parents need to convey that they will support the child through these experiences and that he or she can eventually get past them. Talking about these experiences is a beginning step toward lessening their intensity. The memories that haunt children in nightmares and intrusive thoughts generally stem from the nonverbal dissociated realm of traumatic memory (van der Kolk et al., 1996). By talking about these experiences, children translate traumatic memories into narrative memory, giving them explicit form, meaning, and perspective. This is a precursor to "working through" these experiences.

In addition to providing external supports, adults can help children learn ways to lessen their own anxieties. Generating a list of alternate coping strategies from relaxation techniques to seeking out someone to talk with provides the child with ways to regulate his or her own feelings of fear and anxiety. Self-help strategies include identifying triggers and planning for ways to gain self-control over responses, deep breathing, physical exercise, and positive self-talk (Matsakis, 1992). Teaching self-protection skills can also increase a child's feelings of safety and mastery.

Help the Child Process Traumatic Experiences

As a child is helped to process the traumatic experiences he or she has endured, dual therapeutic goals are achieved. These include decreasing emotional tension and increasing purposeful thinking related to past experiences and to coping in the present. First, the worker must help the child reconnect with the past by reconstructing important events. The worker facilitates the child's talking about experiences and thoughts and feelings related to these experiences. It is important for the worker to express compassion for the child and empathize with how hard things were for the child. But to move beyond victimization, children need to receive the message that trauma can be overcome.

There are many therapeutic activities and techniques for facilitating children's processing of traumatic experiences. One such activity is a resolution scrapbook (Lowenstein, 1995), originally developed by Hindman (1989). This scrapbook is completed by the child with the assistance of a therapist, and is designed to chronicle the child's experiences. The activities incorporated into the construction of the scrapbook are sequenced from nonthreatening to more threatening in content. Many therapeutic workbooks are designed for children from which activity pages may be incorporated. Work on the scrapbook constitutes a segment of a therapy session, accompanied by some free time for less intense activities. Also included in the scrapbook are activities related to problem solving and self-esteem, as well as letters from significant others explaining difficult issues or affirming their support and the child's abilities. This scrapbook seems similar to lifebooks commonly used with adoptive children, but the resolution scrapbook is focused on chronicling the child's therapeutic mastery of major traumatic events in his or her life.

Another activity, called the "garbage bag," (James, 1989) is used to facilitate the child's chronicling and processing of experiences. In this exercise, the child writes on separate sheets of paper every overwhelming, traumatic experience that he or she can remember and puts them all in a paper bag that the child can decorate. James asks children to put stars by any events that their parents do not know about and supports them later in sharing these with parents. At some point during each therapy session, the child pulls out one or two "pieces of garbage" and talk about his or her thoughts and feelings related to this event. If the child doesn't feel ready to work on this thing yet, he or she can throw it back into the bag and choose another. When the child feels that he or she understands the event and that it no longer causes strong feelings, he or she destroys the piece of paper. Children are asked periodically if they have thought of other events that they want to add to their garbage bag. Thus, the therapist assists the child in disposing of this "big, smelly mess of garbage" so the child won't have to carry it around all the time.

A technique called "testimony" has been found to facilitate recovery from traumatic events. Its use with refugees and others who have been the victims of torture has facilitated the survivor's confronting the details of the event to convey an accurate portrayal of what happened but also to confront its meaning (Cienfuegos & Monelli, 1983; Jensen & Agger, 1988). James (1989) reports using children who have worked through their own trauma experiences as "child graduate assistants" in talking to other children about their experiences and healing work. Also, many survivors of terrible experiences have found meaning in helping others who undergo similar experiences. These activities bring healing to themselves as well as others.

Increase Child's Awareness of and
Ability to Manage Feelings

Healing involves reworking the traumatic experiences both cognitively and on an emotional level. Goals for "getting in touch with feelings" include increasing a child's awareness of feelings and helping the child understand feelings and learn how to manage them. This first goal, which is intrinsic to all work with troubled children, is discussed in Chapter 5. Traumatized children must be helped to identify feelings and to differentiate feelings from thoughts. They need to learn that experiencing an emotion does not mean one has to act on it. Many therapeutic activities, games, and techniques have been developed to facilitate feelings work in children. In the "feelings wall" (Lowenstein, 1995), the child is given an envelope with adhesive labels, each describing a different feeling. The child selects one feeling at a time, and writes on the label a time that he or she experienced this feeling. Once all the labels are completed, the child sticks them on the wall, with more intense experiences higher up on the wall. For adolescents, journal writing may be a valuable activity to assist in identifying and feeling feelings.

It is important to identify fears children may have related to their feelings. According to Matsakis (1992), fear of feeling is related to fear of losing control of oneself and fear of suffering. Children may be helped to examine how others have responded to their feelings in the past and how they have expressed them. The more one gets to know oneself emotionally, the more one can gain mastery over feelings. Mastery does not mean that these feelings disappear, but rather that they can be tolerated and that one can decide on how or whether to act on these feelings.

Facilitate Reality-Based Perceptions
Related to Traumatic Experiences

While helping the child to process traumatic experiences, it is important for the adult to facilitate the child's understanding of these experiences from a reality-based perspective. The search for meaning is a common human reaction to trauma, and one that may continue over many years. Like adults, children struggle with finding answers to questions such as "Why did bad things happen to me?" which includes their conflict over why their parent hurt them or allowed them to be hurt. An activity that James (1989) advocates for facilitating children's awareness that a variety of bad things can happen to different people and that these vary in intensity is the "List of Bad, Mean, Rotten Things That Can Happen to Kids." In this activity, children individually or in a group write down a number of different negative things that can happen to people. Some outrageous things are often included, such as being stolen by aliens, as well as other experiences that would be thought to be worse than those the child experienced. Then the child arranges these along a continuum from the very worst thing that could happen to the least bad thing. Children's discussion of why some things are worse than others helps them to put some of their own experiences into perspective.

Adults need to educate children about the effect that hurtful experiences can have on people and the importance of getting rid of the really painful feelings through healing work. Through many modalities, including stories and music, children can come to understand that other adults, children, and even animals have had similar experiences. Sometimes universalizing how others have understood and felt about similar experiences facilitates children's putting their own experiences into perspective and reducing their feelings of alienation and shame. Likewise, they can learn a reality-based perspective by identifying with aspects of others' experiences. Play acting with puppets can enable children to act out similar experiences and explore specific aspects of these experiences that are troubling. As children talk about their own experiences, adults need to assist them in reframing elements that may be distorted, especially related to the child's apparent lack of choice and subsequent feelings of guilt and blame.

Some therapists advocate the use of metaphorical storytelling as conducive to emotional healing. Stories can be created to fit the circumstances of individual children's experiences and to teach specific lessons that children need to learn. Metaphorical storytelling is a way to teach problem solving and to empower children to recognize their own strengths and resilience. Brohl (1996) gives instructions on how to create a metaphorical story to fit the child's own experience. Davis (1988) advocates having parents read selected therapeutic stories to children again and again or having the therapist tape the story for children to take home. Davis describes her therapeutic stories as using Erickson's metaphorical technique, attributing their success to their effect on the unconscious mind (or, for others, the right brain). These nonthreatening stories teach new attitudes and belief systems and impart messages of love, power, and healing.

Achieve the Child's Understanding
That It's Not His or Her Fault

One primary piece of putting traumatic experiences in a reality perspective is helping the child understand that the trauma was not his or her fault, that it was not something he or she deserved to have happen. Simply telling the child that it is not his or her fault does not counteract the intensity of guilt and self-blame the child may feel. It will take a variety of experiences to counteract the negative, self-blaming messages a child has internalized. One of the most effective modalities for reducing feelings of shame, stigma, or difference is support groups for children. Hearing other children's stories and the differences and similarities in experiences helps an individual child to put his or her own experience in a broader perspective. The child can sometimes identify with the healthy messages he or she hears from other survivors. Likewise, biographical stories of children or adults who have survived traumas offer hopeful, nonblaming messages. One book recommended for children is *I Know I Made it Happen,* by Blackburn (1991). In helping the child move from feeling responsible for his or her traumas, adults must be sure to help the child construct an alternative explanation that provides meaning.

In addition, children need to be helped to establish boundaries in relation to indiscriminate disclosure of painful events in their lives. They need to learn about privacy and the need for people to decide with whom they may want to share their "private" business. Discussion of what types of things might be considered private helps to distinguish privacy from secrecy related to shame.

One element that may facilitate the beginning of a child's not blaming himself or herself is the focused expression of anger related to those who have hurt the child. Whether through symbolic play, writing, or physically attacking a punching doll, children need to be helped to put a form to their anger to move beyond their pervasive feelings of rage. A therapeutic activity called "Clay Bombs" was developed by James (1989) for this purpose. James often has the parent present when this exercise is used, and has the parents take a turn at the end. The child makes bombs from mushy clay and throws them from across the room at an outlined picture of his or her abuser. The therapist and child take turns throwing the bombs as they state reasons they are mad, something they hate about the abuser, and so on.

With older children, therapists may use letter writing as a vehicle for helping the child express anger. In some situations, letters may be shared with actual perpetrators. One therapist reported assisting a teenage boy prior to adoptive placement to write all the things he wanted to tell his abuser, who had sadistically abused him over a period of years. Finally, she allowed this boy to telephone the abuser with the intention of reading the letter. After several attempts to connect, he recorded his feelings on the man's answering machine. The therapist reported that after this experience, the boy seemed as if a burden had been lifted from him.

Assist the Child in Developing Feelings of Mastery

Traumatized children are most likely to have difficulty when they feel they have no control over a situation. Therefore, it is important for adults around them to provide opportunities for the child to make choices and to exercise control rather than taking away all the child's sense of control and insisting on total surrender to the adult's will.

As discussed earlier in relation to fears of closeness, Katz (1986) advocates working with the child to develop the child's awareness of fears and needs that lead to negative survival behaviors. He helps children acknowledge and understand their need to control that underlies many problem behaviors. Through this process, Katz helps children learn less destructive ways to gain power and control. For example, he might teach a child positive ways through which the child's actions can produce results in the environment, such as teaching the child how to be good at something and how to get people to like and respect him or her. Some strategies that Katz uses include arts and crafts such as origami and teaching children skills for joke telling—good eye contact, a pleasant expression, talking in a positive manner, and actual jokes to use. Helping them succeed at specific goals and be good at something strengthens their feelings of mastery.

Much of the literature on working with abuse victims focuses on moving from a victim to a survivor identity. This concept is illustrated in the words of David Pelzer (1995), whose adaptation to abuse was described earlier. In reflecting on his experience, Pelzer writes:

> The challenges of my past have made me immensely strong inside. I adapted quickly, learning how to survive from a bad situation. I learned the secret of internal motivation. My experience gave me a different outlook on life, that others may never know. I have a vast appreciation for things that others may take for granted. Along the way I made a few mistakes, but I was fortunate enough to bounce back. Instead of dwelling

on the past, I maintained the same focus that I had taught myself years ago in the garage, knowing the good Lord was always over my shoulder, giving me quiet encouragement and strength when I needed it most.

Helping children understand that they are survivors who have the power to make choices and to a large extent determine the course of their own lives is a part of emotional healing. They need to recognize that although their traumatic experiences are a part of their past lives, they can make choices about their future, including what coping strategies they want to repeat or not repeat. In addition, it is important to facilitate the child's orientation to a hopeful future and a survivor identity. A dramatic exercise developed by James (1989) is "The Elderly Child Remembers." In this exercise, the child imagines a future for himself or herself that he or she weaves with past experiences into a chronicle of his or her own life. The child has to imagine himself or herself as an old person who has been successful in taking care of himself or herself, having a career, and raising a family. As a part of the story, the child must talk about how he or she felt as a child and how he or she got stronger and went on to be successful, as well as how he or she feels now when thinking back on his or her childhood. This exercise may be carried out as a dramatic performance complete with props.

Many types of experiences increase feelings of mastery and control in children. Some post-adoption programs provide children with wilderness experiences or physical challenge courses to increase their sense of personal mastery. Developing spiritually also may be a source for children to give meaning to their own lives and connectedness to God and others. In addition, a major part of emotional healing involves challenging the distorted ideas about self and the world that have resulted in children's feelings of powerlessness, vulnerability, and inferiority.

As children work to integrate their traumatic experiences, they will be better able to acknowledge their history without distorting it or feeling overwhelmed by it. This does not mean that the past no longer causes painful feelings. As with working through loss, healing from trauma is something that may be shelved for a while, only to resurface in a later developmental stage or when experiencing another traumatic event. Children's ability to deal with the trauma at that time is strengthened by the healing work they have already completed. The poem in Figure 6.1, written by an 11-year-old girl served through the Illinois project, illustrates this type of integrative healing work.

Figure 6.1.

Other Strategies and Techniques for Intervention
With Traumatized Children

A variety of treatment modalities has been advocated for emotional healing among adults and children alike, many of which can be used by parents for helping their children. Activities that build on children's creative abilities, from artistic expression to writing stories or performing plays, can be used to promote emotional healing. *Movement therapy* involves a range of activities. Body movements can be soothing or expressive, whether they involve swinging, rocking, or dancing or focused activities such as punching a pillow, martial arts, or playing sports. *Breathing therapy* involves relaxation techniques. Children can be taught to close their eyes and do deep breathing or to visualize comforting scenes when they feel stress.

Just as traumatized children are detached from their true emotions, they also have little awareness of bodily sensations relating to their emotions. Body work, which expands awareness of bodily sensations, is often a part of helping children connect to their feelings. Children who have experienced painful abuse often feel cut off from their bodies and detach themselves from both pleasurable and painful physical feelings. Sometimes *touch therapy* is used to help reconnect to positive physical sensations. Hugging, holding, a pleasurable bath or massage, having hair brushed, and other positive experiences involving touch are conducive to bodily and emotional healing.

Pet therapy also is useful in helping children, but child-pet interactions need to be supervised if the child has episodes of cruelty or harsh treatment of animals. Dogs and other animals have been used widely in therapy with humans, from children to the elderly. One recent article (Arnold, 1995) reports on the benefits of therapy dogs in working with survivors of childhood trauma who are dissociative. Relationships with pets also facilitate the development of empathy in children and offer them the experience of receiving the unconditional love that a pet can give.

Therapeutic rituals of healing and commemoration of one's life also are meaningful in work with children. One such ritual used in a support group curriculum for adopted children (Al-Aidy, Haines, & Studaker, 1992) acknowledges the contributions of the many people who have influenced their lives, the losses they have endured, the painful things that happened to them, the progress they have made, and the hope that lies ahead. This candle-lighting ceremony is an example of a healing ritual for special needs adoptees. As children light candles in a darkened room, the following script is read:

> The first candle is for our birth parents. We light it in honor of the gift they gave us—the gift of life.
>
> The second candle is for our foster parents and others who cared for us.
>
> The third candle is for the memories that were especially hard for us. This candle is for thinking about those adults who should have cared for us but didn't. Maybe they hurt us. The light reminds us that we are going to be able to look at sad memories, too. Because it is a part of the past.
>
> The fourth candle is for the people we had to leave behind—a grandmother or grandfather or maybe birth brothers or sisters. These are sometimes sad memories, too, but the light reminds us that we are getting strong enough to look at those things, too.
>
> The fifth candle is for our adoptive parents—the parents we have now, the parents helping us to grow and who are learning to help us light our past so we can understand.
>
> The sixth candle is the best of all—it is for ourselves and our future— its light for all the wonderful things we're going to do as we grow up.
>
> Look at all those beautiful lights—shining and hopeful just like our children.

Chapter 7

I JUST WANT TO KNOW MORE ABOUT WHO I AM

Identity Issues

The interplay between adoption and identity formation is a theme in most treatises on adoption. Adoption is seen as a complicating factor in identity development, particularly if little is known or shared about the child's history. A further complication is the interplay of loss and trauma with identity issues, the case for most children adopted through the child welfare system.

This does not mean, however, that adoption automatically poses great risks for identity confusion in the adopted person. Rather, adoption is another aspect of identity that must be folded into the sense of self.

Adoptive parents often minimize the extent to which their children think about adoption and wonder about their past. For example, an adoption preservation worker reported meeting with an adoptive mother who stated that she didn't think her daughter really thought much about adoption. Although the mother acknowledged that her child faced many problems, she believed that adoption was something that didn't have much effect on the child. As the conversation continued, the 9-year-old girl returned from school, entered the living room, and stopped short at seeing the visitor. When the mother introduced her to the worker, the child stated, "That's not who I thought you were going to say she was." When her mother asked who she thought the visitor might be, the little girl replied, "My [birth] mother."

SELF-INTEGRATION AND
IDENTITY CONFUSION

Identity is one of those terms central to human understanding yet elusive in definition. Erik Erikson (1968), the major identity theorist, discusses identity in existential terms. He speaks of the search for and achievement of a sense of wholeness, an emergent redefinition based on the sum of all the identities that is yet greater than the sum of these, and a synthesis of a self formed from the sexual, ethnic, and occupational selves. Erikson describes the emerging sense of self as filtered through self-awareness and interaction with the family, community, and larger society. Identity not only incorporates a progressive continuity between the selves one has been, but also with the self that one promises to become. This sense of wholeness, completeness, and self-acceptance we call *self-integration.*

Self-integration is predicated on the resolution of conflicts in earlier stages of life. It is the process of struggle that yields the payoff of self-awareness and self-understanding, as well as a road map for one's future. In Erikson's (1968) model, stages of identity development are closely interwoven, with each building on the foundation achieved in preceding stages. Healthy or largely positive resolution in earlier stages increases the likelihood of satisfactory achievement in the current stage.

The counterpoint to self-integration is identity confusion (or what Erikson, 1968, calls role confusion). This state is described as "a split of self-images—a loss of centrality, a sense of dispersion and confusion and a fear of dissolution" (pp. 122-123). Confusion can result from familial, social, or psychological demands greater than those that can be managed by the individual. It also can result from unresolved conflicts from earlier developmental stages. For example, a child for whom basic trust is absent and who has not had the opportunity to develop autonomy or a sense of mastery over the environment will have to struggle harder to achieve a sense of identity (Erikson, 1963).

Confusion in identity is related to the construct of external locus of control. The person experiencing role confusion feels as if life is something that happens rather than something one influences. The vagaries of life experienced by children who come to adoption through the child welfare system can complicate identity development.

Identity confusion also can lead to negative identity—committing to a group whose values are in contradiction to those of one's parents or society at large. Belonging somewhere, having some sense of "fit," is better than the alienation and loneliness of being nobody.

Adolescence is the ground for identity development. Physical changes, expanded cognitive abilities, societal and family expectations, and internal drives all coalesce to make the adolescent ripe for considerations of self. Although elements of identity construction exist at earlier stages, it is in adolescence that "push comes to shove." As Josselson (1987) notes, "It is at adolescence that the emerging person first has the cognitive capacities to puzzle about the meaning of life, to ponder the mysteries of existence, to recognize the arbitrariness of the universe" (p. 205). For the adopted adolescent, musing about the mysteries of existence must incorporate the mysteries of the past. It is at adolescence that questions about "why was I adopted?" and "how am I like and not like the people who created me?" come to the fore.

ADOPTION AND IDENTITY

That adoptees will struggle with identity-related issues is a point nearly universally accepted in the adoption practice literature. The phenomenon of adoption is thought to present parents and children with a unique set of psychosocial tasks. The tasks "interact with and complicate the more universal developmental tasks of family life" encountered by all families (Brodzinsky, 1987, p. 25).

Despite this belief, there has been limited empirical examination of identity formation in adopted people. Most adoption studies have focused on parental satisfaction with adoption, measured through surveys. The perceptions of adoptees have not been systematically or comprehensively studied. Among studies that have examined identity, there are conflicting findings. For example, Simmons' (1980) study comparing a nonclinical sample of adopted and nonadopted young adults placed before 18 months of age found adoptees to be less well socialized, with lower self-esteem. Others have found no differences on identity measures between adopted and nonadopted adolescents or young adults (Goebel & Lott, 1986; Norvell & Guy, 1977).

Stein and Hoopes (1985) conducted a study that investigated adoption and identity. It compared 50 adopted and 41 nonadopted adolescents on a variety of standardized identity measures and responses on a semistructured interview. All the adopted children were placed prior to age 2, with most placed in infancy. The researchers found few differences between adopted teens and their nonadopted peers, challenging the idea that the adoptee has greater difficulty with the tasks of adolescence. Hoopes (1982) argues that reliance on clinical studies and anecdotal data has led us to overstate the significance of identity issues in adopted adolescents and young adults.

The Search Institute (Benson et al., 1994) examined aspects of adoption adjustment in a large number of adoptive families. The study presented data on 881 adolescents in 715 families. The children were placed for adoption at 18 months of age or younger. Using surveys and data from the Child Behavior Checklist (CBC), the study found very positive results related to identity, attachment, child mental health, and family functioning. Despite this, 27% of adolescents agreed with the statement "Adoption is a big part of how I think about myself"; 16% reported not being strongly attached to either parent; and 25% were experiencing problems in mental health.

This study (Benson et al., 1994) brings into question the belief that adolescence for adopted children is necessarily a complicated drama of identity confusion and angst. It is important to note the study's limitations, however. Fifty percent of those families found and invited to participate did not. Second, the study examined only those who were placed in infancy or early childhood. Finally, the use of surveys precluded the collection of qualitative data on adoptees' perspectives.

Given the limited study on adoption and identity formation, it seems the jury is still out on whether adoptees are particularly vulnerable to identity confusion. Some adoptees clearly do struggle deeply with identity issues. How are these issues resolved? Others struggle less. Why? We need to continue to examine the relationship between adoption and identity. The majority of studies to date have focused on children adopted early in life. Is identity formation more complex for those adopted at older ages or for those for whom adoption, identity, and maltreatment issues are intertwined?

Harold Grotevant (1997) has given much consideration to the interaction of adoption and identity formation. He points out that most investigation of identity has focused on domains of choice—beliefs, occupation, and affiliation. He argues that aspects of identity that are assigned rather than chosen—such as gender, race, and adoption—need to be considered as well. Grotevant calls for a more thorough and sophisticated understanding of identity that explores how people make sense of being adopted. This rich understanding is best developed through analysis of narrative—the stories adopted people tell about their lives as adopted people.

For most children receiving adoption preservation services in the Illinois project, identity was an important issue. Identity concerns were noted by workers in 63% of cases where this issue was rated. As reported in Chapter 4, for younger children, identity issues were most common among 7- to 8-year-olds. Identity issues were most common among early adolescents, peaking at ages 15 to 16, where 85% were rated as having problems related to identity.

The higher prevalence of identity issues among adoptees placed in infancy as opposed to later placement is surprising. The reasons for this finding are unclear. Perhaps more information is available to families who adopt older children. They may have lengthy case records, more contact with foster parents, or access to workers who can provide more information on their children. With children lacking their own memories of earlier history, it may be easier to suppress discussion of adoption and the child's past.

IDENTITY ISSUES THROUGHOUT
THE LIFE SPAN

Although adolescence is a time where identity issues come to the fore, identity issues have salience across the adopted person's lifetime. Because identity formation is a process, not an end in itself, there are many opportunities for the reconsideration of self (Bosma, Graafsma, Grotevant, & deLevita, 1994; Brodzinsky, 1987; Denuth, 1991). As noted by Bosma et al. (1994), "the possibility for reformulation of identity exists across the life span whenever individual or contextual changes occur" (cited in Grotevant, 1997). Thus, identity is not a static state but an ongoing, dynamic process. At certain, somewhat predictable points in the life cycle of an individual and a family, internal and sociocultural forces move the adopted person toward or away from considerations of self.

One young adult talked about adoption as something that shifted from being foremost in her mind to being background noise. She put it this way: "At some times in my life I feel adopted with a capital 'A.' It's the most important thing about me. But other times it's not so important. It's adoption with a small 'a,' one of lots of factors that describe who I am."

In the preschool years, awareness of pregnancy and childbirth lead children to approach parents with questions about their own birth. Parental explanations of how the child's life is different from others (he or she does not live with the mommy whose tummy he or she came out of) will probably not be understood. As one adoption preservation worker noted, one little girl told her that everybody lived with a mommy different from the one that "started them."

When children enter school, they will deal with adoption outside the family for perhaps the first time. Children may be faced with questions they cannot answer and get confusing messages from peers. For example, classmates told one adopted child that her adoptive parents were not her real parents and she shouldn't call them mommy and daddy. During this period, children may begin to understand how babies are made. This reinforces the idea that the adoptive parents are not the people who created the child. The child may begin to wonder how this separation came about and what the birth parents (particularly the birth mother) are like.

Difference is reinforced by school assignments. Family trees, discussion of ethnic backgrounds, and assignments about genetics all pose dilemmas for the child. Do children use the information from the adoptive family, knowing it's not really their history? Or do they use what little information they may have and reveal to all that they are adopted? One adopted child discussed how distressing something as simple as drawing a picture of one's family could be. She reported feeling dishonest when she drew a picture of her adoptive family because she knew she had an older brother somewhere as well as birth parents.

Children in early and middle school years have the cognitive ability to reconsider adoption. As Brodzinsky (1987) notes, "For the first time, they have the capacity to reflect on the reasons (or possible reasons) why they were given up for adoption" (p. 35). Children consider why they were given up or taken away, and begin to question whether adoption was the only alternative available. The story often told to relinquished children, that "your mother loved you so much she wanted you to have a better life," begins to sound false. Giving away something you love is not a logical solution to an 8- or 9-year-old.

Children who were removed from inadequate parental care may begin to reconsider pat stories as well. They wonder why, if their birth parents were unable to care for them, someone didn't help their birth parents do a better job. And if birth parents were unable to provide adequate care, what about grandparents, aunts and uncles, or other family members? When old answers are called into question, the child may substitute new ones. Was he unlovable? Is there a dark secret about the family that no one is telling? Was he stolen from his birth family? Fantasy among children is common. Many theorists argue that all young children experience episodes of doubt that their parents are their real parents. This is generally a brief period, helpful to the child as he or she comes to terms with conflicting feelings of love and hate for parents. Some theorists have speculated that this *family romance* is prolonged for adopted children. Adopted children have the opportunity to split the images of parents, assigning positive attributes to one set and negative attributes to the other. If the bad parents are the birth parents, the child must struggle with fears that he or she will be like them. If the bad parents are the adoptive parents, the child may struggle mightily to accept their care. If children are unclear about the circumstances of adoption, they may question whether membership in the adoptive family is only temporary. Brodzinsky's (1987) interview with a 9-year-old boy illustrates this thinking: "Well, if my parents gave me up because they were too young or too poor to care for me, what's stopping them from coming back now and asking for me back . . . they're older and grown up and maybe have more money now" (p. 35).

Fantasy is common among young children, enabling them psychologically to try out explanations to life's knotty questions. Adopted children in the early and middle school years may wonder if other adults in their environment are actually their parents. Several report they suspect that a favorite teacher, a neighbor, or the parent of a friend is actually their birth parent. This is particularly common if the adult bears some resemblance to the child.

Birthdays begin to take on special significance as the child comes to realize that someone "out there" gave birth to him or her and may be wondering about the child on that day. Even in families where adoption is rarely discussed, the child may feel tension as birthdays approach— feeling pressure to celebrate happily but struggling with sadness or curiosity.

Times of loss take on additional significance as well. Death of a family member, acquaintance, or pet; divorce; a move; or the end of a friendship may all trigger feelings of loss related to the separation from the birth family.

The physical, cognitive, and social changes of adolescence open the door to pondering the meaning of adoption. Now capable of abstract thinking, the adolescent is able to think in more complex ways about being different from others. Adopted adolescents may ponder what life would have been like had they remained with their birth families or in what ways they may have "missed out" by being adopted.

As most children go through puberty, they can look to biological relatives as they question what the end result of their physical evolution will be. In adolescence, many adoptees become keenly aware of their lack of biological connectedness. This lack of biological referents may lead to anxiety. The comfort provided by "genetic expectancy" goes beyond the physical. Attributes of character, skill, and talent are tied to genetic inheritance as well. For the adopted child, there is typically less to identify with or strike out in opposition to. As Dickman (1992) notes, it is hard to be a "chip" without a "block."

"Who am I?" as well as "Who will I become?" are the central questions of adolescence. For some adopted adolescents, the answers to these queries are complicated by lack of knowledge about their origins. This difficulty has been called "genealogical bewilderment" (Sants, 1964). It is characterized by confusion, doubt, and a missing sense of wholeness or belonging.

As teens enter into romantic relationships, questions about the relationship of their birth parents and their sexuality emerge. Many adopted children are told that their parents had children when they were too young to take care of them, then surrendered the child or had the child removed for mistreatment. Adolescents may entertain notions that they would be better parents or that they would never abandon a child.

A fundamental task of adolescence is to begin to separate from the family and move toward independent adulthood. Such separation is promoted by a secure parental relationship. For children who have experienced trauma and loss, this foundation may be less than secure. The ability to trust and to connect with parents emotionally may have been weakened by past experiences. In addition, adopted children must emotionally separate not only from adoptive parents to whom they may feel insecurely attached, but from their images of birth parents as well. Their questions, fantasies, and conflicted feelings regarding birth parents often intensify in adolescence.

If there is conflict in the home, adolescents may use their status as an adopted person to their advantage. Accusations that these are not the real parents, that they don't love the adolescent enough because he or she is adopted, or that they don't trust the adopted adolescent may be used to gain leverage.

Illness, disability, or medical assessment reminds the adopted person once again that he or she is different. Rarely does the adopted child or family have full access to medical and psychiatric history. Common questions about early developmental milestones, immunizations, accidents and injuries, and family history are often impossible to answer. As one young adopted woman put it, "I get that list of questions about family medical history and I mark a big X through it and write 'Adopted.' I hate filling out those forms because they remind me of everything I don't know." In another case, a young teen developed bipolar disorder and had to be hospitalized. Through her mother's perseverance, the family learned that the birth mother had the same diagnosis and that her illness was instrumental in her losing parental rights. The girl was angry that she had to become "sick" to learn this important information.

From adolescence forward, the individual is presented with many opportunities for the reconsideration of self. In late adolescence and young adulthood, the adopted person moves into important life decisions about education, career, and intimate relationships. Brodzinsky (1987) adapts the identity status model of James Marcia (1966) to analyze identity in young adulthood. Marcia classifies young adults in one of four identity statuses: foreclosure, moratorium, diffusion, and achievement. Those in *identity foreclosure* move lockstep into lifestyles and values entirely consistent with those of their parents or other important adults without much consideration of alternatives. Adopted people in foreclosure never allow themselves to consider the importance of adoption in their lives and often identify strongly with their adoptive families. For example, one young adopted woman never referred to her birth mother in any terms but "her" and "that woman." She denied any genetic inheritance from her birth family, bringing in pictures to demonstrate how much she resembled her adoptive family. When asked, she could think of no question she would ask her birth mother. Her goal was to finish college, marry her high school sweetheart, and return to the community where she grew up to live near her parents.

Although those in identity foreclosure appear to have a strong and stable identity, it may come at great cost. Those in foreclosure spend much energy on denying differences from their adoptive families. They may be unprepared to cope with later life challenges where their adoptive status is undeniable. For example, in the young woman described above, the idea that her birth mother might seek her out was a possibility she could not begin to entertain.

A period of exploration of values, occupational goals, sexuality, political and social beliefs, and the like characterizes *identity moratorium*. It is a period of active consideration of alternatives and possibilities. For the adopted person, moratorium includes examining the meaning of adoption in one's life. Adopted young adults may consider how being adopted fits into their overall sense of self. They may ponder what life might have held had they not been adopted. Adopted young adults may consider search and reunion. But moratorium implies a work in progress. The individual is still actively considering possibilities.

Those classified in *identity achievement* have come out on the other side. They have challenged and reconsidered their beliefs and are able to make commitments to particular ideals and goals. They are less vulnerable to the opinions of others because they have worked to develop a personal philosophy.

Young adults in *identity diffusion* have neither explored alternative beliefs and roles nor committed to specific values or goals. They float from job to job and from relationship to relationship, unable to make positive choices or set plans. They lack the active consideration of alternatives of those in moratorium and struggle to come to any conclusions about what course their future should take.

Brodzinsky (1987) notes that clinical observations indicate that adopted young people fall into each of Marcia's statuses. Many adopted young people are able to consider adoption openly and find positive ways of folding this aspect of self into their emerging identity. An atmosphere of support and openness in the adoptive family may expedite this process. Others remain in moratorium, perhaps because they lack necessary information about their past or because they lack social support for examining the meaning of adoption in their lives. Still others avoid considering the importance of adoption in their lives. The tendency toward identity disclosure is likely greater in homes where there was limited discussion of adoption or denial that adoptive families are in any way different from others. The adopted young adult may feel incapable of examining the loss inherent in adoption and avoid considering its implications. Further, he or she may sense parental discomfort or vulnerability related to adoption. The result may be acceptance of the adoptive family's values and lifestyle without considering alternatives. For those adopted people who have strained or distant relationships with their adoptive families, diffusion may result. In such young people, there has been no exploration of adoption issues and no commitment to a set of values or to goals.

As Brodzinsky (1987) notes, empirical investigation is in order to determine the "fit" of the identity status model with adoptive identity, as well as determining the distribution of adoptees across identity statuses. We need to know what aspects of adoption practice, family style, and social support enhance identity achievement.

When adopted persons attains adult status, they may consider searching for information about their birth family. At 18 or 21, they may feel entitled to a fuller story. They may feel more comfortable searching for the original family because the search may be done without the knowledge of the adoptive parents.

The interest of adoptees in learning more about their pasts falls along a continuum. Some are quite comfortable knowing what they know, and have little curiosity about their families of origin. Others feel incomplete and long for more information or even reunion with their birth families. Studies on search indicate that the majority of those who search are women and that search behavior peaks in young adulthood (Schecter & Bertocci, 1990). Many theorists consider search to be much more than the actual process of finding one's birth family, however. It is an internal process beginning in childhood as the child becomes aware of the meaning of adoption. Although there are no reliable figures on search, it is believed that a minority of adopted people engage in active search of the type that leads to reunion with birth family members. Many more express interest in knowing more about the circumstances of their adoption and their history. Young adults are not entitled to comprehensive information in most states, however. The desire to have more information conflicts with society's rules about who is entitled to information about the adopted person's origins.

Entering into long-term relationships is yet another point where adoption gains prominence. Adoptees may fear they are marrying someone to whom they are related. At the very least, the adopted person must inform the partner of the adoptive status. They may fear having children because so much in their background is unknown. If an adopted woman does become pregnant, she may experience anger at not being kept by her own parents or not being properly cared for by them. She may eagerly anticipate having a child who looks like her and to whom she is related by blood, yet such feelings may make her feel disloyal to her adoptive family.

As adopted adults form their own family, they must incorporate "being adopted" into the new family saga. At some point, adoption must be explained to their own children. Medical background becomes important once again. Further, adopted adults may feel renewed sorrow and confusion at an inability to answer basic questions for their children.

At midlife, and particularly at the time of the adoptive parents' deaths, adoption looms large. The loss of adoptive parents can trigger feelings of loss related to the original parents. Thus, mourning one's parents becomes more complex. The death of adoptive parents may hasten an adoptee's decision to seek birth family members or information. The adopted person is reminded that time is running out. He or she may feel freer to pursue information knowing that the adoptive parents can no longer be hurt.

In old age, this sense of urgency may increase. The adopted person may want to ensure that what can be known will be known for the sake of children and grandchildren. The adopted person understands that birth parents are likely deceased, but may want fuller information about the past or contact with siblings or other family members, before it is too late.

BARRIERS TO IDENTITY ACHIEVEMENT

How the adopted person comes to terms with the meaning of being adopted is a function of individual personality, family environment, and the larger culture. When the family is conflicted or negative about adoption or the child's birth family, the adoptee has a harder time coming to a healthy resolution of identity issues. Incorporating "being adopted" into one's sense of self also is more difficult when the larger culture gives messages that adoption is an inferior way to form a family or that adoptees should be grateful for being rescued by adoption.

Although it is rare in modern adoption practice for families to be advised to keep adoption a secret, the subject is still a loaded one in many families. Sorting through conflicted feelings about "who I am" and "who I want to be" is complicated further when the children's histories contain well-guarded secrets. For example, in one family served by the Illinois project, grandparents adopted their daughter's three children. Because their mother had engaged in behavior intolerable to her parents, they had never told the children of her existence, and the children were led to believe that the grandparents were their birth parents. After much discussion with the adoption preservation workers, the parents decided to disclose the family secret. At a family session, they shared the information with all three children. The older children had long suspected something was amiss, but were afraid to express their fears. The oldest child expressed great relief at learning the truth. She had memories of living in a different house and being cared for by a different mother, and had thought she was "crazy." Most families are much more open about adoption. But barriers to discussing adoption can remain both within and outside the family. In some families, adoption is referred to but not really discussed. The unstated message is "Everything's okay. If we discuss it, then our family is not okay." Kirk (1981) discusses lack of openness as the rejection of difference, which leads to problems in adjustment for the adopted person. He argues that acknowledgment of difference allows the parent entry into the child's reality of loss and pain. Families in which acknowledgment of difference is demonstrated would be expected to offer better conditions for identity achievement. Brodzinsky (1987) adds the concept of *insistence on difference,* where adoption assumes the blame for a variety of family difficulties, thus complicating identity achievement.

A family's orientation to adoption is likely more subtle and multi-faceted than Kirk's (1981) dichotomy. Further, the family's stance may change over time. The degree of openness of family communication about adoption issues has been found to be a predictor of overall adjustment in adolescents, however (Stein & Hoopes, 1985). Thus, the critical issue may be a family's refusal or inability to discuss adoption rather than simply acceptance that adoptive families are fundamentally different from other families.

IDENTITY ISSUES IN CHILDREN PLACED ACROSS RACE

If Grotevant (1997) is correct that "layers of difference" make identity consolidation more complex, then children adopted across race or ethnicity have more identity challenges. They face the dual tasks of coming to terms with the difference of being adopted and being raised by parents of a different race or ethnicity.

It has long been the position of groups such as the National Association of Black Social Workers that children are best served when they are adopted within race. Transracial adoption is seen as reducing children's connection with their heritage. Further, it is held that nonminority parents are less able to prepare children for the challenges of racism in the larger culture. Adoptions across race increased in the 1970s, but

were curtailed sharply in the late 1970s and 1980s. The recent passage
of the federal Interethnic Placement Act, mandating that a difference in
race cannot deny or delay placement, will likely lead to an increase in
white adults adopting minority children, however.

For many children adopted by parents of a different race or ethnicity,
adoption can never be a private matter. That is, most people will assume
the child is adopted when they see the child with the family. In some
ways, this is a benefit. It is hard for a family with white parents and
children of a different race to deny or hide the child's adoption.

In the Illinois Adoption Preservation Project, 14% of children studied
were adopted transracially. On measures related to identity problems in
this study, no differences were observed between children adopted
within race and children adopted transracially. Studies on transracially
placed children, including longitudinal studies, support the view that
transracial placement does not necessarily lead to identity confusion
(Grow & Shapiro, 1974; McRoy, Zurcher, & Lauderdale, 1983; Simon
& Alstein, 1992).

Although research indicates that the majority of children adopted
transracially appear to adjust well to adoption and have secure identities, some children struggle mightily. Consider the complexities involved in the case of Sean, 18.

My mom, I guess, didn't want me because my father was black. I think it
was sort of a one-night stand. Anyway, my parents take in strays—they've
taken in kids from all over—they wanted to adopt a child who needed a
home. So, they adopted me because my father was black and that made
me "special." So, I'm supposedly black or half-black anyway, except I
don't look black in the slightest. And obviously, I think about that . . . I
started thinking about this more as I went to high school—all that identity
stuff. I got into quite a lot of trouble then, but not because I was adopted,
just because I didn't want to think about things. . . . One of the things I
wondered was, "Am I really black?" "If I have a kid will that kid be black?"
So, I still haven't settled all this in my own mind.

As this young man considers who he is, he reflects on his origins and
his future. If his father wasn't black, and his birth mother had realized
that, would she have kept him? If his birth father wasn't black, would
his adoptive family have chosen him? What implications does all this
have for the children he may create?

For Emily, adopted from Korea as an infant and now 21, being of a different race from her family was always more important than the fact that she was adopted. As a young child, she lived in an urban area, and her family associated regularly with other families who had adopted children from Asia. When she was about 8, her family moved to a rural area where she and her adopted brother were the only non-Caucasian children in sight. Emily often felt alienated and lonely. Her love for her parents kept her from sharing this pain with them, however. Her high school friends nicknamed her "Chink," a name she laughingly pretended to accept even while it caused her great pain. For her brother, dating was a particular problem. He was well liked but never able to establish a serious dating relationship.

It is important to look beyond general patterns of coping or mal-adjustment and consider what factors contribute to positive adjustment in the child placed transracially or transculturally. Studies indicate that parental sensitivity to race or culture, respect for the child's cultural heritage, living in integrated areas, and exposing the child to positive aspects of his or her heritage are important in promoting positive self-image and adjustment.

Important, too, is rethinking the sense of the family's identity. As one adoptive mother put it, "when you as white parents adopt a child of another race, you are no longer a white family or a white family with a child of a different race. You become a multiracial family."

STRATEGIES FOR ASSISTING IN
IDENTITY DEVELOPMENT

Identity is related to meaning making. Identity formation involves an active process of consolidating the past with the present and anticipating the future. In this way, the same work that helps children and families come to terms with loss and trauma can help with identity. By reviewing the past, the worker helps the family make sense of what has happened, find meaning in past events, and develop the capacity to talk together. In this section, we explore some aspects of meaning making that promote discussion of identity.

The good news is that families play a central role in healthy identity development. For example, Cooper, Grotevant, and Condon (1984), in observational research, found that family connectedness (as indicated by support, cohesiveness, and acceptance of members) and individuality (as reflected by healthy expression of disagreements) enhanced identity formation.

Making Identity Issues "Normal"

Most adoptive parents are not adopted people. It is difficult for those who have access to full information about their heritage and history to understand what it is like to lack it. One task of adoption preservation work when identity issues are present is to help parents reframe the child's curiosity about his or her past. Parents need to know that such curiosity is common and normal and does not imply a rejection of the adoptive family. As is the case with many aspects of adoption, parents need to understand that identity questions are part of adolescence generally, not unique to the adopted child. It may help parents to know that many adoptive parents feel unsettled with what sometimes appears to be a sudden resurgence in interest about roots.

Being open about the circumstances of the child's adoption can be difficult for parents, particularly when the child has come to adoption because of maltreatment. Yet children who are denied information (or given pat, superficial explanations) will provide their own. Families need to be encouraged to discuss issues related to adoption and the child's past regularly, repeating important elements many times. To do so often, with sensitivity to the child's needs and level of understanding, removes some of the drama. One adopted young woman describes her family's approach:

> My parents never sat us down and gave us "the talk." We just always sort of knew. It was something that was just there—stories about when they first saw us or the day we came home with them. For a lot of years we celebrated out adoption day—which as a little kid I liked because we got more presents. And as we grew up it was still that way—casual comments like "Tomorrow's your birthday and I'll bet your birth mother is thinking about you tonight."

Another aspect of openness is discussing with children what others may think about adoption. Parents can help the child explain his or her status to the larger world, which adoption expert Kay Donley (1984) calls the "cover story." The story is a brief and straightforward description of how the family came to be. It can also be a strategy for deflecting discussion if the child feels uncomfortable. As they grow, children need to know that some people have misperceptions about adoption. By gently preparing children for some of these misperceptions, parents demonstrate their understanding of some of the challenges of being adopted and their commitment to help the child face these challenges.

Permitting Exploration

One of the challenges facing every parent of an adolescent is encouraging independence without cutting the child loose. Adolescence is when the child must begin to separate from the family and develop skills for independent adulthood. Children typically experiment with lifestyles or behaviors somewhat different from those of their parents. They may dress in new and provocative ways; try smoking, drinking, or drugs; and connect with new sets of friends. For adoptive parents who harbor fears about the background of their child, this can be a particularly frightening time. They may clamp down on the child's activities, becoming restrictive and controlling. They may deny the child's need for more autonomy. If the child acquiesces, there may be family harmony at the expense of the child's growth.

For families served by the Illinois project, passive acquiescence was not the issue. In these families, control battles were common. Although some children engaged in defiance through deception, many engaged in open rebellion.

For some children, adolescence involves changing peer groups. In several cases in the Illinois project, this change involved affiliation with children from families of a lower social class or with very different values. This "downward drift" needs to be examined further. Do adopted adolescents seek out relationships with people they imagine to be similar in behavior, outlook, and income to their families of origin? Do children with learning problems or emotional difficulties feel more comfortable among those with limited aspirations? Or is this primarily a way for adolescents to distance themselves from the adoptive parents, as part of the process of individuation?

Providing Opportunities to Succeed

Self-esteem and identity are linked concepts. The child who struggles with developing a positive identity often feels inferior, inadequate, and not valued by others. Therapists like Michael Katz stress the importance of validating adoption as something valued. Katz (1986, 1990) uses a variety of strategies to help children reframe their negative notions about adoption. A first step is to help children recognize that one can truly love and be loved by parents other than one's birth parents. Has the child ever had a treasured pet? Does he or she feel love for the pet? What evidence does the child have that the pet loves him or her? Through this simple example, children can begin to think about the genuineness of love in adoption.

A second step is to help the child identify people of courage and strength who are adopted. Both real and fictional examples abound. Katz (1986, 1990) reminds us that Moses, Jesus, and St. Nicholas were adopted. Characters in *Anne of Green Gables,* the *Wizard of Oz, Heidi, Star Wars,* and *Annie* are examples. Contemporary figures such as Dave Thomas, CEO of Wendy's; Scott Hamilton, the Olympic medal winning ice skater; former President Gerald Ford; and the Reverend Jesse Jackson are all adopted.

Stories of hardship and triumph can be used as metaphors for adoption. Katz (1986, 1990) uses the story of the Pilgrims, who could not stay in their original home but came to a new place facing many obstacles and had to accept the help of others to survive.

Finally, Katz (1986, 1990) argues that children need to be helped to separate their sense of worth from their difficulties. He notes that self-esteem is tied to approval from significant others. For many adopted children, behavior problems at home and school result in many negative messages from important adults. Katz works with parents to help them find language specific to the child's behavior and not the child's personhood. He emphasizes the child's need to receive messages that he or she is a good child who deserves a good life, even if he or she is now having serious problems.

Another way to assist children in developing a positive sense of self is to help them identify strengths and talents. For many children in the Illinois project, regular opportunities for demonstrating their capacities were limited. School was a source of tension and difficulty for many. Outside activities such as scouts, community sports, after-school activities, and the like were stressful for children whose social skills lagged behind their physical development or whose behavior barred them from participating. Yet such children are the ones who are in the greatest need of opportunities for mastery and success. Finding ways for children to shine is another strategy for helping them develop a positive sense of identity.

For some children, an important step is to find appropriate educational placements. Children who are constantly frustrated in school often improve when settings that meet their needs are found. For the

Whitman family, introduced in Chapter 3, a change in the school setting to one that worked with children with significant learning disabilities and behavior problems resulted in "unbelievable progress."

Another strategy is to adapt existing community opportunities to meet the needs of children. In one project, children were assigned mentors to accompany them to scouts, sports, and after-school activities. The one-on-one attention of the mentor allowed the child to succeed in activities. Children also benefited from having an older "buddy" who came to know them well and enjoyed their company.

Many children have talents or abilities that are hidden by their behaviors. In the Illinois project, therapists assisted family members in identifying what children did well and finding opportunities to act on these talents. Children may be given chores to perform that increase their sense of mastery. One child who had serious problems with hyperactivity was able to take excellent care of the family pet, a rowdy dog who needed lots of exercise and rough play. In the Whitman family, Katie was helped by a rehabilitation specialist at her school to find a job at a senior citizens' center. She received much positive feedback from her supervisor, who reported that Katie was very compassionate and patient with her clients. Mrs. Whitman reported that this had done wonders for Katie's self-esteem and her sense of responsibility. One site in the Illinois project created a children's choir so children could learn the discipline of practice and the rewards of performance. The choir brought adopted children together, giving them an activity where they could succeed and of which both children and their parents could be proud.

Adoption Stories and Lifebooks

Most families develop an adoption story when their child first comes to them. In infant adoptions, the story often includes the waiting parents' anticipation, the bravery of the young mother in choosing a better life for her child, and the joy experienced by the parents when they first took home the baby. Less is known about the adoption stories in families adopting older children or children who have been maltreated. All families must develop some explanation for how the child joined the family, however.

In many families, the story remains static. But children can be helped to incorporate being adopted into their sense of identity if the story becomes fuller, containing more nuance and specificity as the child matures. As noted by Brodzinsky et al. (1992), the idea that your mother loved you so much that she gave you away may satisfy a young child. But to a child of 9 or 14, the idea that if you love something you give it away is harder to accept. Helping children incorporate being adopted into their sense of self may be facilitated by exploring the family's adoption story. Revisiting stories means that adoption is recognized as an important piece of the family's history, one that deserves periodic review.

Older children need to be able to construct their own adoption story rather than just receive it from others. To do so, they need information about their histories. They also need assistance in interpreting the information they receive and folding it into their understanding of self.

For children who have come to adoption through the child welfare system, the sense of past can be extremely fragmented. For many children, chaos and lack of permanency are hallmarks of their early life. Shifts in household composition and many changes in residence are common. Moves and changes once the child enters care can compound this fragmentation. For many foster children, keeping track of where they lived, with whom, and for how long is difficult. Further, physical reminders of the past—pictures, letters, toys—are often lacking or are misplaced as the child journeys from placement to placement, the garbage bag "suitcase" in hand. For all children, both those adopted in early infancy and those adopted later, the adoption story must acknowledge the child's life before adoptive placement. One goal of identity work is to retrieve information about the past, aid the child in interpreting it, and help the child incorporate it into his or her emerging sense of self.

Adoption stories can be facilitated through the use of lifebooks. The purpose of a lifebook is to collect and present the child's history using pictures, letters, and other artifacts. Lifebooks are more than a chronology of the child's life; they provide information and explanation. Lifebooks differ in their approach. Some are primarily factual, giving names, dates, and brief information about the changes in a child's life. They provide the raw data for the child's adoption story. Others are more interpretive—presenting facts in context and providing explanation. For example, a lifebook might include a picture of the first foster family the child lived in. A caption would explain who the child stayed with, the length of time the child stayed there, and other important information such as the school attended, foster siblings who shared the home, the family's pets, a description of the house, and the developmental achievements of the child while in the care of this family. Specific examples that anchor the experience are important to include.

Through the process of constructing a lifebook, the child's understanding of the facts of his or her life are elicited and included. For a child who remembers pieces of an experience, a caption might read,

> This is the Miller House at 308 E. Beecher Street in Peoria, Illinois. Anthony lived here from the time he was $4\frac{1}{2}$ until just after his fifth birthday. Anthony came here because his mother was in the hospital to get help with her drug problem. Anthony doesn't remember why he had to leave the Millers. Mrs. Miller and Anthony's social worker, Ms. Livingston, remember that Anthony had to leave because Mrs. Miller had problems with her heart and couldn't take care of children anymore. All the children had to go to different homes. Although Anthony doesn't remember much about leaving Mrs. Miller's, he thinks he probably felt sad. He wonders what happened to Martin, the little boy he shared a room with who was about a year older.

Such entries include as much information as can be retrieved from available sources—including the names of other children who lived in the home (with pictures, if possible). But because the lifebook is constructed with the child rather than for the child, the child's memories and interpretations can be included.

Lifebooks are particularly important in helping the child understand transitions. Why did he leave home in the first place? How did she end up in this adoptive home? When was the last time he saw his siblings?

Developing or reviewing and updating lifebooks is an activity requiring much tact and skill. The lifebook needs to be factual. But how thorough? This is a problem of special concern for children whose histories include maltreatment. Should the lifebook include the details of severe abuse? Or should it skim the surface, suggesting rather than explaining maltreatment? A list of the harms done to Anthony and by whom is quite different from "Anthony's mom had a problem with drugs and sometimes left Anthony with people who didn't take good care of him or even hurt him." There is no simple answer here. The age and developmental stage of the child need to be considered, as well as the child's expressed desire for more information. Because lifebooks are often public family documents, on the order of baby albums, the family may want to include brief descriptions, saving the specifics for other documents to which the child can gain access as questions arise.

When lifebooks already exist, they can be an important way to gain a sense of the child's understanding of events. Reviewing and updating the lifebook with the child can illustrate the child's knowledge of the events of his or her life. It can also provide a window into understanding those events. Some workers include a "things I wish I knew" section to give children a way to express curiosity about questions the lifebook cannot answer. Others include a section on "what I would like my birth family to know about me."

Despite the fact that lifebooks have been promoted as an important part of preparing children for adoption for many years, many adopted children do not have them. For example, in a study comparing children whose adoptions were consummated with children whose adoptions disrupted, Smith and Howard (1991) found evidence that lifebook work had been done with children in only about one third of the cases.

Other Strategies for Identity Work

For some children, revisiting is another strategy for helping the child remember the past and fold it into his or her sense of self. Visiting the hospital where one was born, the neighborhood of early childhood, the schools or houses where the child lived can all help the past become more real. Workers often take pictures of the child at the hospital or in front of the school for the child to keep. Revisiting also may include contact with important figures from the child's past. A case example using revisiting as well as other techniques is included at the end of this chapter.

Pictures or letters from birth family members or foster parents can make the past real for the child and assist in making sense of it. Juanita, a young adopted woman, shared her feelings about the importance of such contact:

> One day my mother let it slip that she knew the name of the woman who had taken care of us before we were adopted. I was able to find her—she's still doing foster care all these years later. She remembered me and my sister and was glad to know what had happened to us. But the most important thing is that she remembered my birth mother! She talked about how she came to visit us and that she would play with us and bring us presents. She talked about how very young she was and how she was almost like a child herself.

For this young woman, learning more about her early life was of great importance. She learned about herself as a very young child, and could imagine herself and her sister in this, their first home. More important, she learned that her birth mother had been part of her early life. She had already known that her birth mother was only 15 when she was born and that she struggled with mental illness. From her foster mother, Juanita learned that her birth mother, despite her problems, had been part of her early life.

Rituals are a way to help the child understand the many aspects of his or her personal history. Many families celebrate adoption days or acknowledge the adoption on the child's birthday. For example, they might offer a prayer for the birth family as part of their family prayer before a birthday dinner. Guidebooks have been developed for the development of rituals that communities can use to honor and support adoptive families. One such example is Mary Martin Mason's (1995) *Designing Rituals of Adoption for the Religious and Secular Community.*

Support groups are another avenue for addressing identity issues. They provide children access to others who have been adopted. They are safe places to discuss feelings about being adopted and curiosity about one's past. Support groups are discussed further in Chapter 9.

Filling in the Blanks

Information is scant and there is no way to retrieve it for some children. This may be the case for children adopted abroad and sometimes for children who entered the child welfare system at very young ages and had no further contact with their families. Angela was adopted from Korea. Very little is known about her early life. She was found in a park at about age 3, along with a little boy presumed to be her brother. In this part of Korea, it was not unusual for single mothers who could no longer care for their children to leave them in a public place and then watch until the children were found by the police and taken to safety. Angela and her brother arrived at an orphanage without any identifying information. After about a year, they were placed for adoption with an American family who traveled to Korea to bring them to the United States. Angela does not know anything about her early history. She has no real memories of her life before the orphanage. She does not know her birth date or her original name, or anything about the circumstances of her surrender. She struggled with feelings of deep sadness about this void in her understanding. A trip to Korea with her family following her high school graduation made her country of origin more real to her. But because so little is known about her early life, Angela continues to harbor a fear that she was lost rather than abandoned.

For children like Angela, there simply are no available facts. Some adoption preservation workers have attempted to fill in these gaps with informed speculation. Together the parents, child, and worker could develop a list of possibilities to explain how the child became available for adoption. For children about whom little is known, it is particularly important for parents to be able to help their child grieve the fact that so much is missing.

Another strategy for children with very little information about their past is to have the children write letters to the unknown or unavailable parent, sharing aspects of their lives and asking the questions they would like to have answered. Although such letters cannot be delivered or answered, they provide insight into the child's feelings, helping adoptive parents and workers know more about areas to work on with the child. Some therapists suggest that children answer their own letters, taking on the role of the parent. Through this process of imagining the birth parents' response, children may come to better understand their attitudes toward adoption and feelings about having limited access to their own past.

ASSISTING IN THE SEARCH

The interest of adoptees in learning more about their pasts falls along a continuum. Some adoptees are quite comfortable knowing what they know and have little curiosity about their families of origin. Others feel incomplete and yearn for more information and sometimes reunion with their birth families. Many adopted teens and young adults are reluctant to express such feelings for fear of hurting their adoptive parents. For adoptive parents, a child's desire to search can feel like a betrayal. This may be particularly true for parents who have adopted children who were hurt in their birth homes. Why would children want to find the parents who hurt them so?

Helping parents understand the child's need for information about the past as a means to coming to terms with identity issues is a central aspect of intervention. Those in the Illinois project worked hard to educate parents about search and to put this in a context that did not diminish the adoptive parents' importance to the child. This was commonly accomplished by involving the parent fully in the process. The adoptive parent assisted in gathering information, was fully apprised of progress related to search, and was often the conduit for information from the worker to the child. Workers sought to convince parents of their central role in helping the child manage feelings as the search process unfolded and prepared them for the child's fantasies and hopes related to search. They conveyed and reinforced the message that the child both needed to search and needed the adoptive parents to help with this complicated task, just as the child would need his or her parents for any other major undertaking.

In the small number of families where search was undertaken, children did seem to benefit from fuller information and the opportunity to contact some family members. It was very complicated emotionally for both children and their adoptive parents, however. Workers helped families understand that search is not an ending but a beginning, raising questions as well as answering them, and requiring families to make sense of what is learned.

KINSHIP AND FOSTER PARENT ADOPTION

Identity issues for children adopted by kin or by foster parents may be less difficult. This is something that we assume but do not know, as our investigation of many aspects of children's lives after adoption is limited. Adoption by kin has the advantage of keeping the child connected to the family of origin and may allow the child access to information about the circumstances of separation from birth parents. Kinship adoption is more likely to keep the child tied to culture and community than is placement outside the family. Further, kinship adoption might provide the child with the opportunity to have contact with a birth parent and to develop a relationship. Birth parents may assume a role in the child's life even if they lack the capacity to continue to parent the child.

Foster parent adoption offers some of the same potential benefits. The foster parents may know the birth parents, particularly if foster parents were involved in supervising visits of the birth parent and the child. They may have access to considerable information about the child's past, provided by the placing agency. They may have been party to administrative case reviews and other proceedings where information about the original family was discussed as planning for the child took place. If they have cared for the child for any length of time, they know the child well and are indeed part of the child's history. Because the child is already living with the family, it is assumed that the child will more easily join with the family as a permanent member.

The assumption that kinship or foster parent adoption makes identity development less complex makes sense. But it is important not to overlook the difficulties that such adoptions can create. In kinship adoption, the child must make the transition from being nephew to being son, from being granddaughter to being daughter. Kinship adoption still involves loss. For children whose birth parents are rejected by the adopting family or who are blamed or criticized, problems of divided loyalty can emerge. As in adoption by strangers, competition with children who are the birth children of the adoptive parents may be another complication.

Foster parent adoption raises potential difficulties as well. For some children, the adoption revives deep sorrow as they consider that they have lost their birth family forever. This can be further complicated in families where other foster children in the family continue to have contact with family members. In such families, adopted children may question their status. Is their situation really permanent when other children come and go? For children who do understand their status, the shift from being a foster child to being an adopted child may allow them to explore painful issues that have never been faced. Children may act out behaviorally as they revisit past loss and trauma in the safety of the adoptive home. To adoptive parents, it may seem that the adoption made their child worse. Therapists help parents reframe the child's problematic behaviors as evidence that the child finally feels secure enough to face the past.

The national effort to increase adoption of waiting children will lead to an increase in adoption by kin and by foster parents. Anecdotal reports from the Illinois project suggest that foster parent adoptors are less likely to receive extensive preparation and training than families where the child and parents are not known to one another. It is important for us to assess the needs of foster and kin adoptive families rather than assuming that all will be well because parents and children already know one another.

The meaning people make of being adopted and how they fold this aspect of their lives into their sense of self vary markedly from one adopted person to the next. For some adopted children, it is a struggle to come to terms with the fact that they could not be raised by the people who created them. Recognition of the importance of adoption to identity formation and the emergence of adoption issues in tandem with developmental stages is critical to intervention with adopted children and their families. Following is an intervention targeted toward helping children develop continuity between their past and present.

RECONSTRUCTING THE PAST:
AN INTERVENTION

Jenny (14) and Erin (12) were sisters by birth. When their parents sought adoption preservation services, the parents informed the worker that the girls had suffered both abuse and neglect as infants, were sexually and physically abused in a previous foster home, and had been sexually molested by a teenage male relative. Despite this history, the girls had never been involved in counseling. The adoption preservation worker described her intervention as follows:

I first met with Jenny and Erin at a local park under a shade tree. I quickly discovered they knew almost nothing about their birth history or birth family. They didn't know where they had been born or what nationality they were. They assumed they were Hispanic because of their skin tone and some of their features. They believed they had been born in the Southwest but had no idea why they thought that, nor any evidence to support this belief. They knew they had been abused and neglected as young children, but didn't know any of the details about their removal from their birth parents. They spoke of being in "lots of foster homes" and knowing they were sometimes moved because they had been bad.

During the first session, Jenny described a memory that she wasn't sure was fact or a dream, but she believed had happened. The four children had been abandoned on a bus. She could see Erin as an infant, wearing only a diaper, lying on the floor of the bus with a broken leg. She remembered "seeing Erin lying there with her mouth wide open—screaming for hours and hours." Erin had no such memory and didn't believe she had ever had a broken leg.

I believed my first task was to help Jenny and Erin learn more about their history and to help fill in the huge gaps of missing information and understanding. It was my belief that these girls could not move forward until they were able to make some sense of the past. The girls appeared open and willing to share with me whatever they could.

Our second meeting was held in the conference room at my office building. I presented the girls with 12-foot rolls of heavy paper— 2-feet wide, in a variety of colors—and a big box of bright crayons and assorted markers. I announced we were going to create time-lines to help them, and me, sort out where they had come from and where they had been. They didn't seem to grasp the concept of a timeline and, when asked, I suggested sort of a gently winding path, a foot or more wide, and utilizing the full 12 feet of paper. They would then divide the path in 13 or 14 sections, allowing one section for each year of their lives thus far. As they began to understand and got involved in creating their personal "paths," they informed me that they might as well not make sections for the first 5 or 6 years of their lives because they wouldn't have anything to put in them. I casually replied, "we'll see about that," and they included all the sections. Much time was spent creating and decorating their time lines, but about all each girl put on her path that first day was her age and when she was adopted— Jenny (9) and Erin (8).

In successive sessions, as we talked about their past and tried together to sort things out, a memory or comment by one of the girls would trigger an additional memory of the other, and their excitement at remembering grew. "Didn't one of our foster moms have a horse?" "Oh, yeah, and remember . . ." "Was that where those kids used to pick on us?" and "Remember how mean we were to . . ." Their past began to take form. As they colorfully and creatively added bits and pieces to their timelines, they had a great deal of trouble figuring out when and at what ages various things had taken place. The girls struggled with trying to put memories of events in chronological order, and the confusions sometimes led to frustration.

At this point, I revealed the department's placement history, which I had recently obtained. The girls were amazed to learn they had been in nine different homes! They discovered they were about 18 months and 2 when they entered the system, so of course couldn't remember some of the first homes they had lived in. By figuring out the locations, dates, the length of each placement, and their ages at the time, they began to be able to form a sense of where they had been; but they still couldn't put places, events, and people together in a meaningful way. They did, however, begin to conclude that they had probably not been born out of state due to the locations of their foster homes. Learning facts about the places they had lived continued to trigger memories, both good and bad, of past people and events. Yet even as their history began to take shape, the girls did not always appear confident that the story being developed with their timelines was congruent with their personal experiences. As they struggled with the facts, I decided it was time to take a trip.

With their parents' permission, I suggested to the girls that we take a road trip and drive past each of their former foster homes. They were astonished at the prospect of such an undertaking—"We could really do that?"—and were more than eager to get started. Together we mapped out a drive route—a total of 200 miles—and set the date. I took along a camera to provide a permanent, visual record of each home. Being teenagers, they sometimes acted bored during the drive, and as we approached a town in which they remembered living, they doubted we would find the house. I replied, "I don't know; I guess we could look at a phone book map." As I drove into the town, one of the girls suddenly cried, "Look, there's that store we used to go to!" and the other chimed in, "Keep going this way; I know we're going the right way!" and, "Can we drive by our school?"

Each remembered landmark caused more excitement. We found the home and then found their school. As I parked the car, they questioned why I was stopping and were surprised when I suggested we go into the school and look around. The pleasure on the faces of those too cool, teenage girls as they found and showed me their first and second grade classrooms made the entire day worthwhile. We also took time to swing on the playground swings, and it was wonderful to see the girls able to reexperience this childhood joy.

The girls took turns taking photos at each stop, including a picture of the one particularly abusive home. I had worried and talked with them in advance about their desire to stop at or pass by that town, but they were insistent that it not be left out of the journey. At the end of the day, 8 hours later, we were able by prearrangement to visit with one of the last families they had lived with prior to their adoption. The girls had talked about some "terrible" things they had done in that home, and were eager for the family to see how they had "turned out." It was a very gratifying experience for the girls to have the opportunity to apologize for their behavior and to hear that the past had been "long forgiven and forgotten." They delighted in filling those parents in on their current lives, reliving shared memories, and catching up on the lives of the other children who had been in the home with them. Even though they were tired, it was hard for the girls to leave the comfort of those loving people who had provided them a home and could share part of their past with them.

The timelines soon became filled with more fully developed memories, dates, people, and events. Hopefully the combination of concrete evidence (the photos), experiences (the trip), and recreating the past (the timelines) will assist these previously abused and abandoned children in moving forward into the future. (C. Blackburn, personal communication, 1998).

Chapter 8

A PLACE TO TURN WHEN THERE'S NO PLACE ELSE TO GO

An Overview of Adoption Preservation Services

Adoption preservation services have the hallmarks of any good intervention—they are based on the understanding of the family in the context of its environment, are tailored to family needs, and restore or improve the functioning of members. Workers connect families to additional resources, and terminate with care. They are supportive and nonblaming. They are knowledgeable and dedicated advocates. They are able to instill hope and help families regain optimism. Yet families describe adoption preservation services as being something more and something better than traditional services. This chapter explores the distinctive aspects of adoption preservation services that make them so useful to struggling adoptive families. Intervention with the Whitman family (introduced in Chapter 3) is presented to illustrate adoption preservation services and strategies.

PHILOSOPHY OF ADOPTION PRESERVATION

Although there is as yet no comprehensive body of research to guide adoption preservation, several basic premises underlie practice. As noted in the Introduction, adoption preservation work is based on the belief in adoption as a remedy to the problem of children unable to be cared for in their original families. Adoption preservation services are predicated on the idea that children deserve to grow up in families, and that society should invest in adoptive families to promote their positive functioning.

Second, adoption preservation work is undergirded by a presumption of functionality. There is a belief in the family's capacity to change, despite sometimes entrenched patterns of struggle and dysfunction. Most families do not want to live as they are, but lack skills, knowledge, and resources. The philosophy of adoption preservation holds that adoptive families are worth preserving and deserve expert services and support to this end.

Third is the understanding that adoption is a complex personal and social phenomenon. As noted by longtime adoption advocates such as Watson and Kirk, adoption is different. It is not a better or lesser way to form a family, but an alternative way. To assume that adoptive families are the same as families formed through birth is to underestimate adoption's complexity. But to assume that adoptive families are inherently troubled is to underestimate the power of families to cope and grow.

In what ways is adoption different? Adoptive families are formed through loss. The adopted child must contend with loss of birth family and sometimes loss of culture or racial or ethnic affiliation as well. The adoptive parents may have losses related to infertility. They may experience loss of the family they imagined as well. The child they have may not match the child they envisioned. Yet these losses are often undiscussed in the family and unrecognized in the larger environment. In families where children are adopted through the public child welfare system, children frequently have experienced maltreatment and trauma. The manifestations of the abuse and neglect in early life may not appear until many years later. Further, adoptive families must contend with misinformed and sometimes negative valuations of adoption in the larger culture.

In sum, adoption is a good but not simple solution to the problem of children needing families. If our society believes in adoption as a legitimate way to form families, we must provide support and expertise to strengthen adoptive families.

Where do these beliefs lead in terms of intervention? Adoption preservation services should be family centered, ecological, developmental, and strength based. *Family centered* means that adoption preservation services work with the family system. The behavioral and emotional problems of the child are the reason most commonly given by parents for seeking services. Adoption preservation services do not simply "fix the child," however. Workers enter into the family system and develop a sense of problems from each member's perspective. They help the family consider its unseen members—the original family of the adopted child. They help promote family cohesion. They help the family restructure interaction patterns and work together for change. Although acknowledging that the problems exhibited by the child are often what led the family to services, adoption preservation workers help the family as a whole.

Ecological means that families are considered in the context of their environments. The goal is to improve the interaction between the family and its environment by building on and strengthening the family's adaptive capacities and working for change in the systems with which the family interacts. Thus, adoption preservation work concerns itself not only with parent-child relationships but also with marriage, extended family and friends, school, church, work, neighborhood, and social service systems. The ecological perspective moves away from the illness or pathology model to one that views problems from a more holistic perspective.

A *developmental perspective* means the effect of developmental changes on individual family members and the development of the family as a whole are carefully considered. Both normal developmental challenges and particular challenges of adoption (and the interaction of the two) are examined. For example, in many families adolescence poses challenges as the child struggles with physical changes, emerging sexuality, and the need to separate from the family. But for an adoptive family where the birth mother had children as a teenager, the legacy of the original family may lead the parents to set rigid and strict limits on their adolescent daughter. Interaction of adoption-related issues and issues of adolescence need to be examined.

A *strength-based approach* recognizes that families, no matter how incapacitated at the time of referral, have positive attributes that can be brought to bear to improve family functioning. Intervention involves uncovering such strengths in present functioning and in the current environment. It also involves identifying previous effective methods of coping and sources of support used in the past that might be mobilized in the present. A strength-based approach takes into account that families typically arrive at services at times of great difficulty and stress. Their current style is not necessarily representative of their abilities as a family. Where strengths are lacking, the goal is to create a stronger family by teaching necessary skills, improving communication, and connecting the family to resources. In troubled families, this strength-based approach can lead to a restoration of hope and a renewed commitment to work together as a family.

CENTRAL ELEMENTS OF
ADOPTION PRESERVATION WORK

Adoption preservation work includes different emphases and approaches beyond the basic building blocks of intervention. Serving struggling adoptive families requires careful engagement. In many families, an extended period of outreach and active listening is needed to engage the adoptive family and establish a relationship of trust. Workers often begin by working primarily with the adoptive parents. Struggling adoptive parents are often guarded initially and fearful of being seen as inadequate. Their initial distrust may stem from previous experiences where they felt blamed for their children's problems or excluded from therapeutic efforts.

Workers in the Illinois project reported that this prolonged period of careful listening and slow acceptance was different in character from other engagement work. Parents often felt the need to discuss at length the difficulties of raising a troubled child and their previous attempts to find solutions. Empathic responses by workers were accepted, but information sharing or initial problem-solving suggestions were not well received at this stage. Workers stated that parents often needed to vent their feelings, with minimal interruption. Although basic crisis intervention theory poses that workers can use the disequilibrium inherent in crisis to begin quickly working for change, adoption preservation workers found they had to allow an extended period simply to listen.

Engagement is enhanced by meeting with the family in its own territory (the family home) and at the family's convenience. Meeting with the family in the home allows for all family members to be included in assessment and problem definition. Transportation problems, child care needs, and the logistics of organizing the schedules of a large family can be diminished. Work in the home may be shifted to the office or another setting as the intervention continues.

Initially, some workers found they formed conclusions about parents that were incorrect. The parents' need to express frustration, often in terms that were negative toward children, led workers to see parents as unyielding, insensitive, and blaming. As the worker-parent relationship grew, workers changed their perspective. Although some parents remained extremely negative, most were able to move to a more balanced view and commit to working toward change once the worker had acknowledged the severity of their frustration and disappointment.

Beyond allowing parents to vent without challenge, workers sought to validate the efforts of parents and reduce their sense of blame for children's problems. As discussed in Chapter 2, many adoptive parents feel judged and blamed by helping professionals. An important task of adoption preservation work is reducing parental guilt and blame. Parents seeking adoption preservation services often struggle with feelings of failure and incompetence. Their strategies generally have been ineffective. Such attitudes are underscored by attitudes of family, friends, and the systems from which they have sought help. For many parents, school is a particular source of stress. As one mother put it, "A good day is one where I don't get a call from the principal. A good week is when nobody gets sent home from school." As families struggle to cope but are unsuccessful, they may settle into negative, rigid patterns of interaction. There is little satisfaction or joy. Home life is dreaded. The goal is to help parents understand that they are not the cause of many of their child's difficulties, but that they can be a force for positive change. For example, workers recognize the many positive steps parents have taken to meet children's needs. They acknowledge that such efforts might have worked with another child (i.e., they were reasonable steps to take) but do not work with this particular child.

De-Escalation of Crisis

Many families come to adoption preservation services in crisis. For some, the crisis state results from a single, serious incident: A child is expelled, a child is accused of a crime, a child is found to be sexually involved with other children. For others, it is "one more thing" that moves the family from coping (if only barely) to capitulating.

In either case, parents feel unable to cope. Crisis intervention, then, is an aspect of much adoption preservation work. Workers respond quickly, spending as much time with the family as necessary to reach stability. They ask, "What do you need to make it tomorrow? Through the weekend? Until Johnny's appointment at the residential treatment center?" They marshal resources, provide emotional support, and work on small tasks on the way to achieving larger goals. They may offer a contrary view to the one the family presents, one that is more hopeful. "I see strengths you may not be able to see right now."

In the Illinois project, all programs offer 24-hour assistance. For families who feel they are unable to cope for one more day, knowing emergency help is available at any time is a great relief. It is interesting that families do not routinely call on workers beyond usual hours. The knowledge that they can call seems to give parents the stamina to continue.

Increasing Parental Entitlement

Adoption preservation work is conducted with great sensitivity to the parents' tentative sense of entitlement. As Bourguinon and Watson (1987) note, families formed through adoption may be undervalued in society. Societal attitudes may convey that parents are not "real" parents, merely "adoptive" parents. There is lingering stigma about adoption, including notions that it is an inferior way to become a family. Families, friends, even professionals may refer to a couple's "natural" children as opposed to their adopted (and therefore unnatural?) children. We lack rituals to acknowledge adoption and even language to explain it. For example, what does the adopted child who has searched and found her original family call them?

Thus, adoption preservation work should increase the parents' sense of entitlement. It should strengthen parents' belief in their right and ability to act decisively on behalf of their children. It should increase their sense of competence. Parents need to be included as allies in the therapeutic process. Their expertise and understanding of their child must be acknowledged.

Another critical aspect of adoption preservation work is thorough assessment. Many children have had multiple and conflicting tests and diagnoses. Others have had little investigation into health, learning, or emotional problems. Adoption preservation work requires sifting through what is known about the child and arranging for additional information to be obtained when necessary. In some cases, there is a great deal of information about the child, but it has not been synthesized or explained to parents. Beyond assessment, then, adoption preservation workers make sense of information.

A diagnosis can sometimes help a parent reduce self-blame or anger at the child. For example, parents may feel deep frustration when their child appears to ignore instructions or take repeated risks. A diagnosis of attention deficit disorder or fetal alcohol syndrome renders the child's behavior understandable. Behaviors attributed to willfulness may be reinterpreted as beyond the child's control. But obtaining a diagnosis is insufficient. Assessment involves both interpretation and developing a plan of action based on new information.

Retrieving and Interpreting Children's History

Perhaps one of the most important aspects of adoption preservation work is helping families retrieve information about their child's past. In the Illinois project, adoption preservation services were provided by private agencies under contract with the state Department of Children and Family Services. Because of this connection, workers were able to retrieve information from long-closed files if the child was adopted through the child welfare system. A wealth of information often can be found in these, including the details of maltreatment, a listing of the child's many placements, pictures, even letters from surrendering parents, and information on the whereabouts of siblings. For some children and parents, the files hold information that is entirely new to them.

Reframing Children's Behaviors

Retrieving information is often the first step in helping parents understand their children's current behavior. Another central part of adoption preservation work is helping parents and children make sense of children's behavior. Many parents find behaviors such as lying or stealing to be particularly repugnant. Beyond the embarrassment such behaviors can cause parents is a deeper sense of betrayal and breach of trust. With children who have experienced loss, trauma, and maltreatment, such behaviors provide ways to maintain a sense of control or to protect themselves from harm. Keeping others at bay emotionally can be very useful if those others are untrustworthy or dangerous. Joining a safe, nurturing family is no guarantee that the child will be able to relinquish behaviors that were essential to his or her sense of well-being in the past.

For many adoptive parents of children with special needs, traditional methods of discipline have proven ineffective. For example, one father was particularly upset at his child's lying. He used many punishments, including making his 10-year-old son write "I will not tell lies" 100 times, denying privileges, and requiring his son to confess to lies he had told to others. His son's failure to change his behavior was very

Table 8.1

Behavior Worksheet

Behavior I Hate	Why It Bothers Me	What It Might Mean
1. Lying	• I value honesty.	• No one ever taught her to be honest.
	• Parents should be able to trust their kids.	• She learned to lie to keep from getting hurt.
	• It embarrasses me. (Others may think I'm not a good parent.)	• Lying helps her feel like she's in charge of things— she needs to be in control.
	• I'm afraid she may not have a conscience.	• She's afraid to tell the truth.

frustrating. This father valued honesty, and his son's constant lying felt like rejection of the father's core beliefs. When asked, the father revealed that the child's lies were often obvious and were about things of little apparent importance. His son didn't just lie to escape punishment, but often lied for the sake of lying.

Workers help parents reconsider the meaning of behavior. When parents come to understand such behaviors as survival behaviors (that is, ways of coping with powerlessness and fear tied to previous maltreatment), they can begin to move beyond anger and condemnation to empathy. One approach is to ask parents to identify the behavior that makes them "craziest" and explore what it is about that behavior that makes it so difficult to tolerate. Another technique is to ask parents to list behaviors that they find particularly troubling and, in a second column, to list why these behaviors are so troubling. Then parents are asked to think of alternative explanations related to the child's history. Such a worksheet (see Table 8.1) serves as the basis for developing a plan of action, one that is less blaming of the child.

Once the list is developed, workers can help parents reframe their child's behaviors. For example, "Lying is not about hurting me per se, it's about gaining control. It's a way she used to protect herself in the past. It keeps me off balance, which is the way she was used to living.

It keeps me at a distance." Or, "He had so little security when he was very little. Stealing and hoarding food are about having enough and feeling safe." Reframing the child's behavior in light of the past can make coping with such behaviors more possible. With older children, interpreting their behavior with them and connecting it to past experiences can help them understand their behaviors as well.

Sometimes a parent is so angry at a child's behavior that the third column is negative and blaming ("She lies because she has no moral values." "She's a rotten kid."). In such cases, the worker and parent brainstorm together to come up with alternative explanations, always anchoring them to the child's past experiences.

Reestablishing Parental Control and Dealing With Control Battles

Parents of children who have experienced significant loss and trauma need a broad repertoire of skills. Struggling parents need to be helped to see their struggles as skill deficits, not incapacity. The adoption preservation worker encourages parents to try new approaches and to join with the therapist in testing hypotheses about parenting, based on the needs of the child. As parents learn to assess situations and as they gain skills, ineffective cycles are altered.

Troubled children may seek to gain a sense of control by recreating the chaos of earlier life. Gaining power can feel critical to survival. Experience from the Illinois project suggests that when it comes to control battles, adopted children with needs for power will always prevail!

An interesting dynamic emerged from discussions with families and workers. In many families, the child was masterful at identifying the behavior that drove the parents mad and then doing it repeatedly. Families became locked in all-encompassing power struggles. Most of the family's energy and focus were spent on battles of will. As parents grew more and more frustrated with their inability to control their child's behaviors, they went to greater lengths to exert control. For example, parents of a teenage daughter were asked by the worker to identify the essential rules that needed to be abided by in their home. They listed 79 "essential" rules!

Adoption preservation work involves helping families identify control problems, step back from incidents that trigger a power struggle, and try new strategies to resolve conflicts. Perhaps most important is helping parents acknowledge their child's need to control and to help them pick the issues on which they will stand firm. The irony is that by relinquishing some control, parents regain control. When they decide whether to confront or demand rather than just reacting, they change the dynamics of the interaction.

In some cases, parents are astonished at the absurdity of some interactions when they are able to step back and reconsider them. For example, one mother related her constant struggles with her child at dinner time. She would come home from work tired and frazzled and hurry to get dinner on the table. Her 9-year-old son, Sam, would come into the kitchen demanding a cookie. When told to wait for dinner, he would repeat and repeat his demand. "I'm starving! Why can't I have a cookie? You never let me have anything to eat when I'm hungry. I can't wait another minute. I want a cookie. Give me a cookie!" From there the battle escalated. He demanded a cookie, she ordered him to wait 10 minutes until dinner was ready. He demanded half a cookie. She, her anger rising at his refusal to obey, ordered him to leave the kitchen. He refused. She insisted. He demanded a quarter of a cookie, an eighth of a cookie, the crumb of a cookie.

Were this only an occasional battle, the family could manage. But every discussion followed this course of demand, order, and stalemate, ending with the mother screaming at the child. The mother reported "feeling like an idiot" when she denied her child a cookie crumb, but the larger issue was winning the battle. To give in was to relinquish control. The worker helped the mother learn to pick her battles. If every discussion becomes a scene, then children can neatly sidestep responsibility. The problem is not "I did something wrong" but "Mom is an irrational witch." The strategy was to have the mother withdraw from the fight. She would give her answer once and once only. Beyond this she would remain calm, turning on the radio and humming a little tune as she finished preparing dinner. Initially, the child became even more demanding. But Mom refused to enter into the fray. Eventually, she built in some preemptive actions—sitting with Sam and offering a few bites of a healthy snack before she started making dinner, giving him tasks to help her, and the like. As the fights diminished, opportunities for positive interaction increased. From these dinnertime episodes the family learned to identify patterns of escalation. They learned to stop the slide into battles by using a code phrase—"Is this a cookie crumb conversation?"

Parents receiving adoption preservation services often request help with managing children's behavior. Developing plans rather than acting in the moment, avoiding reacting in anger, and establishing consistent and reasonable consequences are recommended and practiced. Some programs recommend resources such as the *1-2-3-Magic!* curriculum (Phelan, 1996) or Cline and Fay's (1990) *Parenting with Love and Logic.* Two practical and helpful books specific to adoptive parenting are Delaney and Kunstal's (1993) book on parenting children in foster care and adoption, *Troubled Transplants,* and *Adopting the Hurt Child: Hope for Families with Special Needs Kids* by Keck and Kupecky (1995). In addition, programs often host speakers or workshops on behavior management in the context of adoption.

An important related issue is to help the adults in the household present a united front. Children can be masterful at pitting parents or other adults against one another. Doing so is another way to gain control. Parents need to be helped to see patterns of divide and conquer and to work together.

Exploring Adoption Issues

Part of adoption preservation work involves helping families consider how adoption has affected their lives. Most adoptive parents are not adopted people. They must learn ways to understand their children's sense of loss and help them grieve past losses. They may be unfamiliar with the effect of maltreatment experienced by their children. One mother stated, "I had no idea that something that happened to her before she could even talk would hurt her this way. I figured if I loved her enough and kept her safe, everything would be all right." Another mother noted that she had agreed to adopt a child who had been sexually abused but had had no understanding of how such harm would play out over the course of her child's life.

Part of family education is to enable families to see adoption as a lifelong process. Young children may think of adoption as something special and positive. As they mature, they come to understand that adoption is something unusual and may perceive this difference as negative. Brodzinsky and others have argued that adoptive families face predictable crises in development, with adolescence posing particular challenges (Brodzinsky, 1987; Brodzinsky, Singer, & Braff, 1984; Silin, 1996).

Acknowledging the Original Families

An important aspect of adoption preservation work is acknowledging and coming to terms with the legacy of the child's birth family. Families are helped to honor the child's legacy from the birth family while understanding their limitations. For both parents and children, it is important to separate what was inherited, what comes from the environment, and what is created by the interaction of the two. In some cases, this is facilitated by finding out more about the child's history. In others, it may go so far as to involve search and reunion.

Adoptive parents need to be helped to acknowledge that every birth family gives something positive to a child. Being able to respect attributes of those who have hurt a child or cared for the child poorly is no small task. One mother described her internal struggles this way:

> There are times when I almost hate Maria's birth family. When I think about the abuse she endured as such a little girl—how no one helped her or protected her—when I see her struggle to make friends, to manage the pressures of school and all the rest—I really feel such anger at them! They've made her life so hard and, therefore, mine as well. But if they hadn't hurt her, she wouldn't be my daughter. I work hard to think about how limited they were in intelligence, that they were poor, that her mother in particular had it pretty rough. But it's not easy to understand or to forgive what they did to Maria.

Yet it is impossible for the child to disassociate from his or her family of origin completely. If they were all bad, what are the chances that he or she is not? How then to acknowledge the loss or harm experienced by children while respecting the original family? Information about the child's past can be used to provide balance. The parent may have cared for the child well in the early years but became neglectful after other children were born. Parents may have provided for some of the child's needs even if others were unmet. Even when parental care was uniformly lacking, the genetic inheritance of the family can be recognized. The child's beautiful brown eyes, musical talent, athletic prowess, math ability, or other assets can be acknowledged as gifts from the birth family.

Once when we were presenting a workshop, a participant shared the story of his sister's adoption of a child. The little boy was abandoned, and there was no information about his family of origin. Almost defiantly, the uncle asked, "What good can you find to say about a mother who leaves her baby in an alley?" The adoption preservation workers had already dealt with such dilemmas and provided an answer: "This mother chose to give her child life."

Parents may choose to withhold information about the past to protect their child. But difficult information is better than no information. Children often develop elaborate fantasies about their separation from their birth parents, such as being lost or kidnapped. Children need to know the truth in a form appropriate for their developmental level. Parents must work to achieve the delicate balance between honoring their child's original family and acknowledging that family's hardships and limitations.

For some children, the need to know about or even reconnect with their original families is compelling. When the need is great, adoption preservation workers may help with search and reunion work. The idea of search is often very frightening to adoptive parents; yet their assistance in helping a child search and in coping with feelings during the process can strengthen the parent-child relationship. Adoption preservation work has involved family meetings to discuss members' fantasies and fears, assistance in locating information, and joint sessions with birth and adoptive family members.

Revisiting Adoption Stories

Children who have been adopted have one fundamental difference to explain to themselves and the world—why they are not being raised by the people who created them. Families develop stories to explain important events. The stories a family uses to explain adoption are important for workers to consider. Examining adoption stories can reveal how the family perceives adoption and ways in which perceptions may vary among family members. Comparison of parental and child stories and examination of the stories children tell at different stages of development indicate that discrepancies between parents and children's understanding are likely (Brodzinsky, Schecter, & Brodzinsky, 1986; Krementz, 1982).

Examining a family's adoption stories is a way to understand a family. What is the story told by each member of the family? Are stories similar? Have they changed over time? Are stories open to discussion, or is the story given by the parents the one the child is expected to accept? Parents report they are often advised to wait to discuss adoption until the child asks. The problem is that parents may give the message that this is a taboo subject, one that is too uncomfortable to mention. Workers help families examine their adoption stories and revise them in ways that fit the child's level of understanding. More discussion of adoption stories is included in Chapter 7.

Advocacy, Empowerment, and Linkage

Adoption preservation work frequently involves both advocacy and linkage. Adoptive families may have rights in the legal, educational, mental health, or child welfare systems that they are unaware of or unsuccessful in exercising. Adoption preservation workers provide information about services and rights. They accompany or represent the family at case conferences and hearings. They explain adoption issues to those who are unfamiliar with their importance. They connect families to services that can support them for the long haul. They teach parents how to obtain resources for their children. Teaching parents how to be effective advocates for their children empowers parents.

Empowerment is a central goal of adoption preservation. It is defined by workers as the state achieved by parents who develop a sense of control over their lives and feel more effective as parents. It is common for parents receiving adoption preservation services to feel overwhelmed and powerless. Such feelings may result in parents' feeling that placement or dissolution of the adoption is the only remedy. Workers further empowerment by stressing that the parent is in charge of the family. They reassure the parent that they will not do anything without parental knowledge and permission. This approach is particularly important because it adds to parental entitlement.

Direct Work With Parents

As the previous paragraphs suggest, much of adoption preservation work involves direct work with parents. The goal is to strengthen parental ability and build confidence. Adoption preservation services don't fix troubled children, they strengthen families and improve their ability to manage for themselves.

Work with parents may involve helping them reevaluate expectations. For many parents in the Illinois project, their dreams of raising a child were greatly out of sync with their daily experiences. Part of adoption work is helping parents discuss their expectations about adopting. Struggling adoptive parents often insist that they were misled about their child's past or unprepared for the realities of adoption. In some cases, this is true. But in others, the parents' hopes and desires obscured the information they were given. The anger parents express toward adoption agencies is often a reflection of their disappointment about their relationship with their child.

The adoption preservation worker allows parents to express their disappointments and frustration. Parents are helped to grieve the loss of the child they anticipated raising or the family they imagined they would be. For parents who adopted due to infertility, this is a particularly important area. Work with parents also may involve helping them see the connections between adoption and the child's stage of development and previous history.

Those who become adoptive parents after being foster parents of a child are often particularly surprised when problems emerge. The child they thought they knew so well seems to have been replaced by, in one parent's words, "his evil twin!" The movement from foster care to adoption may allow the child the security to act out fears and insecurities. It may lead other children to push limits—"Will they really keep me?" Some children can handle the somewhat less intense demands of being a foster child. Becoming a permanent member of a family may call up fears and insecurities that the child could keep hidden as a foster child. Finally, moving from foster care to adoptive status underscores the permanent loss of the birth family to the child. It is not surprising that the transition from being a foster son or daughter to being an adopted child may lead to emotional upheaval for some children.

Adoptive parents need to be helped to understand that adoption-related issues may lie dormant only to reemerge at later developmental stages or in response to changes in the family. Children who have experienced loss may be particularly sensitive to additional losses. They may have fewer emotional reserves to draw on when the family faces stress or changing circumstances. Moving, divorce, death of a loved one may all have pronounced effects on the loss-sensitive child.

Family Work

Much of adoption preservation work involves working directly with parents. To a lesser extent, it involves direct work with children. In many families, family counseling is equally important. In family sessions, members can discuss roles, compare perceptions, express their feelings (with the benefit of a referee), and develop new strategies for solving problems. In such sessions, the adoption preservation worker may set ground rules and model ways to talk about family issues.

Family sessions also can be used for joint problem solving. For example, several families report a kind of noncompliance that drives the rest of the family crazy: dawdling. A child may take an inordinate amount of time to get out of bed, dress, eat breakfast, gather school supplies, and get out the door. This is not a case of occasional procrastination, but a pattern of behavior that is deeply entrenched and keeps the family in an uproar. Parents typically have tried the usual techniques: setting the alarm for an earlier time and prodding the child; coaxing and rewarding attempts to get ready; overseeing every aspect of the child's preparation; and finally demanding, threatening, yelling, and punishing. The more the parent pushes, the slower the child becomes, whining that it's too hard to get ready. Every morning begins in anger.

In a family struggling with this issue, the worker begins by asking the family as a family to name the problem and to list everything they can think of that they have tried to solve it. Although the parent may list the problem as "Tameka's taking forever to get ready for school," Tameka might name it as "It's too hard to get ready in the morning. I'm tired and nobody will help me and there's too much to do." or "Mama being mad and yelling every morning." An older sibling might list, "Tameka being slow and Mama acting crazy and everybody being late." What we have here are three different perspectives on the problem. The worker summarizes each family member's point of view and then brainstorms with them about ideas to make the morning routine go more smoothly.

Because procrastinating can be a way of taking control, typical behavioral approaches may be unhelpful. Tameka is a little girl who never received much nurturing before her adoptive placement. In many ways, she is much younger than her years. Although most children her age can be expected to dress themselves and prepare for the day, Tameka may not be up to the task. The worker might make the following suggestion:

> It makes everybody upset when Tameka has trouble getting ready in the morning. The things we've tried so far haven't made it any easier. Before Tameka came to this family she didn't have anyone who took very good care of her. Maybe we should treat her like a much younger little girl for a while and give her lots of help.

This approach is similar to one suggested by Delaney and Kunstal (1993). They recommend *infantilizing strategies* for children who were poorly nurtured. By treating the child as a much younger child, expectations diminish and so do frustrations. Tameka's mother may wake her, dress her, brush her teeth, and even feed her breakfast. Tameka will receive far more touch, cuddling, and interaction. Her mother will know that Tameka is making progress, and no one will be late. Ultimately, Tameka will begin to assert her need to do things herself, but probably only after considerable time behaving as a much younger child. If parents and older siblings can accept that the child's developmental age is much younger than her physical one, they can treat the child as a younger child without being resentful.

Individual Work With Children

Children frequently express strong feelings of pain and confusion to adoption preservation workers. Often, no one else has asked them specifically about their questions or concerns about being adopted, their memories of their original families, or the losses they experienced. Although many children in the Illinois project had received counseling in the past, adoption, loss, and prior maltreatment were rarely addressed.

Some workers fear that individual work with children conveys blaming and neglects family dynamics. Many children benefit from one-on-one time to uncover painful feelings and discuss ways to interact with other family members, however. In the Illinois project, workers reported working directly with children in over 60% of cases.

Permission to speak about adoption is important. Children report they feel adoption is too painful a subject to be broached with parents. For example, one 12-year-old girl (who complained that her adoptive mom wanted to keep her a baby) told her worker she was afraid to talk about adoption because whenever she did, her mother cried. Even when parents are open in their discussion of adoption, children may avoid the topic because they feel to raise it is to be disloyal.

Typically, workers begin by working with parents, then see the adopted children separately or conjointly. Workers note that it is important to explain their role to the child even before they begin individual work with them. Many adopted children harbor fears about being taken away from their parents. Older children may be suspicious about the worker's purpose. As one child put it, "I've been tricked by social workers before."

Individual work with children may involve reviewing the child's memories and examining fantasies in light of what is actually known about the child's past. It also may focus on helping the child make connections between feelings and behaviors, as well as working to develop alternative ways to express feelings that have less destructive consequences. Work with children can entail teaching the child about what adoption is and how children come to be adopted. Often it includes exploring feelings common to adopted children, especially feelings of loss and abandonment.

Concrete aids such as constructing time lines; drawing pictures of birth, foster, and adoptive families; and writing letters to express feelings are used. Despite improvements in adoption practice, many children in the Illinois project had no lifebooks or pictures prior to joining the adoptive family. Constructing or updating lifebooks is a common practice in adoption preservation work.

Workers report that some families have information about their child's past that they did not share with the child. Some are waiting for the child to ask. Others fear their children are too emotionally fragile to know the truth about the past. Parents need to be supported and helped to share what is often painful information. One family had a letter from the birth mother that they had never shared with their teenage daughter. They felt the letter, full of errors and containing conflicting information, made the birth mother look ignorant. After reading the letter with her mother and the worker, the child was able to acknowledge the birth mother's concern for her. She greatly valued having a message from her birth mother.

Helping Parents Take Care of Themselves and Each Other

Parents who come to adoption preservation services often feel as if they are at the end of their emotional rope. When a child's problems are severe, the energy of the family goes to one member. Maintaining the strength to cope with life's ordinary challenges seems impossible. When one is emotionally exhausted, every problem looms large.

Many parents in the Illinois project had become isolated and alienated. Marriages, friendships, work relationships, and connections to extended family were strained. Parents had to be given permission (and sometimes instruction) to spend time with one another away from their children. For single parents, the burdens often were enormous. Respite care for children can enable parents to attend to their own needs. Adoption preservation programs are creative in their strategies for giving family members a break from one another. Some programs assist families in finding and paying for care from skilled providers. Other programs develop small respites for families—special lessons or day camps for children, movie passes or trips supported by local businesses, or funds to pay trusted family members or friends to provide child care for a challenging child. A monthly camp program in one site allows parents to plan a regular break for themselves while their children enjoy activities with other adopted children.

One program provides family respite. It rewards those who have completed a series of support and information group sessions with a family weekend. Arranged like a conference, this activity gives parents and children time together and apart at a resort. Structured activities for parents and children give them the chance to be in the company of other adoptive families.

Careful Termination

Preparing for and facilitating termination is important in any counseling relationship. It is doubly important for children and families for whom loss and abandonment are highly charged issues. In the Illinois project, there is a time limit on services. Families are eligible for 6 months of services, with a possible additional 6 months if indicated. Preparation for termination began in the initial contracting with the family. One worker began with, "We provide intensive services for 6 months, so it is very important that we work hard together in that time."

Workers noted the importance of making sure termination did not occur close to a period of high stress for a family. For example, children's birthdays and holidays are often stressful for families, reviving feelings of loss. Workers planned carefully with families to prepare for termination. Workers linked the family to services if needed and made sure the services were fully in place. They developed action plans for handling upcoming events such as Christmas, the beginning of school, or the next juvenile court hearing. They often observed rituals of parting, acknowledging the family's strengths, progress, and goals.

In preparing for termination with children, workers exercised particular care. They used activities to mark the ending of services such as taking pictures of each other, writing letters, and marking the remaining days off on a calendar. Workers frequently shared with the child how much they thought he or she had grown and what had changed. One worker routinely used the Dr. Seuss (1990) book, *Oh, the Places You'll Go!* in the termination process and then presented the child with his or her own copy.

IS IT EVER TOO LATE?

Adoption preservation workers report that it is particularly difficult to affect change when emotional dissolution has occurred. Emotional dissolution refers to a state in which parents and children are emotionally distant, and parents have lost the capacity for empathy for their child. Such cases often involve adolescents whose emotional and behavioral problems are severe and long-standing. In many cases, attachment had been tenuous at best. Some parents explicitly state their wish to end the adoption. Building or rebuilding empathy in families where there is minimal attachment is very difficult. It is important to note, however, that in many families who appear to have reached emotional dissolution, there is enough of a foundation for positive change to occur. Parents who come to services saying, "All I want is to end this adoption" may actually mean "All I want is for this pain to end and I can't see any other way out."

Some public agency adoption workers have suggested that the message "I want to end this adoption" may be a means to getting needed help. Families who have been foster parents prior to adoption may have learned the best way to get one's message heard is to make strong statements. This is not to suggest that families make such statements lightly. Rather, when feeling duress, they may turn to a strategy that was useful in the past.

It is important for those assessing struggling families to determine the following:

- if the child is at risk for maltreatment given the level of parental frustration or despair;
- if the family can acknowledge empathy, attachment, or mutual satisfaction now or at any previous time in the family's history; and
- if the family has a repertoire of skills and supports that they can tap (even though they may struggle to recognize and use such assistance).

For families where the child is not in immediate danger and some level of previous emotional connection can be identified, workers may enter into a bargain, even with parents who state they want only to end the adoption. For example, a worker might state, "I know you feel as if you can't face one more day the way things are. But you have invested 8 years in this relationship. I'm asking you to work with our program for 2 months. At the end of the 2 months all of us agree to reevaluate whether you can continue."

For some families, estrangement may be so complete as to be irreversible. The Illinois project provides some examples. Nine-year-old Samantha's family was referred for adoption preservation services after Samantha falsely told her teacher her family would not feed her. The subsequent investigation by the state revealed a child who was emotionally isolated from her family, spending very little time in their presence. Her parents and older adoptive brothers were distant and cold after years of trying to develop a bond with the child. In the eyes of the adoption preservation worker, the situation bordered on emotional abuse. Because of the child's age and the degree of emotional disengagement in the home, the state child welfare department agreed to place the child in another home. Adoption preservation services were used to help the parties process the loss and to ease the transition to a new home.

Marcus, 14, was referred to adoption preservation services when his parents refused to pick him up from a psychiatric hospital. The parents had adopted several physically or mentally disabled children in addition to Marcus, who was the most recent member of their family. The parents adopted Marcus because they had previously adopted his birth sister. Marcus's parents felt overwhelmed by this oppositional child who stole, ran away, and sexually perpetrated against other children. Marcus made it clear he did not want to be part of this family, preferring to reconnect with his birth mother. The parents entered adoption preservation services intent on ending the adoption, and were unable to direct their energy to any other goal.

ADOPTION PRESERVATION SERVICES
IN THE WHITMAN FAMILY

In Chapter 3, we introduced the Whitman family, who greeted the adoption preservation worker with the demand that their daughter Katie be removed from their home permanently.

Following years of struggle, Katie's parents were ready to give up after she falsely reported them for abuse a second time. Both parents felt hopeless and exhausted. Katie's mother wanted to end the adoption, and was particularly resistant to receiving adoption preservation services. She didn't want to preserve this relationship—she wanted to end it.

Adoption preservation services offered much that previous services had not. The therapist's first words were like balm on a wound: "Katie's struggles are not your fault. It's not something you're doing or not doing." Further, the therapist shared her belief that the family could progress to a place where there was less anger and pain. She didn't offer miracles—merely hope. To be supported rather than blamed was a wonderful relief.

The worker helped Mr. and Mrs. Whitman understand the link between Katie's behaviors and her past loss and trauma, the first helping professional who had ever done so. They began to understand the meaning of her behavior and how her actions protected her against the pain she felt. Mrs. Whitman stated, "Finally there was someone who understood and didn't judge me as a bad mother."

It was very significant to the Whitmans that the worker was "available like no one else. When something would happen I'd call and she would talk me through it. Often in the past there was no one available to help. We'd hear, 'Do you have an appointment?' or 'The doctor is with someone and will call you back,' but he never would." The adoption preservation worker was available 24 hours a day.

Early on, the worker also spent time with Katie. She emphasized the message that problems in the family could and would get better, and problems could be worked through as a family.

Katie had joined the Whitmans following an adoption disruption from the family she thought was her birth family. Mr. and Mrs. Whitman noted that the first time they heard the word *grief* related to adoption was from the adoption preservation worker. She explained the grief process and made it clear that Katie needed to feel the pain of her losses to heal. They also learned the importance of examining their own grief. They began to acknowledge their sorrow at raising a child so different from the one they had imagined. They also had to learn to accept their inability to undo the damage done to their child in her past. Like so many other parents who have adopted children with special needs, they had to learn that "love is essential, but it is not enough."

Like many families in crisis, the Whitmans experienced little ease, joy, or satisfaction in their daily interactions. Tension was high, and playfulness and humor were nonexistent. One of the early strategies of the worker was to change this pattern. Once, when Katie was being particularly obnoxious to her mother in the worker's presence, the worker joked, "Do you want to tear off her arm and beat her with the bloody stump, or shall I?" Following a stunned silence, the mother began to laugh, and the tension of the moment was broken.

Through the worker's help, the family identified problems in the way they communicated. Katie had become expert at turning one parent against the other. Through much discussion and practice, the Whitmans were able to present a more united front. Further, most of the interaction between Katie and her mother was angry. The worker modeled ways for family members to talk to one another, helping Mr. and Mrs. Whitman listen before reacting.

The worker helped Katie learn how to identify and express her feelings. Early in their work together, Katie had a limited repertoire of emotions—anger and sadness. Both were constant and unanchored. That is, Katie had no idea why she felt so angry or so sad. The adoption preservation worker taught Katie how to put her feelings into words. Together, she and Katie worked toward finding ways for Katie to express her feelings in ways that were not so alienating to her parents.

Undoing years of angry and hurtful communication is not accomplished easily. The worker often told Mrs. Whitman she needed to learn not to take Katie's verbal attacks personally. At first, this angered Mrs. Whitman. "How can you not take it personally when your daughter is telling you she hates you and you're not her real mother?" Over time, though, Mrs. Whitman began to understand the effect of Katie's early experiences. She understood Katie's harsh words in a new way, as anger at her birth and first adoptive mothers. At the same time, there was some reduction in Katie's anger as she began to understand the source of some of her feelings.

Mrs. Whitman, an admitted "control freak," had to practice picking her battles. She learned she couldn't back her daughter into a corner. She had to give her choices and allow her to save face. Taking a deep breath, acting only after thinking, and working on controlling feelings were skills all family members worked to develop. Mrs. Whitman reported, "Now when I'm considering what to fight over, I'll ask myself, will this matter in 5 years? Usually, the answer is no." When battles reduce in number, there is the possibility for positive interludes. Every day is not a war. In this family, the character of daily interactions slowly began to change for the better. An additional important aspect of services was the parent support group Mr. and Mrs. Whitman attended. The isolation and incompetence they had felt were diminished through contact with others who were struggling mightily as well. They also benefited from the suggestions and strategies of other parents.

Despite advances made, all was not smooth sailing for the Whitmans. After the case was first closed, Katie became more violent, cutting herself and threatening greater injury. She was ultimately hospitalized for several weeks. The case was reopened. The situation stabilized, but yet another hospitalization was required several months later. Because of what they had learned, and with the support of adoption preservation services, the Whitmans were able to have their daughter's early life experiences receive proper attention from the staff at the hospital. Better preparation and transition from home to hospital and home again were achieved.

Prior to the reopening of the case, a therapist in the hospital had suggested the Whitmans help Katie find her birth mother. They were quite wary of this, but the adoption preservation worker helped them understand the importance of this to Katie. Further, she helped the Whitmans see the role they could play as Katie's parents. By acknowledging her strong need to know and facilitating her search, they were acting as involved and caring parents. The worker also discussed with Katie her fears and hopes about her original family, and helped her consider best case and worst case outcomes of reunion.

Katie did meet her birth mother and one sibling. The Whitmans believe this has helped Katie make sense of her feelings about her birth family. Like many adopted children, Katie had fantasized that her birth mother would be perfect and would "come in on a white horse and carry her away." In reality, she was a struggling single mother who had three more children after Katie. Mr. Whitman believed that meeting her birth mother allowed Katie to accept her adoptive parents as her parents. Mrs. Whitman was ambivalent. She felt Katie sought more from her birth mother than she would ever get. She stated, "It breaks my heart to see her birth mother talking about her three children, cuddling them, and nurturing them. I want to scream, 'You had *four!*' Why did Katie get abused when the other children were protected?" Although Mrs. Whitman saw some value in the connection, she felt Katie needed much help in managing this complicated relationship.

Although much of adoption preservation work in this case involved family counseling and support, advocacy was another important component. The adoption preservation worker connected the family to resources and helped them fight to get services for Katie. Advocacy in regard to education was of particular importance. With the Whitmans, the worker worked long and hard to get a full educational assessment and push for appropriate educational placement. Finding the right place for Katie made a big difference in her confidence and achievement.

At the end of services, the Whitman family was in a much better place than they were at the initiation of adoption preservation services. The level of anger in the household was much reduced. Katie made what the Whitmans characterized as "unbelievable progress" in her school setting. Mr. Whitman believed she had learned more in the past 2 years than in all the previous years combined. She was taking medication for ADD and depression. She no longer felt the need to injure herself, something she had done to "stop the other [emotional] pain." Perhaps most significant was that Katie could see a change in herself and her family. Mr. and Mrs. Whitman felt Katie understood more about the roots of her feelings and was learning to direct her anger and share her feelings in ways that didn't hurt so much. The family was able to enjoy one another, taking trips, having fun, and acting more like a family.

Scars remained, however. Mr. and Mrs. Whitman believed Katie felt more secure but deep inside still feared they would "boot her out" if she did something bad enough. And although Katie appeared to be more emotionally connected to Mr. and Mrs. Whitman than at any time in her life with them, she was at best "three quarters attached."

For the first time since she joined the family at age 4, Katie was able to express affection, calling her parents mommy and daddy and seeking physical closeness. For Mr. Whitman, this was very satisfying. Mrs. Whitman took pleasure in it as well, but candidly admitted, "Sometimes it's hard for me to accept this affection at this late date." Further, she worried about the appropriateness of Katie's childlike behavior at age 16.

Through adoption preservation services, this family came to see adoption as a lifelong process rather than an event to be overcome. Adoption preservation services led them to a deeper understanding of one another, strengthened their emotional connections, helped them make sense of their child's behaviors, and increased their confidence as parents. Through these services, they also have become more realistic. Mr. and Mrs. Whitman stated that they were much more committed to Katie, and she was as attached to them as she was capable. Katie's last birthday was the first in years where she had not been hospitalized or "out of control." Although the family continued to work hard on important issues, they felt stronger, more capable, and more optimistic.

This family is an example of the many families who seek reach services exhausted, angry, and overwhelmed. The Whitmans credited adoption preservation services for the fact that their family remained together.

Chapter 9

NO LONGER ALL ALONE IN THE TWILIGHT ZONE

Support Groups for Children and Parents

Adopted children and their parents often know no other adoptive families. Further, many adoptive families are not connected to resources that are sensitive to the effect of adoption and the adopted child's history on family functioning. In struggling adoptive families in particular, parents may question their abilities to raise children with complicated needs, difficult behaviors, or emotional struggles. For parents and children confronting the challenges of adoption, support groups can be a powerful source of information, education, support, and validation.

As is the case for many aspects of postlegal services, there is little in the professional literature about the use of groups with families postlegally and even less that empirically examines the role of groups in improving family situations. There is a growing body of information on developing and conducting groups, however. Curricula and other materials developed to help families and children examine issues related to adoption and family life are discussed at the end of this chapter.

Although data on support group experiences are scarce, there are indicators that working with adoptive parents and children in groups has merit. For example, one study (Miall, 1987) found that adoptive parents, particularly adoptive mothers, feel there is significant stigma in the larger society related to adoption, but that in the presence of other adoptive mothers, they feel more comfortable, able to share concerns and to offer one another advice.

Such views are echoed in an early article that examines the responses of adolescents adopted as infants and their adoptive parents to a group experience (Pannor & Nerlove, 1977). Parents (especially mothers) expressed their fears about being adequate parents, revealing that adoptive mothers need to be "perfect." Fears about children's need to find their birth parents were frequently discussed. Therapists worked to reframe search as the child's interest in his or her own past and origins, rather than as a need to abandon adoptive parents and replace them with "real" parents. One father in the group was able to model a way to think about search that reduced fear. He articulated the importance of search for his daughter and his confidence that their relationship would be strengthened if he assisted her and supported her emotionally through this process. For the adolescents, the group provided a place to discuss subjects that they sensed were taboo or at least uncomfortable in the adoptive home. Other issues remained unraised in the family because of the children's own pain in considering them. These included aspects of loss and wondering why they were given up, curiosity about birth parents' attributes, physical appearance and well-being, and satisfaction with the nature of information shared with them by their adoptive parents. At a summing-up session, parents expressed that the group had opened up avenues of communication with their children and had given them a better understanding of their children's feelings. As one mother stated, "There was a veil between us—now it is gone. Maybe getting together in a group by themselves, they could talk about things that they couldn't talk about before."

Groups for adoptive families were part of the postlegal services offered by many projects supported by federal Adoption Opportunities grants. In projects where consumer reactions were gathered, support groups were identified as the single most effective intervention. For example, Iowa's Post-Legal Supportive/Educational Service Project asked families to rate various aspects of service as to helpfulness (Nelson & Parrish, 1993). Contact with other families through groups was rated even more highly than direct postlegal services, although both were rated highly. Fifty-five percent of those responding stated that the group had helped them "a great deal." Among the benefits cited was the ability to express frustrations, joys, and feelings long held in with others who understood.

In the Illinois project, families were asked to complete follow-up forms 6 months after the conclusion of services. Support groups were identified by respondents as one of the most helpful components of adoption preservation services. The knowledge that other families confronted similar problems and that parents' fears were not unique was cited. As one participant wrote, "The most important thing was that it helped me see that others had the same problems, that I was not all alone in the twilight zone by myself." Intervention with people through groups is based on the belief that bringing together people with similar life concerns can be an effective way to foster growth. Available information on group work with adoptive parents and children suggests that such groups combine elements of psychoeducational groups, counseling and interpersonal problem-solving groups, and therapeutic groups as defined by Corey and Corey (1997). Psychoeducational groups seek to educate group members who are relatively well functioning but have deficits in information that limit them. Family life education, with its explications of aspects of child development, is an example. The goal of such groups is increased knowledge and skill, as well as preventing future problems. Therapeutic groups help members diminish the effect of usual but complicated problems of living through interpersonal support and group problem solving. Again, the goal is to help develop competencies so members will be better able to handle similar challenges in the future. Therapeutic groups, in Corey and Corey's formulation, do not refer to the treatment of emotional and behavioral disorders, but rather have as their broad purpose "to increase people's knowledge of themselves and others, help them clarify changes they most want to make in their lives and give them tools necessary to make these changes" (p. 10).

Both psychoeducational and therapeutic groups offer support, providing information and examination of member concerns in a way that increases insight and understanding, and the opportunity to gain and practice new knowledge and skills in a psychologically safe environment that promotes honest communication. For the purposes of this chapter, we label such groups *support groups.*

BENEFITS OF SUPPORT GROUPS
FOR ADOPTIVE FAMILIES

A basic premise of group work is that, if the social-emotional climate of the group promotes a sense of emotional safety, group members will risk disclosure of painful or deeply held concerns (Luft, 1984). Many of the benefits of group participation have particular salience for adoptive families who feel isolated, who have received limited assistance in the larger helping community, and who often feel their feelings are both unusual and unacceptable.

Support groups provide a safe environment for examining complex issues by considering emotions as well as content. One positive aspect of groups is the opportunity for cathartic expression of strongly held feelings, often called *venting,* in the company of others who are likely to have experienced similar strong emotions. Some adoptive parents feel they have no right to complain about children they have been given. The opportunity to express emotions without being judged can be liberating. One parent participating in a support group in the Illinois project noted that the best thing about the group experience was "hearing other parents voice the same concerns and feelings that I have. It is difficult to express your feelings with family and friends if they haven't adopted." In a support group, the expressions of painful feelings may be not allowed but encouraged as a normal parental response.

Support groups typically provide a sense of commonality and community, particularly important to parents feeling overwhelmed and isolated. One parent in the Illinois project stated, "Support groups are much better than family counseling alone . . . You are with people who know what you are experiencing, They have all been there, too." When a group theme is established ("We're all having trouble with our kids"), a sense of common need and common purpose evolves. Once established, this communal sense sets the stage for members to provide compassion, understanding, suggestions, and encouragement, an important aspect of support groups (Gambrill, 1997; Whitaker & Tracey, 1989; Zastrow, 1987). When feelings become understandable and seem more normal, isolation and self-blame can diminish.

Participation in a group can provide families with important information that enhances their ability to gain and use necessary services as well as to impart to members specialized skills and knowledge. Educational groups, which focus primarily on imparting information, are often time limited, specific, and led by professionals with special expertise in the subject area. Educational groups for struggling adoptive parents might focus on basic information related to child development, with an overlay of adoption, rights of the family in the educational system, or developing skills in advocating for one's child. For example, one program in the Illinois project brought in a panel of educational experts to discuss the needs of children and the rights of parents in the special education system. Another agency provided a series of groups on behavior management for parents whose repertoire of skills was depleted. Many support groups in the Illinois project used curricula or other educational materials, which helped families gain understanding and new information about adoption issues. They covered topics that had not been addressed (or assimilated) during preparation sessions for those adopting children with special needs.

Beyond information and support, groups can provide members with the opportunity to examine issues and practice new responses to problematic situations. One important aspect of groups is that they can place issues in context, helping members move from seeing their problems as particular to their child and family to understanding them as common and, in light of their children's pasts, expectable. Thus, group participation can normalize feelings. Gaining insights about the purpose and meaning of behaviors can be the forerunner of a cognitive shift (Corey & Corey, 1997), a new way of understanding that yields new possibilities for behaving. Research by Lewin (1984) and others has found that it is easier to change individual attitudes while in a group than to change a person's attitudes in individual counseling.

In Pannor and Nerlove's (1977) report on early support groups for adopted adolescents and their parents, the authors indicate that the information imparted in the group served to make children's behavior seem more normal as basic child development issues were discussed. The idea of identity struggles as normal (albeit complicated by adoption) allowed parents to differentiate those problems related to adoption from those related to the teen's normal efforts to separate himself or herself from parents. Groups give parents a chance to revisit information about child and adolescent development and consider the interplay of adoption and development. In the Illinois project, parent participants reported benefit from learning about the meaning of loss and importance of grief. Many parents were unprepared for the sorrow and anger expressed (often indirectly) by their children. Making connections between loss and trauma and children's behaviors allowed parents to see behaviors in a new light, one that helped them depersonalize their children's actions. Further, parents gained in their ability to view the child in the context of his or her particular biological makeup, experience, maturity, and developmental stage.

Finding out that other parents were experiencing similar challenges helped parents see their children's behaviors as less unusual. As one mother stated, "It's been kind of amazing when people describe behaviors exactly like what we see. We found that the behaviors that drive us crazy with our kids are real typical of all these children [in the support group]."

Care must be taken that adoption or the child's difficulties are not seen as the cause of all family problems, however, but as one aspect of family challenges (Grotevant & McRoy, 1998). Support groups can help parents understand the interaction between child and family issues. For example, one parent remarked on the fact that the group experience helped her understand her contribution to negative dynamics in her family. "I have known for a long time that she pushes my buttons, but now I understand how I push hers." Gentle feedback from other parents can help parents challenge their idea that a child is beyond help or that the child is the sole cause of family struggles.

Concurrent with shifts in understanding or attitude come new behaviors. Support for embarking on new behaviors comes from the presence of other models of approaching problems, practice in the company of supportive others, and peer pressure to consider alternatives. Insight is a beneficial but insufficient outcome of group membership—the goal is to integrate feelings, thoughts, and knowledge in a way that leads to changed action (Corey & Corey, 1997; Gambrill, 1997). Through group exercises, homework, self-monitoring, and reports to the group, members can try out approaches in a supportive community. "By interacting with others in a trusting and accepting environment, participants are given the opportunity to experiment with novel behavior and to receive honest feedback from others concerning the effects of their behavior" (Corey & Corey, 1997, p. 10). Groups influence behavior even for members who are passive or quiet. Learning in groups is often indirect, involving analogy, indirect interpretation, mimicking, and identification with others. Groups provide the opportunity for members to observe others and apply the pieces of knowledge gained with less stress. Families can explore new behaviors in the group. Getting feedback from other parents in a group setting can be less intimidating than being the sole focus of helping.

Some aspects of the child's experience are immutable, however. Adoptive parents cannot change the prenatal effects of alcohol on their child; an adopted child cannot retrieve the sibling killed at the hands of abusive parents; a family cannot create the ideal family each envisioned when anticipating adoption. Groups can help family members evaluate and change attitudes even when situations cannot be changed. For example, learning how other parents with a child with fetal alcohol syndrome manage can help parents see their child's behavior in a new light. Seeing the child's behavior as less willful and provocative can enable parents to respond with less frustration. Groups also provide the opportunity for positive comparison. Parents reported not having it as bad as other families, realizing that their child had some social skills when compared to others, or recognizing family strengths in comparison to others. The families served by the Illinois Adoption Preservation Project often reported feeling overwhelmed and hopeless. One of the most valuable aspects of the groups was a renewed sense of hope and optimism. Support groups are instrumental in this process. One parent stated,

So then you don't feel like the problem is so unusual, that there's no help for it. No matter how bad things are, [families] survive. We found out that if they can survive, we can survive. No matter how bad things get, we can survive too! There's ways to deal with it.

In the last year of the project, 41 parents attending support groups completed evaluation forms on these groups. They responded to a set of statements beginning with the sentence "As a result of the adoption preservation support group, I . . ." Their responses are reported in Table A.7 in the appendix. The majority of parents reported the support groups were very helpful in increasing their understanding of their family's situation. In particular, families reported feeling less self-blame and guilt, as well as less frustration with their child. As one mother stated,

After being [in the group] the very first time, I went home crying, realizing it wasn't all my fault. The people here told us why they were here, and I was hearing the same kind of stories from most of them. It helped me accept that [my son's] anger, even though it's directed at me, is not because of anything I've done, but because of the incredible pain he has because of things that happened to him as a very young child.

Parents also saw advantages of group participation for their children. The support group evaluation forms included a section on the children's experiences. Again, parents were very positive. They commented on the benefits of their children being in the company of other adopted children and discussing aspects of being adopted. One parent stated, "I think he knows now that it is all right to be adopted. At the beginning of this, I think he was ashamed to be adopted." This is not to say that parents thought the children's groups were stress free. Parents noted that group was a place for children to explore complicated feelings that they had not yet been able to share. Painful issues were discussed, but as one parent noted, "I know the groups were very stressful for [my daughter] due to the topics covered, but she needed to be exposed to the discussion and participate as much as she could."

Parents' evaluation of the benefits of support groups to their children are reported in Table A.8. The majority of parents responding saw support groups as benefiting both themselves and their children.

People adopting children with special needs rarely know all the traumas and losses experienced by their children. Nor can they predict how these will be manifested. Although we have not seen the focus of support groups described in just this way, we see an underlying philosophy of promoting external locus of responsibility and internal locus of control in regard to many aspects of adoption. When parents understand they did not cause the problems with which their child struggles (external locus of responsibility), they are freed from crippling self-blame. Further, they can view the child's behavior more dispassionately. Through the support, information, and skills that come from the group experience, they can feel empowered to manage their child's behavior better, advocate on his or her behalf, and take an active role in shaping his or her future (internal locus of control). Helping both parents and children understand and grieve losses, learn about the limitations resulting from trauma or maltreatment, and examine expectations about what is possible are important aspects of support groups as well as intensive family services. As one mother stated, "We have all grown to understand adoption and ourselves better. We've learned we can't take away our daughter's pain (and that's okay) but we can help her cope with it."

BENEFITS TO CHILDREN

Many of the benefits of group participation discussed above in relation to parents apply to children as well. Groups can provide an opportunity for children to see that their status as adopted children is not unique, and that children often have similar questions and feelings about being adopted. Further, groups provide a place where children can safely talk about issues with others who understand. But, as is the case for adoptive parents, literature about the effects of support groups for adopted children is quite limited.

Issues of status and worthiness, which often complicate the adjustment of adopted children with special needs, is often the target of group support. As noted in a description of a support group by Cordell, Nathan, and Krymow (1985), "children do not feel so different, isolated or worthless when they can see there are other children not living with their biological parents and are coping with a different family unit" (p. 114).

Further, support groups can provide children with a mechanism for exploring their past, a helpful precondition for resolving issues in their current family setting. Although the family can be a natural place for such examination to occur, adoptive children are often reluctant to raise issues in the family deemed tacitly taboo or that they feel may cause pain to their parents.

In those few reports in the literature about support groups for adopted children, the group experience is reported to lead to open sharing and communication of feelings. Cordell and colleagues (1985) developed and conducted a six-session group for children adopted as older children. One series was for adolescents, and one was for preteens. They found that a natural cohesiveness emerged and that "the commonality of the adoption experience was powerful in creating rapport in the groups. Group support was spontaneous, consistent, and genuine" (p. 122). Facilitators had anticipated that the members might avoid particularly painful topics (such as difficulties in establishing trust in close relationships). Group members frequently raised painful memories and questions, however. Often when discussion became intense, the members diffused it through the use of humor. Group leaders found that the members, particularly the girls in these mixed-gender groups, used peer pressure to curb disruptive behavior and to keep the group on task.

Palmer (1990) examined the use of groups with foster children to try to prevent placement disruption. The emphasis of group content was on helping children understand the separations they had experienced. As was the case with the adopted children above, Palmer found that most foster children responded positively to the opportunity to share sad, angry, and confused feelings about separation. Further, workers who had worked with children individually found that children revealed more about themselves in the group setting than in individual contacts, and this information could be used to facilitate one-on-one counseling.

In their study of adolescents adopted as infants, Pannor and Nerlove (1977) found that children had much curiosity about their birth families, although they often felt uncomfortable asking questions of their parents. The chief question raised by children was "Why was I given up?" One child responded, "We were adopted by parents who wanted us and there is no reason to bother [the birth parents] because they didn't want us in the first place" (p. 542). Groups provide the opportunity to explore children's perceptions about their origins and history and allow for the introduction of alternative explanations for the child's situation. This is of particular importance given the reticence of many children to raise such issues in their homes.

Support groups for children involve a variety of activities. Therapeutic exercises allow children to examine their perceptions about adoption and compare them to those of others. Information and educational components can help children gain real knowledge about the adoption process beyond their perceptions. For example, children can learn about the process of termination of parental rights and the law related to search.

In the last year of the Illinois project (when support groups for children were being operated in all sites), a support group evaluation form was given to children over 8 participating in adoption support groups for children. The 48 children who completed the form ranged in age from 8 to 17, with 79% between 11 and 17. Forms were distributed by support group leaders during the last session. This procedure may have compromised the children's responses, although leaders attempted to mitigate this by urging children to give their true views and reassuring them that the forms would go back to the researchers directly.

Children were asked to respond to a series of 10 statements beginning "Because of this group I . . ." circling Yes, No, or Don't Know. Most children did not answer in a set response pattern, but rather used all three responses. Seven children (all 13 to 16) had responses that had 50% or more statements marked in the negative, however. Results are given in Table 9.1.

The first five questions are those benefits with which the majority of children agreed. It is interesting to note that the question with the least agreement and the most ambivalent responses relates to feeling better about being adopted, although most children agreed that they liked spending time with other adoptees.

The significant majority of children responded that they fit in with this group more than others, would like to go to the group again, and liked spending time with other adopted kids. Over half felt they had fewer problems at school and could talk more to their parents about

Table 9.1

Children's Perceptions of Benefits of Groups

Question	Yes	No	Don't Know
Feel like I fit in with this group more than others.	31 (65%)	6 (13%)	11 (23%)
Would like to go to group like this again.	30 (63%)	4 (8%)	14 (29%)
I have fewer problems at school.	29 (60%)	9 (19%)	10 (21%)
I liked spending time with other adopted kids.	28 (58%)	5 (10%)	15 (31%)
Can talk more to parents about things important to me.	26 (54%)	10 (21%)	12 (25%)
I don't feel as worried or afraid.	24 (50%)	17 (35%)	7 (15%)
Get along better with other kids in family.	23 (48%)	17 (35%)	8 (17%)
Can talk more about things that bother me.	23 (48%)	17 (35%)	8 (17%)
I am not so mad all the time.	23 (48%)	14 (29%)	11 (23%)
I feel better about being adopted.	22 (46%)	8 (17%)	18 (38%)

things that were important to them. In more than a third of the responses, however, children reported they did not feel less worried or afraid, did not get along better with other children in the family, and were not able to talk about things that bother them.

Children also were asked two open-ended questions—what they like best and least about the group. Two themes dominate their responses and are often interwoven—identifying with other adopted children and the socioemotional benefits of the group experience—expressing feelings, being understood, accepted, and supported. Sample responses illustrate these views:

> "Now that I know more kids that are my age that are adopted, I feel much better about being adopted and having the same feelings as I do."
>
> "[I liked best] that all of the kids had some of the same problems as I had and they had the same feelings about their problems."
>
> "It was the first time I got to meet somebody adopted and exchange problems."

In response to what they didn't like about the group, most children replied "nothing."

TYPES OF GROUPS OFFERED
FOR ADOPTIVE FAMILIES

Groups for adoptive parents and adopted children can take several forms. They range from highly structured, time-limited groups to open-ended groups mixing education and support to primarily social-educational groups from which natural support systems may emerge. Here we discuss groups tied to curricula and groups that are ongoing and typically less structured.

Curriculum-Driven Groups

Highly structured, curriculum-driven groups tend to meet weekly or every other week for a specific period, usually 6 to 8 weeks. Sessions for children, youth, and parents run concurrently. Such groups combine education, examination of feelings, and exploring ideas about how to incorporate information learned into family interaction.

The most commonly used curriculum in the Illinois project was *Family Preservation: The Second Time Around,* developed by the North American Council on Adoptable Children (Al-Aidy et al., 1992). This curriculum provides a framework for educational support groups for adoptive parents, adopted adolescents, and adopted children of latency age. The curriculum is designed to be presented over 8 weeks. The curriculum suggests groups be led by a mental health professional and an adoptive parent or an adopted adult.

The guidebook for group leaders emphasizes the importance of careful planning. It gives advice on publicity, choosing facilitators, assessing children for participation, and many other such issues. The importance of ground rules that help parents and children feel safe is addressed. Practical advice on setting limits on members who dominate discussion, dealing with one-upmanship, and dealing with conflict is presented. The curriculum also includes a primer on group development and group dynamics.

The curriculum itself is targeted differently for latency age children, adolescents, and parents, although there are common themes. The parent group examines the following:

- Entitlement, claiming, and parents' rights (including the right to parent a child born to someone else)
- Introduction to bonding and attachment and ways of promoting attachment why families choose adoption

- Ways in which children can be fully incorporated into family life
- Unmatched expectations (i.e., the ways in which parental expectations before adopting are different from the reality)
- Child development issues and the effect of adoption on development
- Separation and loss (for both parents and children) and anniversary reactions
- Identity issues for adopted children and ways to help develop a positive sense of self
- How behavior masks feelings
- Ideas to enhance parent child communication
- Behavioral interventions
- Preparing teens for emancipation

The latency age and adolescent groups deal with similar issues, using activities and exercises appropriate to the child's developmental level. Lifebook work, completed for each session, provides a basis for exploring issues. Both children and adolescent groups examine the effect of separation and loss, the need for grief, and what it means to be in a family. Teen groups look more closely at identity, helping teens identify what they have gained from each set of parents. Relaxation exercises and guided imagery help teens examine their thoughts about their birth family. Adolescents explore grief in more detail than younger children, considering the stages of grief. They also discuss the behaviors that can stem from loss and feelings of abandonment. In addition, they talk about managing their own behavior and when and how to ask for help.

Younger children are given a workbook, "The Story That Makes Me Special." Activities from it are assigned throughout the group. For example, after the first session, children are instructed to ask their parents why they were adopted. Parental responses (and children's reactions) are discussed the following week. (It is important to note that such assignments are shared with parents as a regular part of their group sessions.)

The workbook also explores feelings. Children are asked to write responses to such questions as "What makes you happy in your family? Sad? What is the best thing that ever happened to you? The worst? What would you like to change about your life if you could?" Other exercises define what a feeling is, and children practice drawing illustrations of feelings.

The teen journal is similar to the workbook. Teens do journal assignments every week. For example, they write a response to the questions

"What were my birth parents' feelings when they could no longer parent me?" or "Why did my family adopt me?"

The heart story (developed by Foster Kline) is another example of an activity in the curriculum that can lead to discussion of difficult issues. A series of drawings accompanied by discussion helps children examine their wounded hearts. Hearts are filled with love, but in an injured heart, love flows out. When the heart is hurt (the illustration is of a heart pierced by arrows), the heart builds a wall to protect itself. But a wall keeps out love as well as harm. (Children discuss how behaviors can be a kind of wall.) What needs to happen for love to get in? (The facilitator draws a broken wall near a heart.) The problem is, we can't break down a wall without letting in both good and sad. But we can patch our hearts by expressing feelings and learning how to cope with pain and accept love. (The final drawing is of a large, full heart with patches.)

Parents engage in a variety of activities as well. One topic is mismatched expectations. We observed a support group where this topic was discussed. The worker began the session by putting a range of goodies in a brown paper bag and asking parents to identify what they hoped to get. The bag was passed around, and invariably some parents pulled out something they hadn't hoped for—a jellybean instead of licorice, gum instead of chocolate. The worker then moved to a discussion of hopes and expectations about being an adoptive parent and how close their imagined experience had been compared to the reality. Most parents admitted they had experienced a jarring difference. One parent had already raised two adopted children and was now struggling with an adopted teenager. As the discussion progressed, she was able to state candidly, "If I had it to do over again, I wouldn't." Other parents responded with such comments as "I can remember feeling the same way during those teen years, but now it's better." Others, after expressing empathy, encouraged her to figure out how to manage, because "she's yours and you can't give her back." They followed with specific questions about what bothered her most and suggested specific strategies of response, all in an atmosphere of concern and support. The discussion shifted to ways in which their children's expectations might have been mismatched. They noted how hard it was to watch their children struggle in school, have difficulty making friends, and be criticized often by adults for their failure to "act their age." The pain felt by parents and their empathy for their children who were often isolated and judged was apparent. The conversation then moved to ways in which parents could shelter children from constant criticism and provide opportunities to succeed.

When parents and children spend several weeks together exploring complex issues, emotional connections can develop. The curriculum calls for an ending that marks the journey. It suggests a group potluck, attended by parents, children, and facilitators. Certificates are awarded, and the end of the group is marked by a ceremony honoring the child's past and future.

In addition to the curriculum produced by NACAC, there are several other adoption curricula. The Post Adoption Center of Montana developed a training guide called *Bridging the Gap* (Montana Adoption Resource Center, 1992). The guide is divided into four units: "Did You Know it Would be Like This?" covers mismatched expectations, the effect of adoption on self-esteem, and the central issue of loss; "Roots and Wings" explores the effect of genetics and environment in adoption as well as the importance of openness; "Sticking It Out Without Getting Stuck" explores how separation affects attachment over the course of the child's development, how adoptive parenting differs from birth parenting, and how to develop strategies that encourage attachment and trust; "Making It Work" discusses the transition from foster care to adoption for both children and parents, learning what therapy is and how to find the right therapist, and how to connect to other sources of support.

VanSlyck and Dupre-Clark's (1996) *Charting the Course: A Therapeutic Manual for Post-Adoptive Families* is a 10-week curriculum for families in crisis or under great stress. Parents attend one group, and children are divided into groups by age, 13-18 and 8-12. A separate group curriculum for younger children (6-10) and their parents was developed for families who are not in crisis but wish to improve communication and develop a better understanding of adoption issues. Children work on a lifebook as they discuss feelings about adoption. There also is a curriculum for adoptive parents of preschool children. It serves as a refresher to preadoptive training or an introduction for those who did not receive training. This curriculum considers the effect of nature versus nurture, how to communicate with young children, the grief process, and issues parents may face as they raise an adopted child.

Each curriculum manual includes suggestions about operating groups (including the importance of the intake process) as well as specific lesson plans and activities. An appendix of handouts specific to each group is included. Information on a range of issues such as fetal alcohol syndrome, attention deficit disorder and adoption, lying and the adoptee, and logical consequences provide parents with ideas about the meaning of difficult behaviors and strategies of response. Children's group handouts explore feelings and thoughts, help children consider what they have in common, and develop trust. Handouts for older children include open-ended questions to which children respond. Examples include "Things I would like to talk to my adoptive parents about but have been unable to say to them [are] . . ." and "If I had the opportunity to ask questions about my adoptive situation and my birth history I would ask . . ."

Other Group Approaches

Groups based on a curriculum have the advantage of being focused and having exercises designed to promote discussion of issues. They move from introductory discussions to consideration of very challenging issues. As helpful as such groups are, they may restrict participants from exploring issues uppermost in their minds. Further, their time-limited nature may keep them from providing the ongoing support many families desire.

Some programs solve this problem by running a series of groups. For example, a 6-week group might be followed by a short break, with another group (with somewhat different focus) beginning shortly thereafter. In other sites, groups are open ended. Such groups meet on a regular basis to provide advice, support, and empathy. Membership may be fluid, but the group itself is constant. The security of knowing the group is there and that one can attend as one wishes is of great importance to parents. A parent in one ongoing group stated, "We have been attending [the adoption support group] for several years. It is not a 'quick fix' to problems, but [enables] extended growth." Ongoing support groups may meet less often than structured groups. In the Illinois project, such groups met monthly.

Another option is to provide semistructured groups but for a specific time period. A group of parents or children may be brought together for 6 to 8 weeks, with the focus of the group being determined by the group members themselves. The group facilitator may arrange speakers, bring in materials, and lead discussion. Yet another alternative is to focus the group on a particular issue. For example, some programs may run a group on fetal alcohol syndrome and developing strategies to help the affected child. Other common topics are related to behavior management techniques, attention deficit disorder, and parenting the sexually abused child.

Part of the group process is making decisions about the nature of the group. In the Illinois project, sites varied on some dimensions. Most separated children by age, but some separated them by gender as well. Some sites alternated recreational activities and support group meetings for children. One site included the birth children of the adoptive parents in groups. Although most groups met in the evening, one site developed a mother's group that met mornings. Another included dinner along with the group to remove the stress of meal preparation and cleanup for busy families. No matter how groups were structured, parents and children found them very helpful.

Learning that other families have similar concerns and that there are strategies to try to make things better mean many families no longer feel "all alone in the twilight zone."

Chapter 10

PARENTING DEVELOPMENTALLY DISABLED CHILDREN

A significant number of special needs adopted children have developmental disabilities, and approximately half of all children awaiting adoption are developmentally disabled (Coyne & Brown, 1985). These disabling conditions include physical disorders such as cerebral palsy, blindness, spina bifida, and speech and hearing problems, as well as mental handicaps such as mental retardation or severe emotional disturbances. Some of these conditions may be the result of early environmental deprivation that stunted the children's developing minds and other capacities. Others are primarily organically based conditions resulting from genetic conditions, prenatal exposure to toxins, brain injuries, or other physiological factors. This chapter explores some of the concerns and needs present among adoptive families parenting these children.

OVERREPRESENTATION OF ADOPTEES AMONG SPECIAL EDUCATION POPULATIONS

Mentally retarded children constitute the largest proportion of children labeled as *developmentally disabled* (DD), and they are also the largest proportion of adopted DD children. Research indicates that adopted children are overrepresented in special education populations at a rate three to four times their representation in the general population (Brodzinsky & Steiger, 1991). Infant adoptees make up the majority of adopted children in special education classes, particularly in classes for the emotionally disturbed. Brodzinsky and Steiger's (1991) study indicates that in their state, special needs adoptees made up 18% of the adopted children in classes for the emotionally disturbed, 27% of the adoptees in classes for the perceptually impaired, and 45% of the adoptees in classes for the neurologically impaired. These authors estimate that the total representation of adoptees in special education populations is higher than reported due to school personnel's lack of awareness of the adoptive status of many children.

DISABILITIES AMONG CHILDREN SERVED
BY THE ILLINOIS PROJECT

Among the children served by the Illinois project, the majority were identified as having some sort of disability—most commonly an emotional disability (54%). Forty-four percent had been assessed as having attention deficit disorder (ADD) or attention deficit hyperactivity disorder (ADHD); 25% had developmental delays; and 11% had physical disabilities. Of these types of disabilities, emotional disability is most strongly associated with behavior problems and dissolution risk. ADD is associated with behavior problems but not with dissolution risk. Physical disabilities are not related to either behavior problems or risk of dissolution.

Many children had a diagnosed organically based problem that contributed to their difficulties in functioning. Twenty-nine percent of cases were identified as involving some organically based problem with the child. Another 33% of the children were suspected as having organic bases to problems, but this link had not been definitively diagnosed. The most common type of organic problem reported was fetal alcohol syndrome or prenatal drug exposure. Others, in order of their frequency, include brain damage from abuse or other causes, mental retardation, and bipolar disorder or other mental health problems thought to be related to a genetic history of mental illness. The presence of organic problems was associated with both severity of behavior problems and dissolution being raised by parents.

Parents and children displayed varying responses in coping with these conditions. Several children served by the project expressed strong anger at their birth mother for her use of alcohol or drugs that resulted in impairments to them. One boy stated that he wanted to find his birth mother some day just so that he could tell her how angry he felt. Some children's problems were diagnosed as a result of evaluation referrals by the adoption preservation workers. Parents' initial response to a diagnosis often included both relief that there was finally a known explanation and feelings of discouragement that they could help their child. Finding the missing piece to this puzzle is especially important for parents who have attributed the child's problems to their perceived lack of parenting skills. Also, some parents reported feeling duped by adoption workers who had failed to share background information regarding the child. In some cases, adoption preservation services were successful in helping parents find services that met the particular needs of their child, thus stabilizing the adoptive placement when parents had been ready to give up and were seeking to surrender guardianship of their child.

RESEARCH ON ADOPTION OUTCOMES OF DEVELOPMENTALLY DELAYED CHILDREN

Most studies on families adopting developmentally delayed children indicate that the majority of parents express high satisfaction with these adoptions (Coyne & Brown, 1985; Glidden, 1990, 1991; Rosenthal, Groze, & Aguilar, 1991). Rosenthal et al. (1991) indicate more positive outcomes for handicapped children in lower-income families than in families with incomes over $50,000. Parental perception about the accuracy of background information they received on their adopted child is an important predictor of overall satisfaction with the adoption and the effect of the adoption on the family (Rosenthal et al., 1991). Glidden (1991) reports that the families' initial reactions to the placement are positively related to adjustment 5 years after the adoption. Thus, it would seem that parental commitment and satisfaction vary between parents choosing to parent children with identified impairments and those adopting "normal" children who are later identified as significantly impaired. Parental understanding of their child's functioning and needs as well as realistic expectations for their child's capacities are important variables influencing family adjustment.

In spite of the overall positive outcome findings in research on adopted children with developmental disabilities, there are still difficult aspects of these adoptions. In Glidden's (1991) study, 88% of respondents reported some negative effect such as negative behavior changes for children already in the family, more arguments with spouses, financial difficulties, negative reactions from extended family members, and inability to cope with specific problem behaviors. These families' abilities to meet the caregiving demands of their adopted children affect the ongoing functioning of their entire family and the security of their children's adoption. Coyne and Brown (1985) report that most failed adoptions of DD children occur with children age 8 or older, indicating a need for more intensive services to these families. As these children reach school age, the stresses of parenting them become more complex. The remainder of this chapter focuses on critical issues to be addressed in facilitating adjustment in these adoptive families.

PARENTAL ATTITUDES TOWARD CHILDREN WITH DISABILITIES

As reported by the research studies described above, parental attitudes toward their children with disabilities and their feelings surrounding parenting these children are powerful influences on the child's development and overall family functioning. Parents may react differently when they choose to adopt a child with a known disability than when they find out years later that the "normal" child they adopted is in fact limited by significant disabilities. Some children's limitations are evident in early childhood through their slow development or physical symptoms. Some disabilities may not become apparent until the child is school age or older, however.

Negative feelings are common for parents reacting to learning that their child is disabled. Denial, anger, depression, fear, grief, guilt, powerlessness, and disappointment may result. Strong feelings of ambivalence in relation to parenting the child also are common as parents vacillate between strong empathy and love for the child and feelings of rejection. According to Patricia Smith (1997), who is director of the National Parent Network on Disabilities, many parents at their deepest points of depression report feeling a death wish for their child. It is important for parents to have someone to whom they can verbalize their feelings and who can help them know that they are not alone and their feelings are common in this situation. This support may come from a professional, another parent of a disabled child, or a parent support group. It also is important for spouses to be able to talk with each other about how they feel, to understand that they may not view their circumstances in the same way, and to accept the other's feelings.

Parents may at various times need help in working through their feelings related to parenting a child with special needs. Strong anger or unremitting grief can color the parents' relationship with each other, their child, and other children in the family. Also, religious beliefs and other culturally based views may shape parents' reactions and perceptions. Parents may feel that their child's condition is intentionally given to them as a hardship by God. Those who are infertile may feel that "this is what you get" because God intended for them to be childless. Conversely, others may believe that God chose them to parent this child because of their positive parenting capacities. Meanings attached to different disabilities vary along cultural lines. Some types of disabilities may be characterized by stigma. In cultures that place strong emphasis on the family's identity as a group, such as the strong familism of Hispanic cultures, the presence of a disability with a stigma such as mental illness may bring disgrace to the whole family's reputation (Harry, 1992). Parents may need assistance in making sense of the disabling condition that their child has and in understanding the ongoing implications that the disability has for their child's development. In situations where parents feel significant stigma, support groups are particularly effective in helping to reduce these feelings and to move parents toward a more reality-based perception of their parenting role.

In addition, parents' ability to parent a child with special needs is affected by their ability to meet this child's needs in a way that still allows for the needs of other family members. If parenting or any type of caregiving responsibility becomes an overwhelming, exhausting task that prohibits the parents' ability to meet their own and other family members' social and emotional needs, a range of problems may result. For these reasons, obtaining respite services and other supports that assist parents is critical. Suggestions for building an adequate support system and accessing needed resources are discussed at the end of this chapter.

ASSESSMENT AND INFORMATION

A primary need of parents of a special needs child is information regarding their child's capacities and limitations and how this child can maximize his or her potential. If a child has a pattern of symptoms indicative of a disability, the earlier this condition is diagnosed, the earlier appropriate intervention can be accessed. Several different patterns indicative of physical, genetic, or emotional disabilities may overlap. For example, a child may be hyperactive due to emotional problems, attention deficit disorder, fetal alcohol syndrome, or other causes. Often parents may take their child to many different professionals before obtaining an accurate diagnosis of their child's condition.

Many special needs adopted children have multiple and chronic conditions that require specialized medical, educational, and social or psychological services. The common void of information on their prenatal, early childhood, and genetic histories contributes to problems in understanding and meeting their needs. In addition, several conditions found among these children, such as fetal alcohol syndrome or attachment disorders, are not yet clearly understood and recognized by many professionals. Obtaining a thorough assessment and diagnosis of the child's condition is an important prerequisite to obtaining the services that develop the child's capacities. Parents often can benefit from support and advocacy to gain access to specialized diagnostic services. Some adoptive parents have become assertive advocates for their children, yet even the fiercest parent advocate may not be able to find the optimal diagnostic resources for a particular child. Adoption preservation workers can assist parents in researching alternative diagnostic resources and in cutting through red tape to obtain these resources.

Usually the gaps in information on children's genetic, prenatal, and early histories are barriers in developing diagnostic work-ups. Workers can assist adoptive parents in obtaining all known information in past child welfare records on their adopted child. In the Illinois project, many adoption preservation workers routinely requested the child's previous child welfare record from state storage facilities to provide themselves, adoptive parents, and children as much pertinent information as was available.

One postlegal adoption project in Alabama, which was made possible through a special grant from the U.S. Children's Bureau, yielded much data on the importance of specialized diagnostic measures for addressing the needs of DD adoptees. This project was located at the Sparks Center for Developmental and Learning Disorders, affiliated with the University of Alabama at Birmingham. It provided diagnostic and evaluation services to 110 adopted children with developmental delays. These children received a comprehensive battery of evaluation services from an interdisciplinary team of professionals (medicine, nursing, social work, psychology, special education, speech and hearing, and others). In addition to evaluating and staffing cases to assess the needs of these children and families accurately, this clinic provided brief parent counseling, consultation, advocacy, and referral for specialized services. The project found that the clinical evaluations were extremely important to parents who generally were not aware of the developmental levels of their adopted children or their service and educational needs. For many of the children, this evaluation identified medical, neurological, or other conditions that were previously unknown.

Most children evaluated were found to be mildly mentally retarded or of borderline intelligence. For some children, review of their individualized educational program from the school indicated that the current educational plan was not appropriate for the child's abilities and needs. In these cases, appropriate educational goals were recommended. For example, one 12-year-old boy's individual educational plan contained 20 pages of computer-generated goals such as, "Ryan will increase his knowledge of sentence structure so that when given a sentence, he can identify the subject and predicate with 90% accuracy." This child was evaluated as being in the trainable mental retardation range of intelligence, with an IQ in the low 50s. The goals in his educational plan were far beyond his capabilities. As a result of the thorough evaluation, more appropriate educational goals were recommended for this child.

For the 110 adopted children evaluated in the Alabama project, speech and language delays were the most frequently found secondary problem. The overwhelming majority of these children had histories of abuse and/or neglect, and had dual diagnoses of developmental delays and emotional problems. A number also had ADD. The adoptive parents needed assistance in obtaining resources such as special therapies and appropriate academic services. The most frequently expressed need for training by adoptive parents was for behavior management techniques. Parents also expressed the need for a lot of support for problems that occur when children reach the preteen or teen years. Many of these children with borderline IQs were in regular classes and having serious difficulties handling regular academics. Beyond academic challenges, some children needed interventions related to sexual development and appropriate peer relationships. These parents also expressed their need for links to family support groups and respite care.

Once parents have obtained an accurate assessment of their child's condition, capacities, and limitations, they need to obtain as much information as possible that facilitates their understanding of their child and the best ways to maximize the child's learning and development. They need information about the child's disability, available services, and the specific things they can do to help their child. Smith (1997) recommends that parents keep a notebook to save all information given to them and that they write down their specific questions before professional appointments or meetings. Much helpful information resides with other parents of children who have disabilities similar to their own children—thus, identifying these contacts is important. The National Information Center for Children and Youth with Disabilities publishes *A Parent's Guide to Parent Groups* (Ripley, 1993). This organization also has a toll-free number (1-800-695-0285) and publishes state resource lists for individual states.

Another valuable source of information is books written for and by parents. A good resource for identifying the books that might be helpful for a particular family is *The Special Needs Reading List: An Annotated Guide to the Best Publications for Parents and Professionals* (Sweeney, 1997).

Prenatal drug exposure among some special needs adopted children poses particular challenges for many adoptive families. The most common and most injurious of these conditions results from prenatal exposure to alcohol, although other children are affected by drugs such as cocaine or heroin, as well as some prescribed medications. Although not all children affected by prenatal alcohol exposure are mentally retarded, this birth defect is the leading cause of mental retardation in the United States. Fetal alcohol syndrome (FAS) is a medical diagnosis revealed by a cluster of symptoms in three categories: growth retardation, facial and other physical abnormalities, and central nervous system dysfunction. Central nervous system problems caused by prenatal alcohol exposure range from mental retardation and hyperactivity to more subtle symptoms such as learning disabilities or poor coordination. Fetal alcohol effect (FAE) is a label attributed to children with less apparent symptoms in the above three categories. Children with FAE, who may look normal and be of normal intelligence, may have very debilitating problems, however. These may include difficulty processing verbal information, irritability, impulsivity, and difficulty with basic skills such as cause and effect thinking or telling time. Many children with significant effects from prenatal alcohol exposure are diagnosed by an array of other problems before being formally diagnosed as FAS, and it is likely that many more children with these conditions are never formally diagnosed. There are many unknowns in understanding the effect of prenatal drug exposure on children and the evolution of symptoms over the child's development. With supportive interventions, many drug-affected individuals have been able to achieve functional lifestyles as adults. One resource that offers practical information and resources for parents of drug-exposed children is *Bruised Before Birth* (McNamara, 1994).

ACCESSING APPROPRIATE
EDUCATIONAL SERVICES

After parents have achieved an understanding of their adopted child's capacities and needs, making sure their child is placed in an appropriate educational program is of paramount importance. Often the child's emotional problems and the parents' frustrations are compounded when children are left in educational programs where they cannot achieve at a level with other children and they experience continued frustration and failure. At times, parents have to become very assertive in advocating for their child, because school systems may try to avoid the added cost of very specialized placements. Mental health professionals who have worked with the child and family can provide invaluable assistance by supporting parents through this process, attending school staffings, and advocating directly for the child.

It also is important for parents to know their child's educational rights. Workshops and printed materials are available to assist parents in acquiring this understanding. One book developed for this purpose is by Anderson, Chitwood, and Hayden (1997): *Negotiating the Special Education Maze: A Guide for Parents and Teachers.* This resource reviews the six major provisions of the Individuals with Disabilities Education Act (IDEA), supporting children's rights to a free, appropriate public education, and parent involvement in decision making. The six major provisions of this legislation include:

1. All children with disabilities, up to age 21, must be provided a free public education. (The original act covered children ages 6 to 18, but the amendments in 1990 expanded eligible students to include children from birth to 21.) The amendment (Part H) covering family-centered, early intervention for infants and toddlers requires that assessment, planning, and coordination services are free, but a sliding scale fee may be charged for other early intervention services.

2. Children must be evaluated fairly by a multidisciplinary team to determine their appropriateness for special education services. The law requires that parents' permission must be obtained for the initial evaluation, that tests must be nondiscriminatory and given in the child's own language, and that several tests showing a range of strengths and weaknesses must be used. Also, school systems must provide for a child to have an independent evaluation at public expense if parents disagree with the results of the school's evaluation (a part of due process). It is helpful for parents to obtain a copy of the evaluation and to seek clarification for any terms or conclusions that are not understandable prior to the individualized education program (IEP) meeting.

3. Schools must provide, at public expense, individually designed and appropriate educational programs for each child. These programs should be based on an assessment of need for a full range of educational services, including special transportation, speech/language therapy, counseling, occupational or physical therapy, assistive technology (e.g., equipment, communication devices) when necessary, and transitional services for students leaving high school. Schools must develop an IEP for each child being placed in special education. This plan is to be reviewed annually, with a new evaluation and eligibility decision occurring every 3 years. The IEP is developed by a team of professionals and in cooperation with the child's parents.

4. Children with disabilities are to be educated in the "least restrictive" environment possible and are to be educated with nondisabled children whenever appropriate.

5. Parents have the right to due process if they disagree with any decisions of the school system. They also must receive reasonable, written notification prior to any change in their child's educational plan. They have the right to bring an attorney or lay advocate to a due process hearing, to have the child present if desired, to open the hearing to the public, and to appeal the hearing decision to the state education agency.

6. Parents participate as partners in the planning of their child's special education. They also have access to all educational records regarding their child.

Other legal rights for persons with disabilities are guaranteed by the Americans with Disabilities Act (ADA) of 1990 and the federal Rehabilitation Act of 1973. For example, school districts must provide necessary supportive services to students who have disabilities but do not qualify for special education services. If a child has a disability, he or she must be given any aids, equipment, or "reasonable accommodations" that facilitate his or her education. Such accommodations might include things such as being given extra time for written work, sitting in the front of the class, having tests given orally, or using a tape recorder to record lectures in secondary school classes.

Those working with families of special needs children recommend ways for parents to maximize their participation in planning and advocating for their children's education. They urge parents to gather pertinent data on the child's functioning at home through structured observation, which is provided to the evaluation team; to review the child's educational records and provide feedback on any false or misleading contents of the records; to join parent groups that provide support and up-to-date information; and to monitor the child's education by talking with the child and teacher and observing in the classroom (Anderson et al., 1997). It is important for parents to develop advocacy skills that go beyond reactive confrontation to include effective assertiveness. This is characteristically a collaborative orientation in working with educational personnel, negotiation skills, and effective confrontation when needed. Some adoption preservation programs and parent groups provide workshops on effectively advocating for the child within the educational system.

ACHIEVING A BALANCE IN EXPECTATIONS OF CHILDREN

It is important for parents to develop realistic expectations of their child that accept the child's limitations as well as facilitate full development of the child's capacities. If parents expect too much from children, they risk causing the child to feel rejected or incapable. If parents expect too little, children are not encouraged to achieve fully. Facilitating the child's participation in various arenas of family life is important for all children. This includes developing self-care responsibilities, responsibilities at home, relationships with grandparents and other relatives, friendships with other children, and participation in other community systems.

To achieve a realistic balance in expectations, parents first need to view their child as a "kid," with the same needs as all children. No matter what the child's limitations, parents need to learn to enjoy their child and to have fun with their child. It is this pleasurable exchange between parent and child that builds a child's self-esteem and helps the child to feel loved.

Sometimes parents are overly protective of children with disabilities and refuse to allow the child to take risks or venture beyond the circle of family and school. Some parents keep their child with one of them all the time that the child is not in school. One adoptive family with an autistic child would leave him for only 2 to 3 hours a month, when they took the child to a child care program for special needs children. They had explored exchanging care with another adoptive family, but due to their child's limited speech, they did not want to risk the possibility of his being mistreated by another child and not being able to communicate this to them. This couple had not had an evening or weekend alone or a vacation apart from their child for years. Such constant caregiving can put undue stress on a parent's individual mental health or a couple's healthy marital relationship.

It is important to help special needs children assume as much responsibility and develop as much competence as possible. This includes assigning them chores at home that are within their abilities, even if it takes them longer to accomplish these and even if someone else could do them with less effort. Promoting the child's participation in any activity that he or she can possibly do helps the child develop independence and a sense of positive self-worth. Likewise, encouraging children to develop special interests and talents contributes to their self-esteem.

GAINING ACCESS TO SUPPORT SYSTEMS
AND NEEDED RESOURCES

Within the Family

Caring for children with special needs usually is linked with increased or more difficult parenting responsibilities. Whether the child's needs require extra physical care or assistance, frequent transporting to medical or other therapeutic appointments, or intensive supervision and guidance, parents are often expending inordinate amounts of physical and emotional energy in caring for their children. To continue being able to meet the needs of their children and other family members, parents need resources and support. Sometimes this means that parents need to be encouraged to attend to their own needs consciously as well as those of spouses and other children.

Ongoing heavy caregiving responsibilities often take their toll on marital relationships, particularly when one parent is much more committed to the adoption than the other parent. In many family situations, the parent who carries the heaviest burden of child care may feel resentful or unsupported by the other parent. If one parent has negative feelings toward a child or a very low threshold of tolerance for a child's demands, the other parent may try to handle everything to avoid a crisis. In situations when a spouse feels neglected or always a low priority, feelings of resentment and alienation can build. Surmounting such circumstances requires open communication between spouses and sufficient attention to the marital relationship. Both parents need to be able to hear and understand the other's feelings and needs and to help each other in ways that matter. Often, regular, planned respites for parents to spend time together are important outlets.

Attention to other children in the family is very important. Siblings may be enthusiastic and supportive when families first embark on adopting a new child; however, if they perceive that they must "fend for themselves" while parents focus most of their energies on a child with many needs, they will start to have negative feelings. Parents may expect too much from other children, thinking that they are able to take care of themselves and should not make extra demands. Parents need to be able to empathize with their children's feelings and respond in ways that do not alienate siblings. Sometimes this may involve spending individual time with other children in the family or making provisions for other activities that are important to them. Some programs for adoptive families offer sibling support groups, a wonderful resource to help explore feelings and coping strategies.

Within the Community

All parents need emotional and social support for their parenting role from relatives, friends, and others in the community. Sometimes adoptive parents express feelings that others do not understand their situation. This may be particularly true for adoptive parents of special needs children. Family members or friends may think that the adoptive parents are crazy for taking on this child, and may even avoid spending time with the adoptive family because the child has problems. For example, one adoptive mother served by the Illinois project described her extended family's rejection of her child with special needs, which resulted in an ongoing rift in the family:

> My family couldn't handle us taking this child. He was too damaged for them to live with as part of their family. . . . He was too streetwise; he knew too many nasty words; he wasn't grateful. . . . They couldn't live with looking at his pain—he has scars on his body where people put cigarettes out on him. And so they chose not to be part of his life.

Another adoptive mother expressed feelings of emotional distance and a more subtle lack of understanding from others, saying that she could never just complain about her kids as other parents do. She sensed that others thought she was rejecting them or should just be grateful to have them. Ideally, adoptive parents of children with special needs find the understanding, emotional support, and help that they might need within their extended family and social circle. When this is not true, however, they particularly need to be linked with other social supports, such as a buddy adoptive family or an adoption support group.

Some innovative adoption programs use eco-maps or other measures of social support to assess environmental supports that a family has, as well as supports they need. Efforts to strengthen existing supports or to build new supports become a major focus of working with the family. Helping efforts may include educational meetings with significant support persons of the adoptive family so that these individuals better understand the adopted child and the family's needs.

In addition, locating needed resources or strengthening the responsiveness of a resource to which the family is connected may be important aspects of supporting adoptive families. Child care, ranging from baby-sitters and day care to respite care, is an area of need for many adoptive families. Inadequate child care is an ongoing source of stress for many special needs adoptive families, particularly for those whose children have severe behavior problems. Some families with several adopted and foster children may have to make many different arrangements for different children. Unpredictable or unusual needs for child care such as early school dismissals or family emergencies are especially difficult for these families. Linking these families to dependable and affordable sources of child care may be an essential aspect to stabilizing the family. Adoptive parent child care co-ops may exist or be developed to assist adoptive families with child care. Also, accessing child care providers or financial assistance for the child's needs provided through existing state or community social service agencies is possible for many of these children. It is important to determine if families qualify for benefits under organizations for developmentally disabled children, mental health services, wraparound services in some community-based programs, social security, and other relevant social service organizations. Advocacy targeted toward expanding financial support provided through adoption assistance also may be a part of intervention with these families.

Another area of need among many special needs adoptive families is recreational and social outlets for their children. Many of these children are not accepted in organized groups such as scouts, dance classes, and sports teams or in informal play groups of their peers. Developing strategies to find social outlets for these children meets the needs of children and parents alike. In some adoption support programs, older high school or college students work as "recreational companions" for such children by supervising play activities between the adoptee and other children or providing needed individual supervision for the child in an organized group activity. Adoptee support groups or weekend respite camps for adopted children exist in some locations. A camp program for adopted children was developed in Minnesota for special needs adoptees, and has been duplicated in other states. This program offers monthly weekend activities to children, serving as a fun, social outlet for the child and a weekend respite for their parents. Many activities have an adoption theme as well, offering the children a chance to know other adoptees and to develop their understanding of adoption.

CONCLUSION

Families adopting children with developmental disabilities face many adjustments that unfold as the child develops. Even when parents knowingly adopt children with recognized disabilities, they often are unprepared for some of the challenges they face. Professionals who work with these families need to assist them in gaining accurate information on these children's needs and in obtaining the resources necessary to maximize the child's development and the family's functioning. To the extent possible, these families should be linked with other parents of disabled children, who are among the most knowledgeable and effective advocates for empowering adoptive families.

Chapter 11

TOWARD A BETTER FUTURE
Partnerships to Strengthen Adoptive Families

Our understanding of the needs of families adopting children with special needs is just emerging. In the early years of the permanency planning movement, we discovered that children once thought unadoptable could be placed in permanent homes. Not all children placed for adoption remained in their homes, however. Research on disruption as well as practical experience led us to prepare children and families better for adoption and to provide services beyond the placement until finalization occurred. Only recently have we come to understand that legal finalization is not the only hurdle for achieving adoption stability. Examining the needs of families after the point of finalization and responding to those needs is the latest phase in the goal of achieving permanent homes for children.

This book has explored the emotional issues confronting children removed from birth families due to maltreatment and later placed with adoptive families. The effect of trauma and loss is ongoing for these children, presenting adjustment challenges that may require special assistance to understand and unravel. Identity issues also continue to evolve as children grow, affecting their self-image, relationships, and behavior. Likewise, parents and families confront loss, trauma, and identity issues of their own as they seek to facilitate their children's adjustment. All professionals working with adoptive families need to expand their understanding of these issues as well as their expertise in therapeutic interventions with children and families struggling with the ramifications of maltreatment and loss.

CURRENT ADOPTION TRENDS

As we enter the new millennium, there is a renewed emphasis on adoption as a solution to the social problem of children who cannot be cared for in their original families. Our earlier progress in reducing the numbers of children in foster care is fast evaporating, and 1998 figures are expected to surpass 500,000 (NACAC, 1998). In response to this upsurge, the Clinton administration's 2002 initiative set the goal that every state double its number of adoptions by 2002. Emerging from this initiative, the federal Adoption and Safe Families Act of 1997 pushes for quicker permanency decisions and provides financial incentives to states to find adoptive or other permanent homes for waiting children. In addition, the 1994 Multiethnic Placement Act (and its expansion through later interethnic adoption provisions) is likely to increase the number of adoptions. This act forbids the consideration of the adopting family's race, culture, or ethnicity as a factor in delaying or denying a foster or adoptive placement.

Several states have moved aggressively to place more waiting children for adoption. For example, Illinois placed 4,293 children in fiscal year 1998, an increase of 92.6% from the previous year. New York City reported a similar increase in its number of adoptive placements. The placement of large numbers of children for adoption will likely increase the need for post-adoption services to sustain families. The expansion of adoption, although a great benefit for children, requires a comprehensive set of supports so that adoptive homes can truly be permanent homes.

ADOPTION SUPPORT AND PRESERVATION

Although only a small percentage of special needs families are at risk of dissolution of adoption, many other families struggle with very difficult problems for which they can find no effective solutions. Further, most families confront predictable developmental challenges accompanied by difficulties related to the loss and trauma experienced by the child and the interaction of the child's difficulties with the history and dynamics of the family.

Other than the monetary support of adoption assistance, very few adoption-sensitive services have been available to these families nationwide. Children placed through the child welfare system often have been damaged by experiences in their birth families and within the system. It seems unfair that adoptive parents are expected to integrate these children into their families and shepherd them to adulthood with no additional support other than monetary assistance. A few states and private agencies have begun to develop some adoption support and preservation services. Many of these services have been developed with adoption opportunities funds obtained from the U.S. Children's Bureau for 2- to 3-year projects. As grant funds ended, most of these projects have been either discontinued or cut back. The few services that do exist are rarely mandated by law, and often are not uniformly available to all adoptive families. Also, post-adoption services are often aimed at families in crisis. Preventive or supportive services that might allow families to avoid crisis are very limited.

Many adoptive families can guide their children to healthy adulthood without services beyond those available to any family. Some families need a range of services to sustain and strengthen them, however. The need for more thorough adoption preparation of families and children is an ongoing one. Better preparation by itself is not sufficient to address all needs that may arise, however. Many problems may not be manifested until years after the adoption is finalized. Families need to be taught to expect developmental challenges and to be armed through guidebooks, resource directories, and other written materials to know where to turn for different types of help. Given the very positive response of children and parents to support groups, ongoing access to adoption support groups is an excellent strategy for sustaining these families.

The range of services needed to sustain adoptive families includes preventive, supportive, and therapeutic services. Families need preventive services such as education and information to assist them in understanding their child and family situation and in learning the most effective strategies for parenting. They need supportive services such as support groups, advocacy, and respite care to sustain their coping abilities and to obtain needed resources for their family. Finally, they need psychosocial services to address specific difficulties, including specialized assessment services, crisis intervention, a variety of therapeutic interventions, and, for some, residential treatment services.

Development of knowledge on post-adoption practice and development of services for these families is the primary challenge to assure permanency for children removed from their birth families. We believe it is in the best interest of adopted children and their families for special needs adoption to be seen as a partnership among families, private agencies, and the state. We understand that states are pulled by many competing forces, and adoption is a very small part of the resource struggle. Still, we believe there is a moral imperative to provide ongoing services to these often very troubled children and the families who agree to raise them. Our hope and that of adoption professionals across the country is that the emphasis on placing children for adoption is accompanied by a commitment to specialized support and intervention for adoptive families.

APPENDIX

Table A.1
Family Strengths ($N = 331$)

Strength	Percentage
Ability to communicate about concerns openly and directly	74
Parents committed to keeping adopted child	72
Demonstrate warmth toward the adopted child	70
Have previous parenting experience	65
Appropriately open about adoption	65
Have the ability to communicate openly with children	64
Have supportive friendships	64
Demonstrate confidence in the ability to parent	60
Have sustaining religious faith	56
Offer appropriately structured and stable environment	56
Reasonable degree of flexibility in dealing with children	55
Adequate financial base	55
Parents have interests outside the home	54
Have the ability to identify problems and generate strategies for resolution	54
Know and are comfortable with child's preadoptive history	50
Have supportive extended family	50
Demonstrate a tolerance for conflict	45
Have strong marital relationship	44
Demonstrate optimism	43
Have contact with others who have adopted	35

Table A.2
Association Between Strengths Identified and Raising Dissolution

Strength	Chi-Square	Significant Level
Committed to keeping child	40.54	.0000
Demonstrate optimism	25.82	.0000
Demonstrate warmth	18.10	.0000
Tolerate conflict	9.46	.0088
Contact with adoptive families	8.04	.0046
Flexibility in dealing with child	9.27	.0023
Maintain structured environment	10.04	.0182
Parents open about adoption	4.64	.0312
Communicate openly with child	4.33	.0376

Table A.3

Current Feelings About Relationship With Child

(in percentages)

Feeling	Strongly Agree	Agree	Neutral	Disagree	Strongly Disagree
The main problem with my family now is my adopted child's behavior/emotional problems.	46	27	10	7	8
I feel confident I can meet my child's needs.	17	37	20	16	11
I feel that things with my child are "out of control."	22	25	17	22	15
My child seems attached to me and other family members.	28	24	17	17	14
I always feel angry with my child.	3	18	20	37	22
I am able to manage my child's behavior.	1	27	25	29	21
Right now I am feeling pretty hopeless that things can get better.	11	20	19	29	21
I feel close to my child.	33	23	21	17	7
I feel like I have experienced the last straw in my relationship with my child.	10	18	15	25	32
I feel like this child belongs to me.	48	29	9	11	4
My family is breaking apart.	13	15	18	23	31
I feel pleasure in parenting my child.	22	30	15	22	11
I am committed to working through these problems no matter what it takes.	52	26	16	5	2
I think my child needs to be placed outside my home.	9	7	18	21	45
If I could, I would end this adoption.	4	5	14	21	56

Table A.4
Mean Scores of Adoption and CBC Samples

		CBC Normed Samples	
	Adoption Preservation	*Clinical*	*Nonclinical*
Boys: 4-11 (*n* = 50)			
Internalizing	63.1	61.7	50.2
Externalizing	66.2	62.5	49.9
Total problems	67.6	64.4	50.0
Boys: 12-18 (*n* = 62)			
Internalizing	62.5	61.5	50.5
Externalizing	71.8	62.6	50.5
Total problems	69.8	64.0	50.5
Girls: 4-11 (*n* = 28)			
Internalizing	60.4	61.4	50.5
Externalizing	70.0	61.2	50.0
Total problems	68.6	63.8	50.1
Girls: 12-18 (*n* = 64)			
Internalizing	64.6	62.0	50.1
Externalizing	71.8	62.8	50.8
Total problems	70.7	63.8	50.4

Table A.5
Percentage Scoring in Clinical Range on CBC Scales

Withdrawn	39	Somatic complaints	20
Anxious/depressed	35	Social problems	39
Thought problems	50	Attention problems	58
Delinquent behavior	69	Aggressive behavior	62
Internalizing score	64	Externalizing score	85
Total problems score	86	Any summary score	91

Table A.6
Behavior Problem Score by Age at Adoptive Placement

Placement Age	*Behavior Problem Score*
Under 1	14.34
1-2 years	11.25
3-6 years	13.03
7 and up	13.19

Table A.7

Parent Responses on Support Group Items (in percentages)

Item	Strongly Agree	Agree	Neutral	Disagree	Strongly Disagree
Blame myself less	14	47	22	6	10
Understand my child better	22	69	8	2	0
Realized my child's behaviors were more serious than others'	2	26	20	35	18
Get less angry at my child	6	55	30	10	0
Manage child's behavior better	8	39	47	6	0
Realize other adoptive families have same problems	51	47	2	0	0
Feel less able to parent child	0	4	14	47	33
Learned from other parents	35	59	6	0	0
Less confidence in my parenting	0	0	12	52	36
Understand child's need to grieve	22	69	6	2	2
More sharing of information with child	22	49	26	2	2
Feel more overwhelmed	8	20	24	28	20
Child's behavior not so bad	12	45	16	26	2
More confused about adoption	0	6	20	47	28

Table A.8
Parents' Responses Related to Children's Support Groups
(in percentages)

"As a result of my child's participation in the support group she/he . . .":

Item	Strongly Agree	Agree	Neutral	Disagree	Strongly Disagree
Better understands adoption	15	50	35	0	0
Is able to talk to me about concerns	15	29	34	17	5
Is more difficult to handle	3	10	29	39	20
Is helped by being with adoptees	32	46	22	0	0
Is too curious regarding birth family	0	2	27	49	22
Asked more questions regarding adoption	5	40	40	15	3
Is better able to talk to me	12	32	37	20	0
Is more confused regarding adoption	0	10	32	39	20
Behavior is easier to manage	10	24	44	22	0
Better understands feelings	8	40	40	13	0
Is less willing to talk to me	0	0	42	37	22

REFERENCES

Achenbach, T. M. (1991). *Manual for the child behavior checklist/4-18 and 1991 profile.* Burlington: University of Vermont, Department of Psychiatry.

Achenbach, T. M., & Edelbrock, C. (1983). *Manual for the child behavior checklist and revised child behavior profile.* Burlington: University of Vermont, Department of Psychiatry.

Ainsworth, M. D. S. (1969). Object relations, dependency and attachment: A theoretical review of the infant-mother relationship. *Child Development, 40,* 969-1025.

Ainsworth, M. D. S. (1985). Attachment across the lifespan. *Bulletin of the New York Academy of Medicine, 61*(9), 792-812.

Ainsworth, M. D. S. (1989). Attachment beyond infancy. *American Psychologist, 44*(4), 709-716.

Ainsworth, M. D. S., Blehar, M., Waters, E., & Wall, S. (1978). *Patterns of attachment: A psychological study of the strange situation.* Hillsdale, NJ: Lawrence Erlbaum.

Al-Aidy, D. C., Haines, J., & Studaker, P. (1992). *Family preservation: The second time around—A curriculum for adoptive families.* St. Paul, MN: North American Council on Adoptable Children.

Allan, J. (1986). The body in child psychotherapy. In N. Schwartz-Salant & M. Stein (Eds.), *The body in analysis* (pp. 145-166). Wilmette, IL: Chiron.

American Psychiatric Association. (1980). *Diagnostic and statistical manual of mental disorders* (3rd ed.). Washington, DC: Author.

American Psychiatric Association. (1994). *Diagnostic and statistical manual of mental disorders* (4th ed.). Washington, DC: Author.

Anderson, W., Chitwood, S., & Hayden, D. (1997). *Negotiating the special education maze: A guide for parents and teachers.* Bethesda, MD: Woodbine House.

Anthony, E. J. (1983). *The child in his family.* New York: John Wiley.

Arnold, J. C. (1995). Therapy dogs and the dissociative patient: Preliminary observations. *Dissociation: Progress in the Dissociative Disorders, 8*(4), 247-252.

Avery, R. J. (1998). Adoption assistance under P.L. 96-272: A policy analysis. *Children and Youth Services Review, 20*(1/2), 29-55.

Backhaus, K. (1989). Training mental health professionals to work with adoptive families who seek help. *Child Welfare, 68*(1), 61-68.

Barth, R. P., & Berry, M. (1988). *Adoption and disruption: Rates, risks, and responses.* Hawthorne, NY: Aldine de Gruyter.

Barth, R. P., Berry, M., Carson, M. L., Goodfield, R., & Feinberg, B. (1986). Contributors to disruption and dissolution of older-child adoptions. *Child Welfare, 65*(4), 359-371.

Beech Brook. (1995). *Continuum of post legal services for adopted children with emotional and behavioral problems and their families: Final grant report.* Cleveland, OH: Author.

Bennison, K. (1992). No deposit no return: The adoption dilemma. *Nova Law Review, 16,* 909-935.

Benson, P. S., Sharma, A. R., & Roehlkepartain, E. C. (1994). *Growing up adopted: A portrait of adolescents and their families.* Minneapolis, MN: Search Institute.

Berman, L., & Bufferd, R. (1986). Family treatment to address loss in adoptive families. *Social Casework: The Journal of Contemporary Social Work, 67,* 3-11.

Berry, M., & Barth, R. P. (1989). Behavior problems of children adopted when older. *Child and Youth Services Review, 11,* 221-238.

Bhaskaran, D., & Freed, C. R. (1988). Changes in neurotransmitter turnover in locus coeruleus by changes in arterial blood pressure. *Brain Research Bulletin, 21,* 191-199.

Blackburn, L. B. (1991). *I know I made it happen.* Omaha, NE: Centering Corporation.

Boeding, C. (1998). *The love disorder.* Lakewood, CO: Passages.

Bosma, H. A., Graafsma, T. L. G., Grotevant, H. D., & deLevita, D. J. (1994). *Identity and development: An interdisciplinary approach.* Thousand Oaks, CA: Sage

Bourguinon, J., & Watson, K. W. (1987). *After adoption.* Springfield: Illinois Department of Children and Family Services.

Bowlby, J. (1960). Grief and mourning in infancy and early childhood. *Psychoanalytic Study of the Child, 15,* 9-52.

Bowlby, J. (1973). *Attachment and loss. Vol. 2: Separation—Anxiety and anger.* New York: Basic Books.

Bowlby, J. (1980). *Attachment and loss. Vol. 3: Loss—Sadness and depression.* New York: Basic Books.

Briere, J. (1992). *Child abuse trauma: Theory and treatment of the lasting effects.* Newbury Park, CA: Sage.

Brodzinsky, D. M. (1987). Adjustment to adoption: A psychosocial perspective. *Clinical Psychology Review, 7,* 25-47.

Brodzinsky, D. M., Radice, C., Huffman, L., & Merkler, K. (1987). Prevalence of clinically significant symptomatology in a non-clinical sample of adopted and non-adopted children. *Journal of Clinical Child Psychology, 16*(4), 350-356.

Brodzinsky, D. M., Schechter, D. E., Braff, A. M., Singer, L. M. (1984). Psychological and academic adjustment in adopted children. *Journal of Consulting and Clinical Psychology, 52*(4), 582-590.

Brodzinsky, D. M., Schechter, M. D., & Brodzinsky, A. B. (1986). Children's knowledge of adoption: Developmental changes and implications for adjustment. In R. D. Ashmore & D. M. Brodzinsky (Eds.), *Thinking about the family: Views of parents and children* (pp. 205-232). Hillsdale, NJ: Lawrence Erlbaum.

Brodzinsky, D. M., Schechter, M. D., & Henig, R. M. (1992). *Being adopted: The lifelong search for self.* New York: Doubleday.

Brodzinsky, D. M., Singer, L. M., & Braff, A. M. (1984). Children's understanding of adoption. *Child Development, 55,* 869-878.

Brodzinsky, D. M., Smith, D. W., & Brodzinsky, A. B. (1998). *Children's adjustment to adoption: Developmental and clinical issues.* Thousand Oaks, CA: Sage.

Brodzinsky, D. M., & Steiger, C. (1991). Prevalence of adoptees among special education populations. *Journal of Learning Disabilities, 24*(8), 484-489.

Brohl, K. (1996). *Working with traumatized children: A handbook for healing.* Washington, DC: Child Welfare League of America Press.

Bush, M., & Gordon, A. C. (1982). The case for involving children in child welfare decisions. *Social Work, 27,* 309-314.

Carlson, V., Cicchetti, D., Barnett, D., & Braunwald, K. (1989). Finding order in disorganization: Lessons from research on maltreated infants' attachments to their caregivers. In D. Cicchetti & V. Carlson (Eds.), *Child maltreatment: Theory and research on the causes and consequences of child abuse and neglect* (pp. 494-528). Cambridge: Cambridge University Press.

Child Welfare League of America. (1997). Report on adoption statistics. [Internet address: www.cwla.org/cwla/adoption/adoption fact sheet.html/]

Cicchetti, D. (1989). How research on child maltreatment has informed the study of child development: Perspectives from developmental psychopathology. In D. Cicchetti & V. Carlson (Eds.), *Child maltreatment: Theory and research on the causes and consequences of child abuse and neglect* (pp. 377-431). Cambridge: Cambridge University Press.

Cicchetti, D., & Beeghly, M. (1987). Symbolic development in maltreated youngsters: An organizational perspective. *New Directions for Child Development, 36,* 47-68.

Cicchetti, D., Ganiban, J., & Barnett, D. (1991). Contributions from the study of high-risk populations to understanding the development of emotion regulation. In J. Garber & K. A. Dodge (Eds.), *The development of emotion regulation and dysregulation* (pp. 15-48). New York: Cambridge University Press.

Cienfuegos, A. J., & Monelli, C. (1983). The testimony of political repression as a therapeutic instrument. *American Journal of Orthopsychiatry, 53,* 43-51.

Cline, F. (1979). *Understanding and treating the severely disturbed child.* Evergreen, CO: Evergreen Consultants in Human Behavior.

Cline, F. (1992). *Hope for high risk and rage filled children.* Evergreen, CO: Evergreen Consultants in Human Behavior.

Cline, F. W., & Fay, J. (1990). *Parenting with love and logic.* Colorado Springs, CO: Pinon Press.

Cohen, N., Coyne J., & Duvall, J. (1993). Adopted and biological children in the clinic: Family, parental and child characteristics. *Journal of Child Psychology and Psychiatry, 34*(4), 545-562.

Cooper, C. R., Grotevant, H. E., & Condon, S. M. (1984). Individuality and connectedness in the family as a context for adolescent identity formation and role-taking skills. In H. D. Grotevant & C. R. Cooper (Eds.), *Adolescent development in the family* (New directions for child development, No. 22, pp. 43-59). San Francisco: Jossey-Bass.

Cordell, A. S., Nathan, C., & Krymow, V. P. (1985). Group counseling for children adopted at older ages. *Child Welfare, 64*(2), 113-124.

Corey, M. S., & Corey, G. (1997). *Groups: Process and practice* (5th ed.). Cincinnati: Brooks/Cole.

Coyne, A., & Brown, M. E. (1985). Developmentally disabled children can be adopted. *Child Welfare, 64*(6), 607-615.

Crimando, S. (1997). Assisting children who are the victims and witnesses of violence and trauma. *Healing Magazine, 2*(1), 4-7.

Davis, N. (1988). *Once upon a time: Therapeutic stories to heal abused children.* Oxon Hill, MD: Psychological Associates of Oxon Hill.

Delaney, R. (1991). *Fostering changes: Treating attachment disordered foster children.* Fort Collins, CO: Walter J. Corbett.

Delaney, R. J., & Kunstal, F. R. (1993). *Troubled transplants: Unconventional strategies for helping disturbed foster and adopted children.* Portland, ME: National Child Welfare Resource Center for Management and Administration.

Denuth, C. L. (1991). *The biological clock: Key times in an adopted person's life.* (Handout)

DePelchin Children's Center. (1993). *Final report of EMPOWER-EM.* Houston, TX: Author.

Dickman, G. E. (1992). Adoptees among students with disabilities. *Journal of Learning Disabilities, 25*(8), 529-543.

Dickson, L. R., Heffron, W. M., & Parker, C. (1990). Children from disrupted and adoptive homes on an inpatient unit. *American Journal of Orthopsychiatry, 60,* 594-602.

DiGiuilo, J. F. (1987). Assuming the adoptive parent role. *Social Casework, 68*(11), 561-566.

Donley, K. (1984, July). *Adoption disruption.* Symposium conducted at the North American Council on Adoptable Children conference, Chicago.

Droga, J. T. (1997). Realities lost and found: Trauma, dissociation, and somatic memories in a survivor of childhood sexual abuse. *Psychoanalytic Inquiry, 17*(2), 173-191.

Eagle, R. (1993). Airplanes crash, spaceships stay in orbit: The separation experience of a child "in care." *Journal of Psychotherapy Practice and Research, 2*(4), 318-334.

Eagle, R. S. (1994). The separation experience of children in long-term care: Theory, research, and implications for practice. *American Journal of Orthopsychiatry, 64*(5), 421-434.

Egeland, B., & Sroufe, L. A. (1981). Developmental sequelae of maltreatment in infancy. In R. Rizley & D. Cicchetti (Eds.), *Developmental perspectives in child maltreatment* (Vol. 11, pp. 77-92). San Francisco: Jossey-Bass.

Egeland, B., Sroufe, L. A., & Erickson, M. (1983). The developmental consequences of different patterns of maltreatment. *Child Abuse and Neglect, 7*(4), 459-469.

Erich, S., & Leung, P. (1998). Factors contributing to family functioning of adoptive children with special needs: A long term outcome analysis. *Children and Youth Services Review, 20*(1/2), 135-150.

Erikson, E. H. (1963). *Childhood and society* (2nd ed.). New York: Norton.

Erikson, E. H. (1968). *Identity: Youth and crisis.* New York: Norton.

Fahlberg, V. (1991). *A child's journey through placement.* Indianapolis: Perspective Press.

Famularo, R., Fenton, T., Kinscherff, R., Ayoub, C., & Barnum, R. (1994). Maternal and child posttraumatic stress disorder in cases of child maltreatment. *Child Abuse and Neglect, 18*(1), 27-36.

Famularo, R., Kinscherff, R., & Fenton, T. (1990). Symptom differences in acute and chronic presentation of childhood post-traumatic stress disorder. *Child Abuse and Neglect, 14*(3), 439-444.

Fanshel, D., & Shinn, E. (1978). *Children in foster care: A longitudinal investigation.* New York: Columbia University Press.

Farber, E. A., & Egeland, B. (1987). Invulnerability among abused and neglected children. In E. J. Anthony & B. J. Cohler (Eds.), *The invulnerable child* (pp. 253-288). New York: Guilford.

Festinger, T. (1986). *Necessary risk.* Washington, DC: Child Welfare League of America.

Finkelhor, D., & Browne, A. (1985). The traumatic impact of child sexual abuse: A conceptualization. *American Journal of Orthopsychiatry, 55,* 530-541.

Finkelhor, D., & Browne, A. (1986). Initial and long-term effects: A conceptual framework. In D. Finkelhor (Ed.), *A sourcebook on child sexual abuse* (pp. 180-198). Beverly Hills, CA: Sage.

Flango, V., & Flango, C. R. (1995). How many children were adopted in 1992. *Child Welfare, 74*(5), 1018-1032.

Franz, K. (1993). *Final report.* Warren: Northeast Ohio Post Adoption Family Support Project.

Freud, S. (1957). Mourning and melancholia. In J. Strachey (Ed.), *The standard edition of the complete psychological works of Sigmund Freud* (Vol. 14). London: Hogarth.

Frey, L. (1986). *Preserving permanence: A survey of post-adoption services in Massachusetts.* Boston: Massachusetts Department of Social Services.

Fullerton, C. S., Goodrich, W., & Berman, L. B. (1986). Adoption predicts psychiatric treatment resistances in hospitalized adolescents. *Journal of the American Academy of Child Psychiatry, 25*(4), 542-551.

Gabel, S. (1988). *Filling in the blanks: A guided look at growing up adopted.* Ringoes, NJ: Tapestry Books.

Gallagher, M. M., Leavitt, K. S., & Kimmel, H. P. (1995). Mental health treatment of cumulatively/repetitively traumatized children. *Smith College Studies in Social Work, 65*(3), 205-237.

Gambrill, E. (1997). *Social work practice: A critical thinker's guide.* New York: Oxford University Press.

Glidden, L. M. (1990). The wanted ones: Families adopting children with mental retardation. *Journal of Children in Contemporary Society, 21,* 177-205.

Glidden, L. M. (1991). Adopted children with developmental disabilities: Post-placement family functioning. *Children and Youth Services Review, 13,* 363-377.

Goebel, B. L., & Lott, S. L. (1986, August). *Adoptees' resolution of the adolescent identity crisis: Where are the taproots?* Paper presented at the annual meeting of the American Psychological Association, Washington, DC.

Goerge, R., Howard, E., & Yu, D. (1996). *A study of adoption disruption and dissolution: Rates and variables in Illinois' welfare system.* Chicago: Chapin Hall Center for Children.

Green, B. L., Lindy, J. D., Grace, M. C., Glazer, G., Leonard, A., Korol, M., & Windget, C. (1990). Buffalo Creek survivors in the second decade: Stability of stress symptoms. *American Journal of Psychiatry, 60,* 45-54.

Grotevant, H. (1997). Identity processes: Integration of social, psychological and developmental approaches. *Journal of Adolescent Research, 12*(3), 354-357.

Grotevant, H., & McRoy, R. (1998). *Openness in adoption: Exploring family connections.* Thousand Oaks, CA: Sage.

Grow, L., & Shapiro, D. (1974). *Black children, white parents: A study of trans-racial adoption.* New York: Child Welfare League of America, Research Center.

Groze, V. (1996). A 1 and 2 year follow-up study of adoptive families and special needs children. *Children and Youth Services Review, 18*(1-2), 57-82.

Groze, V., & Rosenthal, J. (1993). Attachment theory and the adoption of children with special needs. *Social Work Research and Abstracts, 29*(2), 5-12.

Hajal, F., & Rosenberg, E. B. (1991). The family life cycle in adoptive families. *American Journal of Orthopsychiatry, 61*(1), 78-85.

Harrington, R. (1993). *Depressive disorder in childhood and adolescence.* Chichester, UK: Wiley.

Harrison, J. (1988). Making life books with foster and adoptive children. In C. E. Schaefer (Ed.), *Innovative interventions in child and adolescent therapy* (pp. 377-399). New York: John Wiley.

Harry, B. (1992). *Cultural diversity, families, and the special education system: Communication and empowerment.* New York: Teachers College Press.

Hartman, A. (1991). Every clinical social worker is in post-adoption practice. *Journal of Independent Social Work, 5*(3-4), 149-163.

Hartman, A., & Laird, J. (1989). Family treatment after adoption: Common themes. In D. Brodzinsky & M. Schecter (Eds.), *The psychology of adoption* (pp. 221-239). New York: Oxford University Press.

Herman, J. (1997). *Trauma and recovery.* New York: Basic Books.

Hewitt, S. K. (1994). Preverbal sexual abuse: What two children report in later years. *Child Abuse and Neglect, 18*(10), 821-826.

Hindman, J. (1989). *Just before dawn.* Ontario, OR: Alexandria Associates.

Hoopes, J. L. (1982). Prediction in child development: A longitudinal study of adoptive and non-adoptive families. *The Delaware Family Study.* New York: Child Welfare League of America.

Howard, J., & Smith, S. (1995). *Adoption preservation in Illinois: Results of a four-year study.* Springfield: Illinois Department of Children and Family Services.

Howard, J., & Smith, S. (1997). *Stengthening adoptive families: A synthesis of post-legal adoption opportunities grants.* Normal: Illinois State University.

James, B. (1989). *Treating traumatized children.* Lexington, MA: Lexington Books.

James, B. (1994). *Handbook for treatment of attachment-trauma problems in children.* New York: Lexington Books.

Jensen, S. B., & Agger, I. (1988). The testimony method: The use of testimony as a psychotherapeutic tool in the treatment of traumatized refugees in Denmark. *Refugee Participation Network, 3,* 14-18.

Jernberg, A. (1979). *Theraplay: A new treatment program using structured play for problem children and their families.* San Francisco: Jossey-Bass.

Jernberg, A. M. (1990). Attachment enhancing for adopted children. In P. V. Grabe (Ed.), *Adoption resources for mental health professional* (pp. 271-279). New Brunswick, NJ: Transactions.

Jernberg, A. M. (1993). Attachment formation. In C. E. Schaefer (Ed.), *The therapeutic powers of play* (pp. 241-265). Northvale, NJ: Jason Aronson.

Jerome, L. (1986). Overrepresentation of adopted children attending a children's mental health centre. *Canadian Journal of Psychiatry, 31*(6), 526-531.

Jerome, L. (1993). A comparison of demonography, clinical profile and treatment of adopted and non-adopted children at a children's mental health centre. *Candian Journal of Psychiatry, 38*(4), 290-294.

Jewett, C. L. (1982). *Helping children cope with separation and loss.* Harvard, MA: Harvard Common Press.

Josselson, R. (1987). *Finding herself: Pathways to identity development in women.* San Francisco, CA: Jossey-Bass.

Kadushin, A. (1988). *Child welfare services.* New York: Macmillan.

Kardiner, A., & Spiegel, H. (1947). *War, stress, and neurotic illness.* New York: Hoeber.

Kates, W. A., Johnson, R. L., Kader, M. W., & Grieder, F. H. (1991). Whose child is this? Assessment and treatment of children in foster care. *American Journal of Orthopsychiatry, 61,* 584-591.

Katz, M. (1986, August). *Understanding and helping adopted and foster children with emotional problems.* Presentation at conference of North American Council on Adoptable Children, Toronto.

Katz, M. (1990). *Understanding and helping adopted and foster children with emotional problems* [Videotape]. VIDTEK Productions.

Katz, M. (1991). Using intensely positive sensory stimulation to help adopted children with attachment, control and identity problems. *Roots and Wings,* 22-27.

Kaufman, J. (1991). Depressive disorders in maltreated children. *Journal of American Academy of Child and Adolescent Psychiatry, 30*(2), 257-265.

Kaye, K. (1990). Acknowledgement or rejection of differences. In D. Brodzinsky & M. Schechter (Eds.), *The psychology of adoption* (pp. 121-143). New York: Oxford University Press.

Kaye, K., & Warren, S. (1988). Discourse about adoption in adoptive families. *Journal of Family Psychology, 1*(4), 406-433.

Keck, G. C., & Kupecky, R. M. (1995). *Adopting the hurt child: Hope for families with special-needs kids.* Colorado Springs, CO: Pinon Press.

Keller, M. B., Lavori, P. W., Beardslee, W. R., Wunder, J., & Ryan, N. (1991). Depression in children and adolescents: New data on "undertreatment" and a literature review on the efficacy of available treatments. *Journal of Affective Disorders, 21,* 163-171.

Kirk, D. (1984). *Shared fate: A theory and method of adoptive relationships.* Port Angeles, WA: Ben-Simon.

Kirk, H. D. (1964). *Shared fate: A theory and method of adoptive relationships.* Port Angeles, WA: Ben-Simon.

Kirk, H. D. (1981). *Adoptive kinship: A modern institution in need of reform.* Toronto: Butterworths.

Kirschner, D., & Nagel, L. (1988). Antisocial behavior in adoptees: Patterns and dynamics. *Child and Adolescent Social Work, 5*(4), 300-314.

Kiser, L. J., Ackerman, B. J., Brown, E., Edwards, N. B., McColgan, E. B., Pugh, R. L., & Pruitt, D. B. (1988). Post-traumatic stress disorder in young children: A reaction to purported sexual abuse. *Journal of the American Academy of Child and Adolescent Psychiatry, 27*(5), 645-649.

Kiser, L., Heston, J., Millsap, P., & Pruitt, D. (1991). Physical and sexual abuse in childhood: Relationship with post-traumatic stress disorder. *Journal of American Academy of Child and Adolescent Psychiatry, 30*(5), 776-782.

Kotsopolous, S., Cote, A., Joseph, L., Pentland, N., Chryssoula, S., Sheahan, P., & Oke, L. (1988). Psychiatric disorders in adopted children. *American Journal of Orthopsychiatry, 58,* 608-612

Krementz, J. (1982). *How it feels to be adopted.* New York: Knopf.

Kubler-Ross, E. (1969). *On death and dying.* New York: Macmillan.

Landers, S., Forsythe, L., & Nickman, S. (1996). *Massachusetts Department of Mental Health training and adoptive family stabilization project final report.* Boston: Massachusetts Department of Mental Health.

Lazare, A. (1987). Shame and humiliation in the medical encounter. *Archives of Internal Medicine, 147,* 1653-1658.

Leigh, M. (Producer). (1996). *Secrets and lies* [Film]. (Available from 20th Century Fox Home Entertainment, Inc., P.O. Box 900, Beverly Hills, CA 90213-0900).

LeVine, E. S., & Sallee, A. L. (1990). Critical phases among adoptees and their families: Implications for therapy. *Child and Adolescent Social Work, 7*(3), 217-232.

Lewin, K. (1984). Group decision and social change. In G. E. Swanson, T. M. Newcomb, & E. L. Hartley (Eds.), *Readings in social psychology* (pp. 459-473). New York: Holt.

Lewis, D. O. (1992). From abuse to violence: Psychophysiological consequences of maltreatment. *Journal of American Academy of Child and Adolescent Psychiatry, 31*(3), 383-391.

Lifton, B. J. (1988). *Lost and found: The adoption experience.* New York: Harper & Row.

Lipman, E., Offord, D., Racine, Y., & Boyle, M. (1992). Psychiatric disorders in adopted children: A profile from the Ontario Child Health Study. *Canadian Journal of Psychiatry, 37*(9), 627-633.

Lowenstein, L. B. (1995). The resolution scrapbook as an aid in the treatment of traumatized children. *Child Welfare, 74*(4), 889-904.

Luft, J. (1984). *Group processes: An introduction to group dynamics* (3rd ed.). Palo Alto, CA: Mayfield.

Luthar, S., & Zigler, E. (1991). Vulnerability and competence: A review of research on resilience in childhood. *American Journal of Orthopsychiatry, 61*(1), 6-22.

Macaskill, C. (1985). Post-adoption support: Is it essential? *Adoption and Fostering, 9*(1), 45-49.

Magid, K., & McKelvey, C. A. (1987). *High risk: Children without a conscience.* New York: Bantam.

Main, M., & Solomon, S. (1990). Procedures for identifying infants as disorganized/disoriented during the Ainsworth strange situation. In M. Greenberg, D. Cicchetti, & M. Cummings (Eds.), *Attachment in the preschool years: Theory, research, and intervention* (pp. 121-160). Chicago: University of Chicago Press.

Maluccio, A., Fein, E., Hamilton, J., Klier, J. L., & Ward, D. (1980). Beyond permanency planning. *Child Welfare, 59,* 515-530.

Marcia, J. (1966). Identity and validation of ego-identity status. *Journal of Personality and Social Psychology, 3,* 551-558.

Marschak, M. (1980). *Parent-child interaction and youth rebellion.* New York: Gardner.

Mason, M. M. (1995). *Designing rituals of adoption for the religious and secular community.* Minneapolis, MN: Resources for Adoptive Parents.

Massachusetts Department of Mental Health. (1994). *Training and adoptive family stabilization project quarterly report, 1994.* Boston: Author.

Matsakis, A. (1992). *I can't get over it: A handbook for trauma survivors.* Oakland, CA: New Harbinger.

McCann, I., Sakheim, D., & Abrahamson, D. (1988). Trauma and victimization: A model of psychological adaptation. *The Counseling Psychologist, 16*(4), 531-593.

McFarlane, A. C. (1987). Family functioning and overprotection following a natural disaster: The longitudinal effects of post-traumatic morbidity. *Australian and New Zealand Journal of Psychiatry, 21,* 210-218.

McNamara, J. (1994). *Bruised before birth.* Greensboro, NC: Family Resources.

McRoy, R., Grotevant, H., & Zurcher, S. (1988). *Emotional disturbance in adopted adolescents.* New York: Praeger.

McRoy, R., Zurcher, L., & Lauderdale, M. (1983). Self-esteem and racial identity in transracial and inracial adoptees. *Social Work, 27,* 522-526.

Miall, C. (1987). The stigma of adopted parent status: Perceptions of community attitudes toward adoption and the experience of informal social sanctioning. *Family Relations, 36,* 34-39.

Minshew, D. H., & Hooper, C. (1990). *The adoptive family as a healing resource for the sexually abused child: A training manual.* Washington, DC: Child Welfare League of America.

Minuchin, S., & Elizur, J. (1990). The foster care crisis. *Family Therapy Networker, 14*(1), 44-51.

Montana Adoption Resource Center. (1992). *Bridging the gap: Generating adoption preservation—An adoption training guide.* Helena: Author.

Montgomery, L. M. (1935). *Anne of Green Gables.* Boston: Page.

National Resource Center on Special Needs Adoption. (1995). *Adoption support and preservation curriculum.* Southfield, MI: Author.

Nelson, K. A. (1985). *On the frontier of adoption: A study of special needs adoptive families.* New York: Child Welfare League of America.

Nelson, M., & Parrish, C. (1993). *Partnership spreads post-legal supportive/educational services across the Hawkeye state: Final report.* Des Moines: Iowa Department of Human Services.

North American Council on Adoptable Children. (1998). *Achieving permanence for every child.* St. Paul, MN: Author.

Norvell, M., & Guy, R. (1977) A comparison of self-concept in adopted and non-adopted adolescents. *Adolescence, 12*(47), 443-448.

Offord, D. R., Aponte, J. F., & Cross, L. A. (1969). Presenting symptomatology of adopted children. *Archives of General Psychiatry, 20,* 110-116.

Osofsky, J. D. (1995). The effects of exposure to violence on young children. *American Psychologist, 50,* 782-788.

Parkes, C. (1988). Research: Bereavement. *Omega, 18*(4), 365-377.

Parkes, C. M., & Weiss, R. (1983). *Recovery from bereavement.* New York: Basic Books.

Palmer, S. (1990). Group treatment of foster children to reduce separation conflicts associated with placement breakdown. *Child Welfare, 69*(3), 227-238.

Pannor, R., & Nerlove, E. (1977). Fostering understanding between adolescents and adoptive parents through group experiences. *Child Welfare, 56*(8), 537-545.

Partridge, S., Hornby, H., & McDonald, T. (1986). *Legacies of loss-visions of gain. An inside look at adoption disruption.* Portland: University of Southern Maine, Center for Research and Advanced Study.

Pelzer, D. (1995). *A child called "it."* Deerfield Beach, FL: Health Communications.

Perry, B., Pollard, R., Blakley, T., Baker, W., & Vigilante, D. (1995). Childhood trauma, the neurobiology of adaptation, and "use-dependent" development of the brain: How "states" become "traits." *Infant Mental Health Journal, 16*(4), 271-291.

Peterson, A. C., Compas, B. E., Brooks-Gunn, J., Stemmler, M., Ey, S., & Grant, K. (1993). Depression in adolescence. *American Psychologist, 48*(2), 155-168.

Phelan, T. W. (1996). *1-2-3 magic.* Glen Ellyn, IL: Child Management, Inc.

Potok, C. (1985). *Davita's harp.* New York: Knopf.

Prew, C., Suter, S., & Carrington, J. (1990). *Post adoption family therapy: A practice manual.* Salem: Oregon Department of Human Resources.

Project ENABLE. (1994). *Final report.* Austin: Texas Department of Human Services.

Reite, M., & Field, T. (1985). *The psychobiology of attachment and separation.* Orlando: Academic Press.

Reitnauer, P., & Grabe, P. (1985). *Focusing training for mental health professionals on issues of foster care and adoption.* Mercer, PA: Children's Aid Society.

Reitz, M., & Watson, K. W. (1992). *Adoption and the family system: Strategies for treatment.* New York: Guilford.

Ripley, S. (1993). *A parent's guide to parent groups.* McLean, VA: National Information Center for Children and Youth with Disabilities.

Rogeness, G. A., Hoppe, S. K., Macedo, C. A., Fischer, C., & Harris, W. R. (1988). Psychopathology in hospitalized, adopted children. *Journal of American Academy of Child and Adolescent Psychiatry, 27,* 628-31.

Rosenberg, E. B. (1992). *The adoption life cycle: The children and their families through the years.* New York: Free Press.

Rosenberg, K. F., & Groze, V. (1997). The impact of secrecy and denial in adoption: Practice and treatment issues. *Families in Society: The Journal of Contemporary Human Services, 78*(5), 522-530.

Rosenthal, J. A., & Groze, V. K. (1991). Behavioral problems of special needs adopted children. *Children and Youth Services Review, 13,* 343-361.

Rosenthal, J. A., & Groze, V. K. (1992). *Special needs adoptions: A study of intact families.* Westport, CT: Praeger.

Rosenthal, J. A., & Groze, V. K. (1994). A longitudinal study of special-needs adoptive families. *Child Welfare, 73*(6), 689-706.

Rosenthal, J. A., Groze, V. K, & Aguilar, G. D. (1991). Adoption outcomes for children with handicaps. *Child Welfare, 70*(6), 623-636.

Russell, D. E. H. (1983). The incidence and prevalence of intrafamilial and extrafamilial sexual abuse of female children. *Child Abuse and Neglect, 7,* 133-146.

Sanford, L. T. (1990). *Strong at the broken places: Overcoming the trauma of childhood abuse.* New York: Random House.

Sants, H. J. (1964). Genealogical bewilderment in children with substitute parents. *British Journal of Medical Psychology, 37,* 133-141.

Schecter, M. D., & Bertocci, D. (1990). The meaning of the search. In D. M. Brodzinsky & M. D. Schechter (Eds.), *The psychology of adoption* (pp. 62-90). New York: Oxford University Press.

Scurfield, R. M. (1985). Post-trauma assessment and treatment: Overview and formulations. In C. R. Figley (Ed.), *Trauma and its wake: The study and treatment of post-traumatic stress disorder* (pp. 219-256). New York: Brunner/Mazel.

Senior, N., & Himadi, E. (1985). Emotionally disturbed, adopted, inpatient adolescents. *Child Psychiatry and Human Development, 15*(3), 189-197.

Seuss, D. (1990). *Oh, the places you'll go!* New York: Random House.

Shyne, A., & Schroeder, A. (1978). *National study of social services to children and their families.* Rockville, MD: Westat.

Silin, M. (1996). The vicissitudes of adoption for parents and children. *Child and Adolescent Social Work Journal, 13*(3), 255-269.

Silverman, P. R., Nickman, S., & Worden, J. W. (1992). Detachment revisited: The child's reconstruction of the dead parent. *American Journal of Orthopsychiatry, 62,* 494-503.

Silverstein, D., & Kaplan, S. (1988). Lifelong issues in adoption. In L. Coleman, K. Tilbor, J. Hornby, & C. Boggis (Eds.), *Working with older adoptees: A sourcebook of innovative models* (pp. 45-53), Portland, ME: University of Southern Maine.

Simmons, W. W. (1980). A study of identity formation in adoptees. *Dissertation Abstracts International, 40, 12-B, Part I,* 5832.

Simon, R., & Alstein, H. (1992). The case for transracial adoption. *Children and Youth Services Review, 18*(1-2), 5-22.

Simon, N. M., & Senturia, A. G. (1966). Adoption and psychiatric illness. *American Journal of Psychiatry, 122,* 858-868.

Small, J. W. (1987) Working with adoptive families. *Public Welfare, 45,* 33-41.

Smith, P. M. (1997). Parenting a child with special needs: A guide to reading and resources. *NICHCY News Digest, 20,* 1-28.

Smith, S. L. , & Howard, J. A. (1991). A comparative study of successful and disrupted adoptions. *Journal of Social Service Review, 65,* 248-265.

Smith, S. L., & Howard, J. A. (1994). The impact of previous sexual abuse on children's adjustment in adoptive placement. *Social Work, 39*(5), 491-501.

Smith, S. L., & Howard, J. A. (1995). *Evaluation of project DREAM.* Springfield: Illinois Department of Children and Family Services

Sorenson, T., & Snow, B. (1991). How children tell: The process of disclosure in child sexual abuse. *Child Welfare, 70,* 3-15.

Spaulding for Children. (1989). *The children who wait* [Videotape]. Southfield, MI: National Resource Center for Special Needs Adoption.

Stein, J., Golding, J. M., Siegel, J. M., Burnam, M. A., & Sorenson, S. B. (1988). Long-term psychological sequelae of child sexual abuse: The Los Angeles epidemiologic catechment area study. In G. E. Wyatt & G. J. Powell (Eds.), *Lasting effects of child sexual abuse* (pp. 135-154). Newbury Park, CA: Sage.

Stein, L. M., & Hoopes, J. L. (1985). *Identity formation in the adopted adolescent.* New York: Child Welfare League of America.

Steinhauer, P. (1979). How to succeed in the business of creating psychopaths without even trying. In R. Dawson (Ed.), *Training resources in understanding, supporting, and treating abused children* (pp. 153-194). Toronto: Ministry of Community and Social Services, Children's Services Division.

Stone, A. M. (1992). The role of shame in post-traumatic stress disorder. *American Journal of Orthopsychiatry, 62*(1), 131-136.

Sweeney, W. (1997). *The special-needs reading list: An annotated guide to the best publications for parents and professionals.* Bethesda, MD: Woodbine.

Ternay, M. R., Wilborn, B., & Day, H. D. (1985). Perceived child-parent relationships and child adjustment in families with both adopted and natural children. *Journal of Genetic Psychology, 146,* 261-272.

Terr, L. (1991). Childhood traumas: An outline and overview. *American Journal of Psychiatry, 148*(1), 10-20.

Terr, L. (1994). *Unchained memories: True stories of traumatic memories lost and found.* New York: Basic Books.

Tinbergen, E. A., & Tinbergen, N. (1983). *Autistic children: New hope for a cure.* London: Allen & Unwin.

Toth, S. L., & Cicchetti, D. (1993). Child maltreatment: Where do we go from here in our treatment of victims? In D. Cicchetti & S. L. Toth (Eds.), *Child abuse, child development, and social policy* (pp. 399-437). Norwood, NJ: Ablex.

Urban Systems Research and Engineering, Inc. (1985). *Evaluation of state activities with regard to adoption disruption.* Washington, DC: Author.

van der Kolk, B. A. (1996). Trauma and memory. In B. A. van der Kolk, A. C. McFarlane, & L. Weisaeth (Eds.), *Traumatic stress: The effects of overwhelming experience on mind, body, and society* (pp. 279-302). New York: Guilford.

van der Kolk, B. A., McFarlane, A. C., & van der Hart, O. (1996). A general approach to treatment of posttraumatic stress disorder. In B. A. van der Kolk, A. C. McFarlane, & L. Weisaeth (Eds.), *Traumatic stress: The effects of overwhelming experience on mind, body, and society* (pp. 417-440). New York: Guilford.

Ver Ellen, P., & van Kammen, D. (1990). The biological findings in post-traumatic stress disorder: A review. *Journal of Applied Social Psychology, 20,* 1789-1821.

van Gulden, H., & Bartels-Rabb, L. M. (1994). *Real parents, real children: Parenting the adopted child.* New York: Crossroad.

Van Patten, J. (1992). *Enhancing mental health services for adoptive children and families: Final report.* Wichita, KS: Lutheran Social Services.

VanSlyck, B., & Dupre-Clark, A. (1996). *Charting the course: A therapeutic manual for post-adoptive families.* Columbus, OH: Central Ohio Multi-Modal Adoption Services.

Vasaly, S. (1978). *Foster care in five states: A synthesis and analysis of studies from Arizona, California, Iowa, Massachusetts, and Vermont.* Washington, DC: Department of Health, Education, and Welfare.

Verhulst, F. C., & Versluis-den Bieman, H. J. M. (1995). Developmental course of problem behaviors in adolescent adoptees. *Journal of the American Academy of Child and Adolescent Psychiatry, 34,* 151-159.

Warren, S. (1992). Lower threshold for referral for psychiatric treatment for adopted adolescents. *Journal of the American Academy of Child and Adolescent Psychiatry, 31*(3), 512-517.

Watkins, C. (1992). *Case management issues in fostering and adopting the unattached child.* [Televideo conference, Springfield, IL]

Watson, K. (1992). Providing services after adoption: The public child welfare agency must take the lead to meet the lifelong needs of the adoption triangle. *Public Welfare, 50,* 4-13.

Weiss, R. (1988). Loss and recovery. *Journal of Social Issues, 44*(3), 37-52.

Welch, M. G. (1988). *Holding time.* New York: Simon & Schuster.

Werner, E. E. (1989). High-risk children in young adulthood: A longitudinal study from birth to 32 years. *American Journal of Orthopsychiatry, 59,* 72-81.

Wertlieb, D., Weigel, C., Springer, T., & Feldstein, M. (1989). Temperament as a moderator of children's stressful experiences. In S. Chess, A. Thomas, & M. E. Herzig (Eds.), *Annual progress in child psychiatry and child development: 1988* (pp. 238-254). New York: Brunner/ Mazel.

Whitaker, J. K., & Tracey, E. M. (1989). *Social treatment: An introduction to interpersonal helping in social work practice* (2nd ed.). New York: de Gruyter.

Zaslow, R. W., & Menta, M. (1975). *The psychology of the Z process: Attachment and activation.* San Jose, CA: San Jose State University Press.

Zastrow, C. (1987). *Social work with groups.* Chicago: Nelson-Hall.

INDEX

Adolescence:
  and identity, 59, 163-167
  and parental fears, 57
  worsening behaviors in, 56-57
Adopted children:
  and developmental adjustments, 7-9
  behavioral and emotional problems
    of, 9-12, 75-77
  developmental disabilities in, 230-233
  overrepresentation in special educa-
    tion and mental health services,
    28-29
Adopting the Hurt Child (Keck &
  Kupecky), 197
Adoption:
  adjustment to, 8
  and attachment, 96
  and behavior problems, 79-80
  and developmental disabilities, 233
  core issues in, 31-34
  impact of loss and, 8
  impact of trauma and, 8
  lifelong process of,7, 32
  mastery and control and, 36-37
  outcomes of, 9-10, 11
  powerlessness and, 36-37
  range of professionals in, 37-42
  search and, 167, 214
  secrecy in, 5,6, 27

statistics on, xii, 3, 246
stigma and, 56, 213
trends in, 3-7, 169, 246
Adoption and Safe Families Act, 246
Adoption Opportunities grants, 31, 214
Adoption practice, 1-2, 27
  and placement of children with spe-
    cial needs, 1-3
  changes in, 6-7
  limited history of children and, 27
  matching in, 26
Adoption preservation services:
  and de-escalation of crisis, 191-192
  and exploring identity issues, 197
  and prolonged engagement, 190
  and reducing control battles, 195-197
  and reframing child behavior, 193-195
  and reviewing child history, 193
  careful termination in, 205
  central elements of, 190-205
  increasing entitlement through,
    192-193
  philosophy of, 187-190
Adoptive families:
  and social services, 28-31
  common themes in, 58-64
  dynamics in troubled, 53
  exhaustion in troubled, 64
  grief and, 14

ABOUT THE AUTHORS

Susan Livingston Smith is Professor of Social Work at Illinois State University, and a licensed clinical social worker who has been practicing, teaching, and doing research in child welfare for 30 years. She has published studies related to child abuse—its etiology, investigation, and impact—as well as to special needs adoption. As Co-Director of the Center for Adoption Studies, she continues to strive to advance our understanding of the needs of children in the child welfare system and ways of facilitating their healing as they grow up in adoptive families.

Jeanne A. Howard is Co-Director of the Center of Adoption Studies and Associate Professor of Social Work at Illinois State University. She has been interested in child welfare since her internship with the Illinois Department of Children and Family Services over 20 years ago. Concern about what became of children who entered the child welfare system sparked her research into visitation by parents of children in care, adoption disruption, and the functioning of children and families after adoption finalization.